C-1741 CAREER EXAMINATION SERIES

THIS IS YOUR **PASSBOOK®** FOR ...

POLICE OFFICER, SUFFOLK COUNTY POLICE DEPT. (SCPD)

NATIONAL LEARNING CORPORATION®
passbooks.com

NLC®

National Learning Corporation

212 Michael Drive, Syosset, NY 11791
(516) 921-8888 • www.passbooks.com
E-mail: info@passbooks.com

PUBLISHED IN THE UNITED STATES OF AMERICA

PASSBOOK® SERIES

THE *PASSBOOK® SERIES* has been created to prepare applicants and candidates for the ultimate academic battlefield – the examination room.

At some time in our lives, each and every one of us may be required to take an examination – for validation, matriculation, admission, qualification, registration, certification, or licensure.

Based on the assumption that every applicant or candidate has met the basic formal educational standards, has taken the required number of courses, and read the necessary texts, the *PASSBOOK® SERIES* furnishes the one special preparation which may assure passing with confidence, instead of failing with insecurity. Examination questions – together with answers – are furnished as the basic vehicle for study so that the mysteries of the examination and its compounding difficulties may be eliminated or diminished by a sure method.

This book is meant to help you pass your examination provided that you qualify and are serious in your objective.

The entire field is reviewed through the huge store of content information which is succinctly presented through a provocative and challenging approach – the question-and-answer method.

A climate of success is established by furnishing the correct answers at the end of each test.

You soon learn to recognize types of questions, forms of questions, and patterns of questioning. You may even begin to anticipate expected outcomes.

You perceive that many questions are repeated or adapted so that you can gain acute insights, which may enable you to score many sure points.

You learn how to confront new questions, or types of questions, and to attack them confidently and work out the correct answers.

You note objectives and emphases, and recognize pitfalls and dangers, so that you may make positive educational adjustments.

Moreover, you are kept fully informed in relation to new concepts, methods, practices, and directions in the field.

You discover that you arre actually taking the examination all the time: you are preparing for the examination by "taking" an examination, not by reading extraneous and/or supererogatory textbooks.

In short, this PASSBOOK®, used directedly, should be an important factor in helping you to pass your test.

POLICE OFFICER, SUFFOLK COUNTY POLICE DEPARTMENT (SCPD)

DUTIES

Patrols assigned area in a radio-equipped car, on motorcycle or on foot to prevent and discover the commission of crimes; answers calls and complaints involving automobile accidents, domestic disturbances and other misdemeanors or felonies; directs traffic, enforces traffic laws and arrests traffic violators. At scenes of crime, administers first aid, conducts preliminary investigations, gathers evidence, obtains witnesses and makes arrests; testifies in court on arrests made. Performs related work as required.

SCOPE OF THE EXAMINATION

The written test will cover knowledge, skills and/or abilities in such areas as:

1. Cognitive abilities;
2. Work styles; and
3. Background information.

HOW TO TAKE A TEST

I. YOU MUST PASS AN EXAMINATION

A. WHAT EVERY CANDIDATE SHOULD KNOW

Examination applicants often ask us for help in preparing for the written test. What can I study in advance? What kinds of questions will be asked? How will the test be given? How will the papers be graded?

As an applicant for a civil service examination, you may be wondering about some of these things. Our purpose here is to suggest effective methods of advance study and to describe civil service examinations.

Your chances for success on this examination can be increased if you know how to prepare. Those "pre-examination jitters" can be reduced if you know what to expect. You can even experience an adventure in good citizenship if you know why civil service exams are given.

B. WHY ARE CIVIL SERVICE EXAMINATIONS GIVEN?

Civil service examinations are important to you in two ways. As a citizen, you want public jobs filled by employees who know how to do their work. As a job seeker, you want a fair chance to compete for that job on an equal footing with other candidates. The best-known means of accomplishing this two-fold goal is the competitive examination.

Exams are widely publicized throughout the nation. They may be administered for jobs in federal, state, city, municipal, town or village governments or agencies.

Any citizen may apply, with some limitations, such as the age or residence of applicants. Your experience and education may be reviewed to see whether you meet the requirements for the particular examination. When these requirements exist, they are reasonable and applied consistently to all applicants. Thus, a competitive examination may cause you some uneasiness now, but it is your privilege and safeguard.

C. HOW ARE CIVIL SERVICE EXAMS DEVELOPED?

Examinations are carefully written by trained technicians who are specialists in the field known as "psychological measurement," in consultation with recognized authorities in the field of work that the test will cover. These experts recommend the subject matter areas or skills to be tested; only those knowledges or skills important to your success on the job are included. The most reliable books and source materials available are used as references. Together, the experts and technicians judge the difficulty level of the questions.

Test technicians know how to phrase questions so that the problem is clearly stated. Their ethics do not permit "trick" or "catch" questions. Questions may have been tried out on sample groups, or subjected to statistical analysis, to determine their usefulness.

Written tests are often used in combination with performance tests, ratings of training and experience, and oral interviews. All of these measures combine to form the best-known means of finding the right person for the right job.

II. HOW TO PASS THE WRITTEN TEST

A. NATURE OF THE EXAMINATION

To prepare intelligently for civil service examinations, you should know how they differ from school examinations you have taken. In school you were assigned certain definite pages to read or subjects to cover. The examination questions were quite detailed and usually emphasized memory. Civil service exams, on the other hand, try to discover your present ability to perform the duties of a position, plus your potentiality to learn these duties. In other words, a civil service exam attempts to predict how successful you will be. Questions cover such a broad area that they cannot be as minute and detailed as school exam questions.

In the public service similar kinds of work, or positions, are grouped together in one "class." This process is known as *position-classification.* All the positions in a class are paid according to the salary range for that class. One class title covers all of these positions, and they are all tested by the same examination.

B. FOUR BASIC STEPS

1) Study the announcement

How, then, can you know what subjects to study? Our best answer is: "Learn as much as possible about the class of positions for which you've applied." The exam will test the knowledge, skills and abilities needed to do the work.

Your most valuable source of information about the position you want is the official exam announcement. This announcement lists the training and experience qualifications. Check these standards and apply only if you come reasonably close to meeting them.

The brief description of the position in the examination announcement offers some clues to the subjects which will be tested. Think about the job itself. Review the duties in your mind. Can you perform them, or are there some in which you are rusty? Fill in the blank spots in your preparation.

Many jurisdictions preview the written test in the exam announcement by including a section called "Knowledge and Abilities Required," "Scope of the Examination," or some similar heading. Here you will find out specifically what fields will be tested.

2) Review your own background

Once you learn in general what the position is all about, and what you need to know to do the work, ask yourself which subjects you already know fairly well and which need improvement. You may wonder whether to concentrate on improving your strong areas or on building some background in your fields of weakness. When the announcement has specified "some knowledge" or "considerable knowledge," or has used adjectives like "beginning principles of..." or "advanced ... methods," you can get a clue as to the number and difficulty of questions to be asked in any given field. More questions, and hence broader coverage, would be included for those subjects which are more important in the work. Now weigh your strengths and weaknesses against the job requirements and prepare accordingly.

3) Determine the level of the position

Another way to tell how intensively you should prepare is to understand the level of the job for which you are applying. Is it the entering level? In other words, is this the position in which beginners in a field of work are hired? Or is it an intermediate or advanced level? Sometimes this is indicated by such words as "Junior" or "Senior" in the class title. Other jurisdictions use Roman numerals to designate the level – Clerk I, Clerk II, for example. The word "Supervisor" sometimes appears in the title. If the level is not indicated by the title, check the description of duties. Will you be working under very close supervision, or will you have responsibility for independent decisions in this work?

4) Choose appropriate study materials

Now that you know the subjects to be examined and the relative amount of each subject to be covered, you can choose suitable study materials. For beginning level jobs, or even advanced ones, if you have a pronounced weakness in some aspect of your training, read a modern, standard textbook in that field. Be sure it is up to date and has general coverage. Such books are normally available at your library, and the librarian will be glad to help you locate one. For entry-level positions, questions of appropriate difficulty are chosen – neither highly advanced questions, nor those too simple. Such questions require careful thought but not advanced training.

If the position for which you are applying is technical or advanced, you will read more advanced, specialized material. If you are already familiar with the basic principles of your field, elementary textbooks would waste your time. Concentrate on advanced textbooks and technical periodicals. Think through the concepts and review difficult problems in your field.

These are all general sources. You can get more ideas on your own initiative, following these leads. For example, training manuals and publications of the government agency which employs workers in your field can be useful, particularly for technical and professional positions. A letter or visit to the government department involved may result in more specific study suggestions, and certainly will provide you with a more definite idea of the exact nature of the position you are seeking.

III. KINDS OF TESTS

Tests are used for purposes other than measuring knowledge and ability to perform specified duties. For some positions, it is equally important to test ability to make adjustments to new situations or to profit from training. In others, basic mental abilities not dependent on information are essential. Questions which test these things may not appear as pertinent to the duties of the position as those which test for knowledge and information. Yet they are often highly important parts of a fair examination. For very general questions, it is almost impossible to help you direct your study efforts. What we can do is to point out some of the more common of these general abilities needed in public service positions and describe some typical questions.

1) General information

Broad, general information has been found useful for predicting job success in some kinds of work. This is tested in a variety of ways, from vocabulary lists to questions about current events. Basic background in some field of work, such as sociology or economics, may be sampled in a group of questions. Often these are principles which have become familiar to most persons through exposure rather than through formal training. It is difficult to advise you how to study for these questions; being alert to the world around you is our best suggestion.

2) Verbal ability

An example of an ability needed in many positions is verbal or language ability. Verbal ability is, in brief, the ability to use and understand words. Vocabulary and grammar tests are typical measures of this ability. Reading comprehension or paragraph interpretation questions are common in many kinds of civil service tests. You are given a paragraph of written material and asked to find its central meaning.

3) Numerical ability

Number skills can be tested by the familiar arithmetic problem, by checking paired lists of numbers to see which are alike and which are different, or by interpreting charts and graphs. In the latter test, a graph may be printed in the test booklet which you are asked to use as the basis for answering questions.

4) Observation

A popular test for law-enforcement positions is the observation test. A picture is shown to you for several minutes, then taken away. Questions about the picture test your ability to observe both details and larger elements.

5) Following directions

In many positions in the public service, the employee must be able to carry out written instructions dependably and accurately. You may be given a chart with several columns, each column listing a variety of information. The questions require you to carry out directions involving the information given in the chart.

6) Skills and aptitudes

Performance tests effectively measure some manual skills and aptitudes. When the skill is one in which you are trained, such as typing or shorthand, you can practice. These tests are often very much like those given in business school or high school courses. For many of the other skills and aptitudes, however, no short-time preparation can be made. Skills and abilities natural to you or that you have developed throughout your lifetime are being tested.

Many of the general questions just described provide all the data needed to answer the questions and ask you to use your reasoning ability to find the answers. Your best preparation for these tests, as well as for tests of facts and ideas, is to be at your physical and mental best. You, no doubt, have your own methods of getting into an exam-taking mood and keeping "in shape." The next section lists some ideas on this subject.

IV. KINDS OF QUESTIONS

Only rarely is the "essay" question, which you answer in narrative form, used in civil service tests. Civil service tests are usually of the short-answer type. Full instructions for answering these questions will be given to you at the examination. But in case this is your first experience with short-answer questions and separate answer sheets, here is what you need to know:

1) Multiple-choice Questions

Most popular of the short-answer questions is the "multiple choice" or "best answer" question. It can be used, for example, to test for factual knowledge, ability to solve problems or judgment in meeting situations found at work.

A multiple-choice question is normally one of three types—

- It can begin with an incomplete statement followed by several possible endings. You are to find the one ending which *best* completes the statement, although some of the others may not be entirely wrong.
- It can also be a complete statement in the form of a question which is answered by choosing one of the statements listed.
- It can be in the form of a problem – again you select the best answer.

Here is an example of a multiple-choice question with a discussion which should give you some clues as to the method for choosing the right answer:

When an employee has a complaint about his assignment, the action which will *best* help him overcome his difficulty is to

A. discuss his difficulty with his coworkers
B. take the problem to the head of the organization
C. take the problem to the person who gave him the assignment
D. say nothing to anyone about his complaint

In answering this question, you should study each of the choices to find which is best. Consider choice "A" – Certainly an employee may discuss his complaint with fellow employees, but no change or improvement can result, and the complaint remains unresolved. Choice "B" is a poor choice since the head of the organization probably does not know what assignment you have been given, and taking your problem to him is known as "going over the head" of the supervisor. The supervisor, or person who made the assignment, is the person who can clarify it or correct any injustice. Choice "C" is, therefore, correct. To say nothing, as in choice "D," is unwise. Supervisors have and interest in knowing the problems employees are facing, and the employee is seeking a solution to his problem.

2) True/False Questions

The "true/false" or "right/wrong" form of question is sometimes used. Here a complete statement is given. Your job is to decide whether the statement is right or wrong.

SAMPLE: A roaming cell-phone call to a nearby city costs less than a non-roaming call to a distant city.

This statement is wrong, or false, since roaming calls are more expensive.

This is not a complete list of all possible question forms, although most of the others are variations of these common types. You will always get complete directions for answering questions. Be sure you understand *how* to mark your answers – ask questions until you do.

V. RECORDING YOUR ANSWERS

Computer terminals are used more and more today for many different kinds of exams.

For an examination with very few applicants, you may be told to record your answers in the test booklet itself. Separate answer sheets are much more common. If this separate answer sheet is to be scored by machine – and this is often the case – it is highly important that you mark your answers correctly in order to get credit.

An electronic scoring machine is often used in civil service offices because of the speed with which papers can be scored. Machine-scored answer sheets must be marked with a pencil, which will be given to you. This pencil has a high graphite content which responds to the electronic scoring machine. As a matter of fact, stray dots may register as answers, so do not let your pencil rest on the answer sheet while you are pondering the correct answer. Also, if your pencil lead breaks or is otherwise defective, ask for another.

Since the answer sheet will be dropped in a slot in the scoring machine, be careful not to bend the corners or get the paper crumpled.

The answer sheet normally has five vertical columns of numbers, with 30 numbers to a column. These numbers correspond to the question numbers in your test booklet. After each number, going across the page are four or five pairs of dotted lines. These short dotted lines have small letters or numbers above them. The first two pairs may also have a "T" or "F" above the letters. This indicates that the first two pairs only are to be used if the questions are of the true-false type. If the questions are multiple choice, disregard the "T" and "F" and pay attention only to the small letters or numbers.

Answer your questions in the manner of the sample that follows:

32. The largest city in the United States is
    - A. Washington, D.C.
    - B. New York City
    - C. Chicago
    - D. Detroit
    - E. San Francisco

1) Choose the answer you think is best. (New York City is the largest, so "B" is correct.)
2) Find the row of dotted lines numbered the same as the question you are answering. (Find row number 32)
3) Find the pair of dotted lines corresponding to the answer. (Find the pair of lines under the mark "B.")
4) Make a solid black mark between the dotted lines.

VI. BEFORE THE TEST

Common sense will help you find procedures to follow to get ready for an examination. Too many of us, however, overlook these sensible measures. Indeed, nervousness and fatigue have been found to be the most serious reasons why applicants fail to do their best on civil service tests. Here is a list of reminders:

- Begin your preparation early – Don't wait until the last minute to go scurrying around for books and materials or to find out what the position is all about.
- Prepare continuously – An hour a night for a week is better than an all-night cram session. This has been definitely established. What is more, a night a week for a month will return better dividends than crowding your study into a shorter period of time.
- Locate the place of the exam – You have been sent a notice telling you when and where to report for the examination. If the location is in a different town or otherwise unfamiliar to you, it would be well to inquire the best route and learn something about the building.
- Relax the night before the test – Allow your mind to rest. Do not study at all that night. Plan some mild recreation or diversion; then go to bed early and get a good night's sleep.
- Get up early enough to make a leisurely trip to the place for the test – This way unforeseen events, traffic snarls, unfamiliar buildings, etc. will not upset you.
- Dress comfortably – A written test is not a fashion show. You will be known by number and not by name, so wear something comfortable.
- Leave excess paraphernalia at home – Shopping bags and odd bundles will get in your way. You need bring only the items mentioned in the official notice you received; usually everything you need is provided. Do not bring reference books to the exam. They will only confuse those last minutes and be taken away from you when in the test room.
- Arrive somewhat ahead of time – If because of transportation schedules you must get there very early, bring a newspaper or magazine to take your mind off yourself while waiting.
- Locate the examination room – When you have found the proper room, you will be directed to the seat or part of the room where you will sit. Sometimes you are given a sheet of instructions to read while you are waiting. Do not fill out any forms until you are told to do so; just read them and be prepared.
- Relax and prepare to listen to the instructions
- If you have any physical problem that may keep you from doing your best, be sure to tell the test administrator. If you are sick or in poor health, you really cannot do your best on the exam. You can come back and take the test some other time.

VII. AT THE TEST

The day of the test is here and you have the test booklet in your hand. The temptation to get going is very strong. Caution! There is more to success than knowing the right answers. You must know how to identify your papers and understand variations in the type of short-answer question used in this particular examination. Follow these suggestions for maximum results from your efforts:

1) Cooperate with the monitor

The test administrator has a duty to create a situation in which you can be as much at ease as possible. He will give instructions, tell you when to begin, check to see that you are marking your answer sheet correctly, and so on. He is not there to guard you, although he will see that your competitors do not take unfair advantage. He wants to help you do your best.

2) Listen to all instructions

Don't jump the gun! Wait until you understand all directions. In most civil service tests you get more time than you need to answer the questions. So don't be in a hurry. Read each word of instructions until you clearly understand the meaning. Study the examples, listen to all announcements and follow directions. Ask questions if you do not understand what to do.

3) Identify your papers

Civil service exams are usually identified by number only. You will be assigned a number; you must not put your name on your test papers. Be sure to copy your number correctly. Since more than one exam may be given, copy your exact examination title.

4) Plan your time

Unless you are told that a test is a "speed" or "rate of work" test, speed itself is usually not important. Time enough to answer all the questions will be provided, but this does not mean that you have all day. An overall time limit has been set. Divide the total time (in minutes) by the number of questions to determine the approximate time you have for each question.

5) Do not linger over difficult questions

If you come across a difficult question, mark it with a paper clip (useful to have along) and come back to it when you have been through the booklet. One caution if you do this – be sure to skip a number on your answer sheet as well. Check often to be sure that you have not lost your place and that you are marking in the row numbered the same as the question you are answering.

6) Read the questions

Be sure you know what the question asks! Many capable people are unsuccessful because they failed to *read* the questions correctly.

7) Answer all questions

Unless you have been instructed that a penalty will be deducted for incorrect answers, it is better to guess than to omit a question.

8) Speed tests

It is often better NOT to guess on speed tests. It has been found that on timed tests people are tempted to spend the last few seconds before time is called in marking answers at random – without even reading them – in the hope of picking up a few extra points. To discourage this practice, the instructions may warn you that your score will be "corrected" for guessing. That is, a penalty will be applied. The incorrect answers will be deducted from the correct ones, or some other penalty formula will be used.

9) Review your answers

If you finish before time is called, go back to the questions you guessed or omitted to give them further thought. Review other answers if you have time.

10) Return your test materials

If you are ready to leave before others have finished or time is called, take ALL your materials to the monitor and leave quietly. Never take any test material with you. The monitor can discover whose papers are not complete, and taking a test booklet may be grounds for disqualification.

VIII. EXAMINATION TECHNIQUES

1) Read the general instructions carefully. These are usually printed on the first page of the exam booklet. As a rule, these instructions refer to the timing of the examination; the fact that you should not start work until the signal and must stop work at a signal, etc. If there are any *special* instructions, such as a choice of questions to be answered, make sure that you note this instruction carefully.

2) When you are ready to start work on the examination, that is as soon as the signal has been given, read the instructions to each question booklet, underline any key words or phrases, such as *least*, *best*, *outline*, *describe* and the like. In this way you will tend to answer as requested rather than discover on reviewing your paper that you *listed without describing*, that you selected the *worst* choice rather than the *best* choice, etc.

3) If the examination is of the objective or multiple-choice type – that is, each question will also give a series of possible answers: A, B, C or D, and you are called upon to select the best answer and write the letter next to that answer on your answer paper – it is advisable to start answering each question in turn. There may be anywhere from 50 to 100 such questions in the three or four hours allotted and you can see how much time would be taken if you read through all the questions before beginning to answer any. Furthermore, if you come across a question or group of questions which you know would be difficult to answer, it would undoubtedly affect your handling of all the other questions.

4) If the examination is of the essay type and contains but a few questions, it is a moot point as to whether you should read all the questions before starting to answer any one. Of course, if you are given a choice – say five out of seven and the like – then it is essential to read all the questions so you can eliminate the two that are most difficult. If, however, you are asked to answer all the questions, there may be danger in trying to answer the easiest one first because you may find that you will spend too much time on it. The best technique is to answer the first question, then proceed to the second, etc.

5) Time your answers. Before the exam begins, write down the time it started, then add the time allowed for the examination and write down the time it must be completed, then divide the time available somewhat as follows:

- If 3-1/2 hours are allowed, that would be 210 minutes. If you have 80 objective-type questions, that would be an average of 2-1/2 minutes per question. Allow yourself no more than 2 minutes per question, or a total of 160 minutes, which will permit about 50 minutes to review.
- If for the time allotment of 210 minutes there are 7 essay questions to answer, that would average about 30 minutes a question. Give yourself only 25 minutes per question so that you have about 35 minutes to review.

6) The most important instruction is to *read each question* and make sure you know what is wanted. The second most important instruction is to *time yourself properly* so that you answer every question. The third most important instruction is to *answer every question.* Guess if you have to but include something for each question. Remember that you will receive no credit for a blank and will probably receive some credit if you write something in answer to an essay question. If you guess a letter – say "B" for a multiple-choice question – you may have guessed right. If you leave a blank as an answer to a multiple-choice question, the examiners may respect your feelings but it will not add a point to your score. Some exams may penalize you for wrong answers, so in such cases *only,* you may not want to guess unless you have some basis for your answer.

7) Suggestions

a. Objective-type questions

1. Examine the question booklet for proper sequence of pages and questions
2. Read all instructions carefully
3. Skip any question which seems too difficult; return to it after all other questions have been answered
4. Apportion your time properly; do not spend too much time on any single question or group of questions
5. Note and underline key words – *all, most, fewest, least, best, worst, same, opposite,* etc.
6. Pay particular attention to negatives
7. Note unusual option, e.g., unduly long, short, complex, different or similar in content to the body of the question
8. Observe the use of "hedging" words – *probably, may, most likely,* etc.
9. Make sure that your answer is put next to the same number as the question
10. Do not second-guess unless you have good reason to believe the second answer is definitely more correct
11. Cross out original answer if you decide another answer is more accurate; do not erase until you are ready to hand your paper in
12. Answer all questions; guess unless instructed otherwise
13. Leave time for review

b. Essay questions

1. Read each question carefully
2. Determine exactly what is wanted. Underline key words or phrases.
3. Decide on outline or paragraph answer

4. Include many different points and elements unless asked to develop any one or two points or elements
5. Show impartiality by giving pros and cons unless directed to select one side only
6. Make and write down any assumptions you find necessary to answer the questions
7. Watch your English, grammar, punctuation and choice of words
8. Time your answers; don't crowd material

8) Answering the essay question

Most essay questions can be answered by framing the specific response around several key words or ideas. Here are a few such key words or ideas:

M's: manpower, materials, methods, money, management
P's: purpose, program, policy, plan, procedure, practice, problems, pitfalls, personnel, public relations

a. Six basic steps in handling problems:
   1. Preliminary plan and background development
   2. Collect information, data and facts
   3. Analyze and interpret information, data and facts
   4. Analyze and develop solutions as well as make recommendations
   5. Prepare report and sell recommendations
   6. Install recommendations and follow up effectiveness

b. Pitfalls to avoid
   1. *Taking things for granted* – A statement of the situation does not necessarily imply that each of the elements is necessarily true; for example, a complaint may be invalid and biased so that all that can be taken for granted is that a complaint has been registered
   2. *Considering only one side of a situation* – Wherever possible, indicate several alternatives and then point out the reasons you selected the best one
   3. *Failing to indicate follow up* – Whenever your answer indicates action on your part, make certain that you will take proper follow-up action to see how successful your recommendations, procedures or actions turn out to be
   4. *Taking too long in answering any single question* – Remember to time your answers properly

IX. AFTER THE TEST

Scoring procedures differ in detail among civil service jurisdictions although the general principles are the same. Whether the papers are hand-scored or graded by machine we have described, they are nearly always graded by number. That is, the person who marks the paper knows only the number – never the name – of the applicant. Not until all the papers have been graded will they be matched with names. If other tests, such as training and experience or oral interview ratings have been given, scores will be combined. Different parts of the examination usually have different weights. For example, the written test might count 60 percent of the final grade, and a rating of training and experience 40 percent. In many jurisdictions, veterans will have a certain number of points added to their grades.

After the final grade has been determined, the names are placed in grade order and an eligible list is established. There are various methods for resolving ties between those who get the same final grade – probably the most common is to place first the name of the person whose application was received first. Job offers are made from the eligible list in the order the names appear on it. You will be notified of your grade and your rank as soon as all these computations have been made. This will be done as rapidly as possible.

People who are found to meet the requirements in the announcement are called "eligibles." Their names are put on a list of eligible candidates. An eligible's chances of getting a job depend on how high he stands on this list and how fast agencies are filling jobs from the list.

When a job is to be filled from a list of eligibles, the agency asks for the names of people on the list of eligibles for that job. When the civil service commission receives this request, it sends to the agency the names of the three people highest on this list. Or, if the job to be filled has specialized requirements, the office sends the agency the names of the top three persons who meet these requirements from the general list.

The appointing officer makes a choice from among the three people whose names were sent to him. If the selected person accepts the appointment, the names of the others are put back on the list to be considered for future openings.

That is the rule in hiring from all kinds of eligible lists, whether they are for typist, carpenter, chemist, or something else. For every vacancy, the appointing officer has his choice of any one of the top three eligibles on the list. This explains why the person whose name is on top of the list sometimes does not get an appointment when some of the persons lower on the list do. If the appointing officer chooses the second or third eligible, the No. 1 eligible does not get a job at once, but stays on the list until he is appointed or the list is terminated.

X. HOW TO PASS THE INTERVIEW TEST

The examination for which you applied requires an oral interview test. You have already taken the written test and you are now being called for the interview test – the final part of the formal examination.

You may think that it is not possible to prepare for an interview test and that there are no procedures to follow during an interview. Our purpose is to point out some things you can do in advance that will help you and some good rules to follow and pitfalls to avoid while you are being interviewed.

What is an interview supposed to test?

The written examination is designed to test the technical knowledge and competence of the candidate; the oral is designed to evaluate intangible qualities, not readily measured otherwise, and to establish a list showing the relative fitness of each candidate – as measured against his competitors – for the position sought. Scoring is not on the basis of "right" and "wrong," but on a sliding scale of values ranging from "not passable" to "outstanding." As a matter of fact, it is possible to achieve a relatively low score without a single "incorrect" answer because of evident weakness in the qualities being measured.

Occasionally, an examination may consist entirely of an oral test – either an individual or a group oral. In such cases, information is sought concerning the technical knowledges and abilities of the candidate, since there has been no written examination for this purpose. More commonly, however, an oral test is used to supplement a written examination.

Who conducts interviews?

The composition of oral boards varies among different jurisdictions. In nearly all, a representative of the personnel department serves as chairman. One of the members of the board may be a representative of the department in which the candidate would work. In some cases, "outside experts" are used, and, frequently, a businessman or some other representative of the general public is asked to serve. Labor and management or other special groups may be represented. The aim is to secure the services of experts in the appropriate field.

However the board is composed, it is a good idea (and not at all improper or unethical) to ascertain in advance of the interview who the members are and what groups they represent. When you are introduced to them, you will have some idea of their backgrounds and interests, and at least you will not stutter and stammer over their names.

What should be done before the interview?

While knowledge about the board members is useful and takes some of the surprise element out of the interview, there is other preparation which is more substantive. It *is* possible to prepare for an oral interview – in several ways:

1) Keep a copy of your application and review it carefully before the interview

This may be the only document before the oral board, and the starting point of the interview. Know what education and experience you have listed there, and the sequence and dates of all of it. Sometimes the board will ask you to review the highlights of your experience for them; you should not have to hem and haw doing it.

2) Study the class specification and the examination announcement

Usually, the oral board has one or both of these to guide them. The qualities, characteristics or knowledges required by the position sought are stated in these documents. They offer valuable clues as to the nature of the oral interview. For example, if the job involves supervisory responsibilities, the announcement will usually indicate that knowledge of modern supervisory methods and the qualifications of the candidate as a supervisor will be tested. If so, you can expect such questions, frequently in the form of a hypothetical situation which you are expected to solve. NEVER go into an oral without knowledge of the duties and responsibilities of the job you seek.

3) Think through each qualification required

Try to visualize the kind of questions you would ask if you were a board member. How well could you answer them? Try especially to appraise your own knowledge and background in each area, *measured against the job sought*, and identify any areas in which you are weak. Be critical and realistic – do not flatter yourself.

4) Do some general reading in areas in which you feel you may be weak

For example, if the job involves supervision and your past experience has NOT, some general reading in supervisory methods and practices, particularly in the field of human relations, might be useful. Do NOT study agency procedures or detailed manuals. The oral board will be testing your understanding and capacity, not your memory.

5) Get a good night's sleep and watch your general health and mental attitude

You will want a clear head at the interview. Take care of a cold or any other minor ailment, and of course, no hangovers.

What should be done on the day of the interview?

Now comes the day of the interview itself. Give yourself plenty of time to get there. Plan to arrive somewhat ahead of the scheduled time, particularly if your appointment is in the fore part of the day. If a previous candidate fails to appear, the board might be ready for you a bit early. By early afternoon an oral board is almost invariably behind schedule if there are many candidates, and you may have to wait. Take along a book or magazine to read, or your application to review, but leave any extraneous material in the waiting room when you go in for your interview. In any event, relax and compose yourself.

The matter of dress is important. The board is forming impressions about you – from your experience, your manners, your attitude, and your appearance. Give your personal appearance careful attention. Dress your best, but not your flashiest. Choose conservative, appropriate clothing, and be sure it is immaculate. This is a business interview, and your appearance should indicate that you regard it as such. Besides, being well groomed and properly dressed will help boost your confidence.

Sooner or later, someone will call your name and escort you into the interview room. *This is it.* From here on you are on your own. It is too late for any more preparation. But remember, you asked for this opportunity to prove your fitness, and you are here because your request was granted.

What happens when you go in?

The usual sequence of events will be as follows: The clerk (who is often the board stenographer) will introduce you to the chairman of the oral board, who will introduce you to the other members of the board. Acknowledge the introductions before you sit down. Do not be surprised if you find a microphone facing you or a stenotypist sitting by. Oral interviews are usually recorded in the event of an appeal or other review.

Usually the chairman of the board will open the interview by reviewing the highlights of your education and work experience from your application – primarily for the benefit of the other members of the board, as well as to get the material into the record. Do not interrupt or comment unless there is an error or significant misinterpretation; if that is the case, do not hesitate. But do not quibble about insignificant matters. Also, he will usually ask you some question about your education, experience or your present job – partly to get you to start talking and to establish the interviewing "rapport." He may start the actual questioning, or turn it over to one of the other members. Frequently, each member undertakes the questioning on a particular area, one in which he is perhaps most competent, so you can expect each member to participate in the examination. Because time is limited, you may also expect some rather abrupt switches in the direction the questioning takes, so do not be upset by it. Normally, a board member will not pursue a single line of questioning unless he discovers a particular strength or weakness.

After each member has participated, the chairman will usually ask whether any member has any further questions, then will ask you if you have anything you wish to add. Unless you are expecting this question, it may floor you. Worse, it may start you off on an extended, extemporaneous speech. The board is not usually seeking more information. The question is principally to offer you a last opportunity to present further qualifications or to indicate that you have nothing to add. So, if you feel that a significant qualification or characteristic has been overlooked, it is proper to point it out in a sentence or so. Do not compliment the board on the thoroughness of their examination – they have been sketchy, and you know it. If you wish, merely say, "No thank you, I have nothing further to add." This is a point where you can "talk yourself out" of a good impression or fail to present an important bit of information. Remember, *you close the interview yourself.*

The chairman will then say, "That is all, Mr. _______, thank you." Do not be startled; the interview is over, and quicker than you think. Thank him, gather your belongings and take your leave. Save your sigh of relief for the other side of the door.

How to put your best foot forward

Throughout this entire process, you may feel that the board individually and collectively is trying to pierce your defenses, seek out your hidden weaknesses and embarrass and confuse you. Actually, this is not true. They are obliged to make an appraisal of your qualifications for the job you are seeking, and they want to see you in your best light. Remember, they must interview all candidates and a non-cooperative candidate may become a failure in spite of their best efforts to bring out his qualifications. Here are 15 suggestions that will help you:

1) Be natural – Keep your attitude confident, not cocky

If you are not confident that you can do the job, do not expect the board to be. Do not apologize for your weaknesses, try to bring out your strong points. The board is interested in a positive, not negative, presentation. Cockiness will antagonize any board member and make him wonder if you are covering up a weakness by a false show of strength.

2) Get comfortable, but don't lounge or sprawl

Sit erectly but not stiffly. A careless posture may lead the board to conclude that you are careless in other things, or at least that you are not impressed by the importance of the occasion. Either conclusion is natural, even if incorrect. Do not fuss with your clothing, a pencil or an ashtray. Your hands may occasionally be useful to emphasize a point; do not let them become a point of distraction.

3) Do not wisecrack or make small talk

This is a serious situation, and your attitude should show that you consider it as such. Further, the time of the board is limited – they do not want to waste it, and neither should you.

4) Do not exaggerate your experience or abilities

In the first place, from information in the application or other interviews and sources, the board may know more about you than you think. Secondly, you probably will not get away with it. An experienced board is rather adept at spotting such a situation, so do not take the chance.

5) If you know a board member, do not make a point of it, yet do not hide it

Certainly you are not fooling him, and probably not the other members of the board. Do not try to take advantage of your acquaintanceship – it will probably do you little good.

6) Do not dominate the interview

Let the board do that. They will give you the clues – do not assume that you have to do all the talking. Realize that the board has a number of questions to ask you, and do not try to take up all the interview time by showing off your extensive knowledge of the answer to the first one.

7) Be attentive

You only have 20 minutes or so, and you should keep your attention at its sharpest throughout. When a member is addressing a problem or question to you, give him your undivided attention. Address your reply principally to him, but do not exclude the other board members.

8) Do not interrupt

A board member may be stating a problem for you to analyze. He will ask you a question when the time comes. Let him state the problem, and wait for the question.

9) Make sure you understand the question

Do not try to answer until you are sure what the question is. If it is not clear, restate it in your own words or ask the board member to clarify it for you. However, do not haggle about minor elements.

10) Reply promptly but not hastily

A common entry on oral board rating sheets is “candidate responded readily,” or “candidate hesitated in replies.” Respond as promptly and quickly as you can, but do not jump to a hasty, ill-considered answer.

11) Do not be peremptory in your answers

A brief answer is proper – but do not fire your answer back. That is a losing game from your point of view. The board member can probably ask questions much faster than you can answer them.

12) Do not try to create the answer you think the board member wants

He is interested in what kind of mind you have and how it works – not in playing games. Furthermore, he can usually spot this practice and will actually grade you down on it.

13) Do not switch sides in your reply merely to agree with a board member

Frequently, a member will take a contrary position merely to draw you out and to see if you are willing and able to defend your point of view. Do not start a debate, yet do not surrender a good position. If a position is worth taking, it is worth defending.

14) Do not be afraid to admit an error in judgment if you are shown to be wrong

The board knows that you are forced to reply without any opportunity for careful consideration. Your answer may be demonstrably wrong. If so, admit it and get on with the interview.

15) Do not dwell at length on your present job

The opening question may relate to your present assignment. Answer the question but do not go into an extended discussion. You are being examined for a *new* job, not your present one. As a matter of fact, try to phrase ALL your answers in terms of the job for which you are being examined.

Basis of Rating

Probably you will forget most of these "do's" and "don'ts" when you walk into the oral interview room. Even remembering them all will not ensure you a passing grade. Perhaps you did not have the qualifications in the first place. But remembering them will help you to put your best foot forward, without treading on the toes of the board members.

Rumor and popular opinion to the contrary notwithstanding, an oral board wants you to make the best appearance possible. They know you are under pressure – but they also want to see how you respond to it as a guide to what your reaction would be under the pressures of the job you seek. They will be influenced by the degree of poise you display, the personal traits you show and the manner in which you respond.

ABOUT THIS BOOK

This book contains tests divided into Examination Sections. Go through each test, answering every question in the margin. At the end of each test look at the answer key and check your answers. On the ones you got wrong, look at the right answer choice and learn. Do not fill in the answers first. Do not memorize the questions and answers, but understand the answer and principles involved. On your test, the questions will likely be different from the samples. Questions are changed and new ones added. If you understand these past questions you should have success with any changes that arise. Tests may consist of several types of questions. We have additional books on each subject should more study be advisable or necessary for you. Finally, the more you study, the better prepared you will be. This book is intended to be the last thing you study before you walk into the examination room. Prior study of relevant texts is also recommended. NLC publishes some of these in our Fundamental Series. Knowledge and good sense are important factors in passing your exam. Good luck also helps. So now study this Passbook, absorb the material contained within and take that knowledge into the examination. Then do your best to pass that exam.

EXAMINATION SECTION

PERSONALITY/AUTOBIOGRAPHICAL INVENTORY

EXAMINATION SECTION

TEST 1

DIRECTIONS: Each question or incomplete statement is followed by several suggested answers or completions. Select the one that BEST answers the question or completes the statement. *PRINT THE LETTER OF THE CORRECT ANSWER IN THE SPACE AT THE RIGHT.*

1. While a senior in high school, I was absent 1.____
   A. never
   B. seldom
   C. frequently
   D. more than 10 days
   E. only when I felt bored

2. While in high school, I failed classes 2.____
   A. never
   B. once
   C. twice
   D. more than twice
   E. at least four times

3. During class discussions in my high school classes, I usually 3.____
   A. listened without participating
   B. participated as much as possible
   C. listened until I had something to add to the discussion
   D. disagreed with others simply for the sake of argument
   E. laughed at stupid ideas

4. My high school grade point average (on a 4.0 scale) was 4.____
   A. 2.0 or lower
   B. 2.1 to 2.5
   C. 2.6 to 3.0
   D. 3.1 to 3.5
   E. 3.6 to 4.0

5. As a high school student, I completed my assignments 5.____
   A. as close to the due date as I could manage
   B. whenever the teacher gave me an extension
   C. frequently
   D. on time
   E. when they were interesting

6. While in high school, I participated in 6.____
   A. athletic and nonathletic extracurricular activities
   B. athletic extracurricular activities
   C. nonathletic extracurricular activities
   D. no extracurricular activities
   E. mandatory after-school programs

7. In high school, I made the honor roll 7.____
   A. several times
   B. once
   C. more than once
   D. twice
   E. I can't remember if I made the honor role

8. Upon graduation from high school, I received 8.____
   A. academic and nonacademic honors
   B. academic honors
   C. nonacademic honors
   D. no honors
   E. I can't remember if I received honors

9. While attending high school, I worked at a paid job or as a volunteer 9.____
   A. never
   B. every so often
   C. 5 to 10 hours a month
   D. more than 10 hours a month
   E. more than 15 hours a month

10. During my senior year of high school, I skipped school 10.____
   A. whenever I could
   B. once a week
   C. several times a week
   D. not at all
   E. when I got bored

11. I was suspended from high school 11.____
   A. not at all
   B. once or twice
   C. once or twice, for fighting
   D. several times
   E. more times than I can remember

12. During high school, my fellow students and teachers considered me 12.____
   A. above average
   B. below average
   C. average
   D. underachieving
   E. underachieving and prone to fighting

13. The ability to ______ is most important to a Police Officer 13.____
   A. draw his/her gun quickly
   B. see over great distances and difficult terrain
   C. verbally and physically intimidate criminals
   D. communicate effectively in circumstances which can be dangerous
   E. hear over great distances

14. I began planning for college 14.____
    A. when my parents told me to
    B. when I entered high school
    C. during my junior year
    D. during my senior hear
    E. when I signed up for my SAT (or other standardized exam)

15. An effective leader is someone who 15.____
    A. inspires confidence in his/her followers
    B. inspires fear in his/her followers
    C. tells subordinates exactly what they should do
    D. creates an environment in which subordinates feel insecure about their job security and performance
    E. makes as few decisions as possible

16. I prepared myself for college by 16.____
    A. learning how to get extensions on major assignments
    B. working as many hours as possible at my after-school job
    C. spending as much time with my friends as possible
    D. getting good grades and participating in extracurricular activities
    E. watching television shows about college kids

17. I paid for college by 17.____
    A. supplementing my parents contributions with my own earnings
    B. relying on scholarships, loans, and my own earnings
    C. relying on my parents and student loans
    D. relying on my parents to pay my tuition, room and board
    E. relying on sources not listed here

18. While a college student, I spent my summers and holiday breaks 18.____
    A. in summer or remedial classes B. traveling
    C. working D. relaxing
    E. spending time with my friends

19. My final college grade point average (on a 4.0 scale) was 19.____
    A. 3.8 to 4.0 B. 3.5 to 3.8 C. 3.0 to 3.5
    D. 2.5 to 3.0 E. 2.0 to 2.5

20. As a college student, I cut classes 20.____
    A. frequently B. when I didn't like them
    C. sometimes D. rarely
    E. when I needed the sleep

21. In college, I received academic honors 21.____
    A. not at all
    B. once
    C. twice
    D. several times
    E. I can't remember if I received academic honors

22. While in college, I declared a major 22.____
    A. during my first year B. during my sophomore year
    C. during my junior year D. during my senior year
    E. several times

23. While on patrol as a Police Officer, you spot someone attempting to flee the scene of a crime. Your first reaction is to 23.____
    A. draw your weapon
    B. observe the person until he or she completes the fleeing
    C. identify yourself as a Police Officer
    D. fire your weapon over the person's head in order to scare him or her
    E. call immediately for backup

24. As a college student, I failed _____ classes. 24.____
    A. no B. two C. three
    D. four E. more than four

25. Friends describe me as 25.____
    A. introverted B. hot-tempered C. unpredictable
    D. quiet E. easygoing

KEY (CORRECT ANSWERS)

PLEASE NOTE: The answers listed are the best answers. However, you are to answer the exam honestly. Your personal answer may differ from the *best* answers.

1.	A	11.	A
2.	A	12.	A
3.	C	13.	D
4.	E	14.	B
5.	D	15.	A
6.	A	16.	D
7.	A	17.	B
8.	A	18.	C
9.	E	19.	A
10.	D	20.	D

21. D
22. A
23. C
24. A
25. E

TEST 2

DIRECTIONS: Each question or incomplete statement is followed by several suggested answers or completions. Select the one that BEST answers the question or completes the statement. *PRINT THE LETTER OF THE CORRECT ANSWER IN THE SPACE AT THE RIGHT.*

1. As a Police Officer, you apprehend three men whom you believe are in the country illegally. However, none of the men speaks English, and you don't speak their language. 1.____
   Your reaction should be to
   A. draw your weapon so that they understand the seriousness of the situation
   B. take them into custody, where they will have access to a translator
   C. attempt to communicate through hand gestures and shouting
   D. call for a translator to come and meet you at your location
   E. pretend you understand their language and apprehend them

2. During my college classes, I preferred to 2.____
   A. remain silent during class discussions
   B. do other homework during class discussions
   C. participate frequently in class discussions
   D. argue with others as much as possible
   E. laugh at the stupid opinions of others

3. As a Police Officer, you are chasing a small group of people who are running away from the scene of a crime. During your pursuit, one member of the group is left behind. You see that she is injured and in need of medical attention. 3.____
   Your reaction is to
   A. fire your weapon at the group members to get them to stop
   B. cease pursuit of the group members and take the woman into custody
   C. continue pursuit of the group members, leaving the woman behind since acting ill is a common trick
   D. radio for backup to stay with the woman while medical help arrives while you continue pursuit of the group members
   E. radio for backup to continue pursuit of the group members while you stay with the woman and wait for medical help to arrive

4. As a college student, I was placed on academic probation 4.____
   A. not at all
   B. once
   C. twice
   D. three times
   E. more than three times

5. At work, being a team player means to 5.____
   A. compromise your ideals and beliefs
   B. compensate for the incompetence of others
   C. count on others to compensate for my inexperience
   D. cooperate with others to get a project finished
   E. rely on others to get the job done

6. As a Police Officer, you confront someone you believe has just committed a crime. After identifying yourself, you notice the suspect holding something that looks like a knife. Your FIRST reaction should be to 6.____
   A. draw your weapon and fire
   B. call immediately for backup
   C. keep your weapon drawn until you get the suspect into a position that is controllable
   D. ask the suspect if he is armed
   E. talk to the suspect without drawing your weapon

7. My friends from college remember me primarily as a(n) 7.____
   A. person who loved to party
   B. ambitious student
   C. athlete
   D. joker
   E. fighter

8. My college experience is memorable primarily because of 8.____
   A. the friends I made
   B. the sorority/fraternity I was able to join
   C. the social activities I participated in
   D. my academic achievements
   E. the money I spent

9. A friend who is applying for a job asks you to help him pass the mandatory drug test by substituting a sample of your urine for his. You should 9.____
   A. help him by supplying the sample
   B. help him by supplying the sample and insisting he seek drug counseling
   C. supply the sample, but tell him that this is the only time you'll help in this way
   D. call the police
   E. refuse

10. As a college student, I handed in my assignments 10.____
   A. when they were due
   B. whenever I could get an extension
   C. when they were interesting
   D. when my friends reminded me to
   E. when I was able

11. At work you are accused of a minor infraction which you didn't commit. Your FIRST reaction is to 11.____
   A. call a lawyer
   B. speak to your supervisor about the mistake
   C. call the police
   D. yell at the person who did commit the infraction
   E. accept the consequences regardless of your guilt or innocence

12. While on patrol, you are surprised by a large group of disorderly teenage gang members. You are greatly outnumbered. 12.____
As a Police Officer, your FIRST reaction is to
   A. draw your weapon and identify yourself
   B. get back into your vehicle and wait for help to arrive
   C. call for backup
   D. pretend you are part of a large group of police in the area
   E. identify yourself and get the group members into a controllable position

13. As a college student, I began to prepare for final exams 13.____
   A. the night before taking them
   B. when the professor handed out the review sheets
   C. several weeks before taking them
   D. when my friends began to prepare for their exams
   E. the morning of the exam

14. As a Police Officer in the field, you confront a small group of people you believe to be wanted criminals. 14.____
Your MOST important consideration during this exchange should be
   A. apprehension of criminals
   B. safety of county citizens in nearby towns
   C. safety of the criminals
   D. number of criminals you must apprehend in order to receive a commendation'
   E. the amount of respect the criminals show to you and your position

15. At work, I am known as 15.____
   A. popular
   B. quiet
   C. intense
   D. easygoing
   E. dedicated

16. The MOST important quality in a coworker is 16.____
   A. friendliness
   B. cleanliness
   C. a good sense of humor
   D. dependability
   E. good listening skills

17. In the past year, I have stayed home from work 17.____
   A. frequently
   B. only when I felt depressed
   C. rarely
   D. only when I felt overwhelmed
   E. only to run important errands

18. As a Police Officer, the BEST way to collect information from a suspect during an interview is to 18.____
   A. physically intimidate the suspect
   B. verbally intimidate the suspect
   C. threaten the suspect's family and/or friend with criminal prosecution
   D. encourage a conversation with the suspect
   E. sit in silence until the suspect begins speaking

19. For me, the BEST thing about college was the 19.____
    A. chance to strengthen my friendships and develop new ones
    B. chance to test my abilities and develop new ones
    C. number of extracurricular activities and clubs
    D. chance to socialize
    E. chance to try several different majors

20. As an employee, my WEAKEST skill is 20.____
    A. controlling my temper
    B. my organizational ability
    C. my ability to effectively understand directions
    D. my ability to effectively manage others
    E. my ability to communicate my thoughts in writing

21. As a Police Officer, my GREATEST strength would be 21.____
    A. my sense of loyalty
    B. my organizational ability
    C. punctuality
    D. dedication
    E. my ability to intimidate others

22. As a Police Officer, you find a group of suspicious youths gathered around a truck which is on fire. 22.____
    Your FIRST reaction is to
    A. call the fire department
    B. arrest them all for destruction of property
    C. draw your weapon and begin questioning them
    D. return to your vehicle and wait for the fire department
    E. instruct the group to remain while you return to your vehicle and request backup

23. If asked by my company to learn a new job-related skill, my reaction would be to 23.____
    A. ask for a raise
    B. ask for overtime pay
    C. question the necessity of the skill
    D. cooperate with some reluctance
    E. cooperate with enthusiasm

24. When I disagree with others, I tend to 24.____
    A. listen quietly despite my disagreement
    B. laugh openly at the person I disagree with
    C. ask the person to explain their views before I respond
    D. leave the conversation before my anger gets the best of me
    E. point out exactly why the person is wrong

25. When I find myself in a situation which is confusing or unclear, my reaction is to 25.____
   A. pretend I am not confused
   B. remain calm and, if necessary, ask someone else for clarification
   C. grow frustrated and angry
   D. walk away from the situation
   E. immediately insist that someone explain things to me

KEY (CORRECT ANSWERS)

PLEASE NOTE: The answers listed are the best answers. However, you are to answer the exam honestly. Your personal answer may differ from the *best* answers.

1. B
2. C
3. E
4. A
5. D

6. C
7. B
8. D
9. E
10. A

11. B
12. E
13. C
14. A
15. E

16. D
17. C
18. D
19. B
20. E

21. D
22. A
23. E
24. C
25. B

TEST 3

DIRECTIONS: Each question or incomplete statement is followed by several suggested answers or completions. Select the one that BEST answers the question or completes the statement. *PRINT THE LETTER OF THE CORRECT ANSWER IN THE SPACE AT THE RIGHT.*

1. While on patrol as a Police Officer, you find a dead body lying in the open. Hiding a few feet away, behind some rocks, you find a suspicious person who is holding items which seem to have been taken from the dead body, including a pair of shoes and some jewelry. 1.____
   You should
   A. apprehend the suspect and bring him to the station for further questioning
   B. arrest the suspect for murder and robbery
   C. arrest the suspect for murder
   D. subdue the suspect with force and check the area for his accomplices
   E. subdue the suspect with force and call for backup to check the area for his accomplices

2. If you were placed in a supervisory position, which of the following abilities would you consider to be MOST important to your job performance? 2.____
   A. Stubborness
   B. The ability to hear all sides of a story before making a decision
   C. Kindness
   D. The ability to make and stick to a decision
   E. Patience

3. What is your HIGHEST level of education? 3.____
   A. Less than a high school diploma
   B. A high school diploma or equivalency
   C. A graduate of community college
   D. A graduate of a four-year accredited college
   E. A degree from graduate school

4. When asked to supervise other workers, your approach should be to 4.____
   A. ask for management wages since you're doing management work
   B. give the workers direction and supervise every aspect of the process
   C. give the workers direction and then allow them to do the job
   D. and the workers their job specifications
   E. do the work yourself, since you're uncomfortable supervising others

5. Which of the following BEST describes you? 5.____
   A. Need little or no supervision
   B. Resent too much supervision
   C. Require as much supervision as my peers
   D. Require slightly more supervision than my peers
   E. Require close supervision

6. You accept a job which requires an ability to perform several tasks at once. What is the BEST way to handle such a position? 6.____
   A. With strong organizational skills and a close attention to detail
   B. By delegating the work to someone with strong organizational skills
   C. Staying focused on one task at a time, no matter what happens
   D. Working on one task at a time until each task is successfully completed
   E Asking my supervisor to help me

7. As a Police Officer, you take a suspected perpetrator into custody. After returning to the field, you notice that your gun is missing. 7.____
   You should
   A. retrace your steps to see if you dropped it somewhere
   B. report the loss immediately
   C. ask your partner to borrow his or her gun
   D. pretend that nothing's happened
   E. rely on your hands for defense and protection

8. Which of the following BEST describes your behavior when you disagree with someone? 8.____
   You
   A. state your own point of view as quickly and loudly as you can
   B. listen quietly and keep your opinions to yourself
   C. listen to the other person's perspective and then carefully point out all the flaws in their logic
   D. list all of the ignorant people who agree with the opposing point of view
   E. listen to the other person's perspective and then explain your own perspective

9. As a new Police Officer, you make several mistakes during your first week of work. 9.____
   You react by
   A. learning from your mistakes and moving on
   B. resigning
   C. blaming it on your supervisor
   D. refusing to talk about it
   E. blaming yourself

10. My ability to communicate effectively with others is _____ average. 10.____
    A. below B. about C. above
    D. far above E. far below

11. In which of the following areas are you MOST highly skilled? 11.____
    A. Written communication
    B. Oral communication
    C. Ability to think quickly in difficult situations
    D. Ability to work with a broad diversity of people and personalities
    E. Organizational skills

12. As a Police Officer, you are assigned to work with a partner whom you dislike. You should 12.____
    A. immediately report the problem to your supervisor
    B. ask your partner not to speak to you during working hours
    C. tell your colleagues about your differences
    D. tell your partner why you dislike him/her
    E. work with your partner regardless of your personal feelings

13. During high school, what was your MOST common after-school activity? 13.____
    A. Remaining after school to participate in various clubs and organizations (such as band, sports, etc.)
    B. Remaining after school to make up for missed classes
    C. Remaining after school as punishment (detention, etc.)
    D. Going straight to an after-school job
    E. Spending the afternoon at home or with friends

14. During high school, in which of the following subjects did you receive the HIGHEST grades? 14.____
    A. English, History, Social Studies
    B. Math, Science
    C. Vocational classes
    D. My grades were consistent in all subjects
    E. Classes I liked

15. When faced with an overwhelming number of duties at work, your reaction is to 15.____
    A. do all of the work yourself, no matter what the cost
    B. delegate some responsibilities to capable colleagues
    C. immediately ask your supervisor for help
    D. put off as much work as possible until you can get to it
    E. take some time off to relax and clear your mind

16. As a Police Officer, your supervisor informs you that a prisoner whom you arrested has accused you of beating him. You know you are innocent. You react by 16.____
    A. quitting your job
    B. hiring a lawyer
    C. challenging your supervisor to prove the charges against you
    D. calmly tell your supervisor what really happened and presenting evidence to support your position
    E. insisting that you be allowed to speak alone to the prisoner

17. Which of the following BEST describes your desk at your current or most recent job? 17.____
    A. Messy and disorganized
    B. Neat and organized
    C. Messy but organized
    D. Neat but disorganized
    E. Messy

18. The _____ BEST describes your reasons for wanting to become a Police Officer. 18.____
   A. ability to carry and use a weapon
   B. excitement and challenges of the career
   C. excellent salary and benefits package
   D. chance to tell other people what to do
   E. chance to help people find a better life

19. As a Police Officer in the field, you are approached by a man who is frantic but unable to speak English. After several minutes of trying to communicate, you realize that the man is asking you to come with him in order to help someone who has been hurt. 19.____
   You should
   A. ignore him, since it might be a trap
   B. call for backup
   C. immediately offer to help the man
   D. return to your vehicle and wait for the man to leave
   E. radio your position and situation to another officer, then go with the man to offer help

20. When asked to take on extra responsibility at work, in order to help out a coworker who is overwhelmed, your response is to 20.____
   A. ask for overtime pay
   B. complain to your supervisor that you are being taken advantage of
   C. help the coworker to the best of your ability
   D. ask the coworker to come back some other time
   E. give the coworker some advice on how to get his/her job done

21. At my last job, I was promoted 21.____
   A. not at all
   B. once
   C. twice
   D. three times
   E. more than three times

22. As a Police Officer, you discover the body of a person whom you suspect to be a gang member. You also suspect that there are several other gang members hiding in the nearby vicinity. 22.____
   Your FIRST reaction should be to
   A. begin a search of the nearby area for the other gang members
   B. return to your vehicle and call for backup
   C. return to your vehicle with the body of the person you found
   D. check whether the person you found is dead or alive
   E. draw your weapon and identify yourself

23. You are faced with an overwhelming deadline at work. Your reaction is to 23.____
    A. procrastinate until the last minute
    B. procrastinate until someone notices you need some help
    C. notify your supervisor that you can't complete the work on your own
    D. work in silence without asking any questions
    E. arrange your schedule so that you can get the work done before the deadline

24. When you feel yourself under deadline pressures at work, your response is to 24.____
    A. make sure you keep to a schedule which allows you to complete the work on time
    B. wait until just before the deadline to complete the work
    C. ask someone else to do the work
    D. grow so obsessive about the work that your coworkers feel compelled to help you
    E. ask your supervisor immediately for help

25. Which of the following BEST describes your appearance at your current or most recent position? 25.____
    A. Well-groomed, neat, and clean
    B. Unkempt, but dressed neatly
    C. Messy and dirty clothing
    D. Unshaven and untidy
    E. Clean-shaven, but sloppily dressed

KEY (CORRECT ANSWERS)

PLEASE NOTE: The answers listed are our preferred answers. However, you are to answer the exam honestly. Your personal answer may differ from our answers.

1.	A	11.	C
2.	D	12.	E
3.	E	13.	A
4.	C	14.	D
5.	A	15.	B
6.	A	16.	D
7.	B	17.	B
8.	E	18.	B
9.	A	19.	E
10.	C	20.	C

21.	C
22.	D
23.	E
24.	A
25.	A

TEST 4

DIRECTIONS: Each question or incomplete statement is followed by several suggested answers or completions. Select the one that BEST answers the question or completes the statement. *PRINT THE LETTER OF THE CORRECT ANSWER IN THE SPACE AT THE RIGHT.*

1. Which of the following BEST describes the way you react to making a difficult decision? 1.____
   A. Consult with the people you're closest to before making the decision
   B. Make the decision entirely on your own
   C. Consult only with those people whom your decision will affect
   D. Consult with everyone you known, in an effort to make a decision that will please everyone
   E. Forget about the decision until you have to make it

2. If placed in a supervisory role, which of the following characteristics would you rely on most heavily when dealing with the employees you supervise? 2.____
   A. Kindness B. Cheeriness C. Honesty
   D. Hostility E. Aloofness

3. As a Police Officer, you are pursuing a suspect when he turns and pulls something out of his pocket that looks like a gun. 3.____
   You should
   A. run away and call for backup
   B. assure the man that you mean him no harm
   C. draw your gun and order the man to stop and drop his weapon
   D. draw your gun and fire a warning shot
   E. draw your gun and fire immediately

4. In addition to English, in which of the following languages are you also fluent? 4.____
   A. Spanish B. French C. Italian
   D. German E. Other

5. When confronted with gossip at work, your typical reaction is to 5.____
   A. participate
   B. listen without participating
   C. notify your supervisor
   D. excuse yourself from the discussion
   E. confront your coworkers about their problem

6. In the past two years, how many jobs have you held? 6.____
   A. None B. One C. Two
   D. Three E. More than three

7. In your current or most recent job, you favorite part of the job is the part which involves 7.____
   A. telling other people what they're doing wrong
   B. supervising others
   C. working without supervision to finish a project
   D. written communication
   E. oral communication

8. Your supervisor asks you about a colleague who is applying for a position which you also want. 8.____
   You react by
   A. commenting honestly on the person's work performance
   B. enhancing the person's negative traits
   C. informing your supervisor about your colleague's personal problems
   D. telling your supervisor that would be better in the position
   E. refusing to comment

9. As a Police Officer, you confiscate some contraband which was being imported by an illegal alien who is now in your custody. Your partner asks you not to turn the contraband in to your supervisor. 9.____
   Your response is to
   A. inform your supervisor of your partner's request immediately
   B. tell your partner you feel uncomfortable with his request
   C. pretend you didn't hear you partner's request
   D. tell your supervisor and all your colleagues about your partner's request
   E. give the contraband to your partner and let him handle it

10. Which of the following BEST describes your responsibilities in your last job? 10.____
    A. Entirely supervisory
    B. Much supervisory responsibility
    C. Equal amounts of supervisory and nonsupervisory responsibility
    D. Some supervisory responsibilities
    E. No supervisory responsibilities

11. How much written communication did your previous or most recent job require of you? 11.____
    A. A great deal of written communication
    B. Some written communication
    C. I don't remember
    D. A small amount of written communication
    E. No written communication

12. In the past two years, how many times have you been fired from a job? 12.____
    A. None
    B. Once
    C. Twice
    D. Three times
    E. More than three times

13. How much time have you spent working for volunteer organizations in the past year? 13.____
    A. 10 to 20 hours per week
    B. 5 to 10 hours per week
    C. 3 to 5 hours per week
    D. 1 to 3 hours per week
    E. I have spent no time volunteering in the past year

14. Your efforts at volunteer work usually revolve around which of the following types of organizations? 14.____
    A. Religious
    B. Community-based organizations working to improve the community
    C. Charity organizations working on behalf of the poor
    D. Charity organizations working on behalf of the infirm or handicapped
    E. Other

15. Which of the following BEST describes your professional history? Promoted at _____ coworkers 15.____
    A. a much faster rate than
    B. a slightly faster rate than
    C. the same rate as
    D. a slightly slower rate than
    E. a much slower rate than

16. Which of the following qualities do you MOST appreciate in a coworker? 16.____
    A. Friendliness
    B. Dependability
    C. Good looks
    D. Silence
    E. Forgiveness

17. When you disagree with a supervisor's instructions or opinion about how to complete a project, your reaction is to 17.____
    A. inform your supervisor that you refuse to complete the project according to his or her instructions
    B. inform your colleague of you supervisor's incompetence
    C. accept your supervisor's instructions in silence
    D. voice your concerns and then complete the project according to your own instincts
    E. voice your concerns and then complete the project according to your supervisor's instructions

18. Which of the following BEST describes your reaction to close supervision and specific direction from your supervisor? 18.____
    You
    A. listen carefully to the directions, and then figure out a way to do the job more effectively
    B. complete the job according to the given specifications
    C. show some initiative by doing the job your way
    D. ask someone else to do the job for you
    E. listen carefully to the directions, and then figure out a better way to do the job which will save more money

19. How should a Police Officer handle a situation in which he or she is offered a bribe not to issue a traffic ticket? 19.____
    A. Pretend the bribe was never offered
    B. Accept the money as evidence and release the person
    C. Draw your weapon and call for backup
    D. Refuse the bribe and then arrest the person
    E. Accept the bribe and then arrest the person

20. At work you are faced with a difficult decision. 20.____
    You react by
    A. seeking advice from your colleagues
    B. following your own path regardless of the consequences
    C. asking your supervisor what you should do
    D. keeping the difficulties to yourself
    E. working for a solution which will please everyone

21. If asked to work with a person whom you dislike, your response would be 21.____
    A. to ask your supervisor to allow you to work with someone else
    B. to ask your coworker to transfer to another department or project
    C. talk to your coworker about the proper way to behave at work
    D. pretend the coworker is your best friend for the sake of your job
    E. to set aside your personal differences in order to complete the job

22. As a supervisory, which of the following incentives would you use to motivate your employees? 22.____
    A. Fear of losing their jobs
    B. Fear of their supervisors
    C. Allowing employees to provide their input on a number of policies
    D. Encouraging employees to file secret reports regarding colleagues' transgressions
    E. All of the above

23. A fellow Police Officer, with whom you enjoy a close friendship, has a substance-abuse problem which has gone undetected. You suspect the problem may be affecting his job. 23.____
    You would
    A. ask the Police Officer if the problem is affecting his job performance
    B. warn the Police Officer that he must seek counseling or you will report him
    C. wait a few weeks to see whether the officer's problem really is affecting his job
    D. discuss it with your supervisor
    E. wait for the supervisor to discover the problem

24. In the past two months, you have missed work 24.____
    A. zero times
    B. once
    C. twice
    D. three times
    E. more than three times

25. As a Police Officer, you are pursuing a group of robbers when you discover two small children who have been abandoned near a railroad crossing. 25.____
You should
   A. tell the children to stay put while you continue your pursuit
   B. lock the children in your vehicle and continue your pursuit
   C. stay with the children and radio for help in the pursuit of the robbers
   D. use the children to set a trap for the robbers
   E. ignore the children and continue your pursuit

KEY (CORRECT ANSWERS)

PLEASE NOTE: The answers listed are our preferred answers. However, you are to answer the exam honestly. Your personal answer may differ from our answers.

1. A
2. C
3. C
4. A
5. D

6. B
7. C
8. A
9. A
10. D

11. B
12. A
13. C
14. B
15. A

16. B
17. E
18. B
19. D
20. A

21. E
22. C
23. D
24. A
25. C

SAMPLE QUESTIONS

BIOGRAPHICAL INVENTORY

The questions included in the Biographical Inventory ask for information about you and your background. These kinds of questions are often asked during an oral interview. For years, employers have been using interviews to relate personal history, preferences, and attitudes to job success. This Biographical Inventory attempts to do the same and includes questions which have been shown to be related to job success. It has been found that successful employees tend to select some answers more often than other answers, while less successful employees tend to select different answers. The questions in the Biographical Inventory do not have a single correct answer. Every choice is given some credit. More credit is given for answers selected more often by successful employees.

These Biographical Inventory questions are presented for illustrative purposes only. The answers have not been linked to the answers of successful employees; therefore, we cannot designate any "correct" answer(s).

DIRECTIONS: You may only mark ONE response to each question. It is possible that none of the answers applies well to you. However, one of the answers will surely be true (or less inaccurate) for you than others. In such a case, mark that answer. Answer each question honestly. The credit that is assigned to each response on the actual test is based upon how successful employees described themselves when honestly responding to the questions. *PRINT THE LETTER OF THE CORRECT ANSWER IN THE SPACE AT THE RIGHT.*

1. Generally, in your work assignments, would you prefer 1.____
   A. to work on one thing at a time
   B. to work on a couple of things at a time
   C. to work on many things at the same time

2. In the course of a week, which of the following gives you the GREATEST satisfaction? 2.____
   A. Being told you have done a good job.
   B. Helping other people to solve their problems.
   C. Coming up with a new or unique way to handle a situation.
   D. Having free time to devote to personal interests.

EXAMINATION SECTION

TEST 1

DIRECTIONS: Each question or incomplete statement is followed by several suggested answers or completions. Select the one that BEST answers the question or completes the statement. *PRINT THE LETTER OF THE CORRECT ANSWER IN THE SPACE AT THE RIGHT.*

1. Which of the following events would typically cause the GREATEST amount of stress in a person's life? 1.____
   A. A major change in financial status
   B. Vacation
   C. Pregnancy
   D Marital separation

2. A local shopping center has experienced a recent rash of shoplifting. Officer Jones is patrolling the mall parking lot frequently. 2.____
   Which situation below should Officer Jones regard as MOST suspicious?
   A. A man running out a store entrance with a shopping bag from the store under his arm
   B. A car parked for a long time near the front entrance of the store
   C. A woman loading a pile of clothes, some with plastic security tags still attached, into the trunk of her car
   D. A young man walking around looking in through the windows of various parked cars

3. An officer is faced with the responsibility of telling a woman her husband has been murdered. While the officers should phrase the news as gently as possible, he or she should also demonstrate empathy nonverbally. 3.____
   The BEST way to do this is to
   A. stand with arms crossed
   B. hold the woman closely
   C. maintain eye contact
   D. tell the woman you understand her pain

4. Cognitive symptoms of anxiety include 4.____
   A. rapid heart rate
   B. feelings of fear of helplessness
   C. poor social functioning
   D. euphoria

5. Which of the following is MOST likely to help a person to improve her attitude? 5.____
   A. Avoiding people who make her feel bad about herself
   B. Learning to become more goal-oriented
   C. Learning to look more clearly at her own faults
   D. Taking charge of an unruly situation

6. A suspect has been handcuffed, but refuses to take a seat in the patrol car after several requests. 6.____
The arresting officer should
   A. tap the suspect behind the knees with the baton, just hard enough so that the suspect's legs will fold and he can be inserted into the car
   B. tighten the handcuffs until the pain compel compliance
   C. try to frighten the suspect with threats
   D. inform the suspect of the consequences for resisting arrest

7. Each of the following is likely to be a cause of stress on the job, EXCEPT 7.____
   A. work overload
   B. differences in organizational and personal values
   C. a narrowly-defined role
   D. time pressures

8. In communicating with people, especially in stressful or high-conflict situations, nonverbal communication is 8.____
   A. more important than the verbal message
   B. less important than the verbal message
   C. universal across all cultures
   D. typically contradictory to the verbal message

9. Problem-oriented police work does NOT 9.____
   A. help officers get to the roots of a crime problem
   B. offer a proactive model for policing
   C. focus on responding to calls for service
   D. have any impact on preventing or reducing crime

10. The difference between assertiveness and aggressiveness is that 10.____
   A. assertiveness is not potentially harmful to others
   B. aggressiveness involves strangers
   C. aggressiveness has to do with achieving goals
   D. assertiveness is always negative

11. As an officer and his partner arrive to investigate a reported domestic disturbance, the husband and wife are still arguing. In the presence of the officers, each spouse makes a verbal threat of physical harm against the other. 11.____
In resolving this conflict, the FINAL step that should be taken by the officers is to
   A. indicate the consequences if this behavior continues
   B. empathize with each of the spouses
   C. present the spouses with problem-solving strategies
   D. describe the behaviors that appeared to cause the disturbance

12. Elements of community policing include 12.____
I. the police
II. the business community
III. the media
IV. religious institutions
The CORRECT ANSWER IS:
A. I, II B. I, II, III C. I, III D. I, II, III, IV

13. In a grocery store parking lot, a pair of officers arrest both the buyer and seller in an alleged drug transaction in a grocery store parking lot. After the suspects have been handcuffed and placed in a patrol car, one of the officers notices a wad of bills on the ground where the transaction took place. The officer pockets the money and decides to keep it, telling herself that the money is "dirty" and that she has more of a right to it than either of the criminal suspects. Legally, the officer has committed a crime; ethically, she has committed a(n) 13.____
    A. rationalization B. kickback C. stereotyping D. deviance

14. Probably the MOST effective way to deal with on-the-job stress is to 14.____
    A. find alternative employment
    B. take early retirement
    C. participate in a personal wellness program
    D. acquire assertiveness skills that will help confront the people responsible for the stress

Questions 15-16.

DIRECTIONS: Questions 15 and 16 deal with the following situation.

A pharmacist has complained to the police department that several drug addicts in his neighborhood have been attempting to obtain drugs legally, usually by passing fake prescriptions.

15. Which of the following people should arouse the MOST suspicion when approaching the prescription counter? 15.____
    A. A middle-aged woman who appears homeless and is poorly groomed
    B. A young African-American male in a hooded sweatshirt on a hot day
    C. A man in his thirties who glances around furtively and brings a large amount of nonprescription items to the counter for purchase
    D. None of the above should be regarded as suspicious on the basis of their appearance alone

16. After refusing to fill several prescriptions, the pharmacist describes or gives each of the prescriptions to an investigating officer. Which of the following MOST warrants investigation? 16.____
    A. A written investigation that is covered with several coffee rings
    B. A prescription written on a Post-It note
    C. A written prescription for pain killers with a date indicating it was written more than a week ago
    D. A prescription that is phoned in by a doctor

17. An individual's personality, whether normal or deviant, will ALWAYS 17.____
    A. refer to the person's deep inner self, rather than just superficial aspects
    B. involve unique characteristics that are all different from another person's
    C. be a product of social and cultural environments, with no biological foundation
    D. be organized into patterns that are observable and measurable to some degree

18. Change in a person's life that is due to personal growth is almost always 18.____
    A. negative B. dramatic C. positive D. minor

19. Residents in an urban neighborhood have complained of a recent increase in gang-related graffiti in their community. 19.____
    Which of the following should be regarded as MOST suspicious by an officer on patrol?
    A. One young man walking down the street and flashing gang signs at passing cars
    B. A pair of teenagers riding their bicycles in a tenement parking lot late at night
    C. A group of teenagers hanging out in a convenience store parking lot, leaning against a wall that is covered with graffiti
    D. A group of teenagers hanging out in a convenience store parking lot. One of the teenagers has a spray paint can.

20. Common symptoms of stress include each of the following EXCEPT 20.____
    A. digestive problem B. sluggishness
    C. sleep problems D. emotional instability

21. The general goal of community policing is 21.____
    A. a lower overall crime rate
    B. conviction of criminals who are caught in the community
    C. fewer violent crimes
    D. a higher quality of life in the community

22. In most settings, the simplest and most effective method of stopping sexual harassment is to 22.____
    A. threaten the person with legal or administrative consequences
    B. ignore it
    C. avoid the person as much as possible
    D. ask or tell the person to stop

23. Of the following types of crime, the one MOST likely to have a widespread impact on a victims community is 23.____
    A. hate or bias crime B. workplace violence
    C. theft D. sexual assault

24. Functional roles of the police include: 24.____
    I. Crime prevention II. Order maintenance
    III. Public service IV. Criminal prosecution
    The CORRECT answer is:
    A. I only B. I, II C. I, II, III D. I, II,III, IV

25. A pre-existing thought or belief that people have about members of a given group—whether the belief is positive, negative, or neutral—is 25.____
    A. ethnocentrism B. a stereotype
    C. self-centeredness D. discrimination

KEY (CORRECT ANSWERS)

1. D
2. C
3. C
4. B
5. B

6. D
7. C
8. A
9. C
10. A

11. A
12. D
13. A
14. C
15. D

16. B
17. D
18. B
19. D
20. B

21. D
22. D
23. A
24. C
25. B

TEST 2

DIRECTIONS: Each question or incomplete statement is followed by several suggested answers or completions. Select the one that BEST answers the question or completes the statement. *PRINT THE LETTER OF THE CORRECT ANSWER IN THE SPACE AT THE RIGHT.*

1. Role expectations for police officers generally 1.____
   A. are consistent across the country, with a strong focus on peacekeeping
   B. change from community to community, depending on the local culture
   C. direct them to be more lenient with juvenile offenders
   D. direct them to be self-reliant in both preventing and investigating crime

2. Officer Shinjo takes a complaint from a woman who says she is being stalked by a man who is a classmate in one of her night business courses. The man has sent her unwanted gifts and left numerous unanswered telephone messages, but she did not become concerned until last night, when she noticed the man following her home from class. She asks Officer Shinjo what to do about the situation. 2.____
   At least part of Officer Shinjo's advice to the woman should include the suggestion that she
   A. immediately apply for a restraining order
   B. create a logbook to document each of the stalking incidents in as much detail as possible
   C. answer one of the man's telephone calls and try to explain that the unwanted attention is making her uncomfortable
   D. call the man herself and threaten legal action if he doesn't stop bothering her

3. Which of the following is an element of self-direction? 3.____
   A. Knowing when to seek help from others
   B. Being able to get from one geographic location to another without a map
   C. Establishing and reaching both short- and long-term goals
   D. Adopting healthier lifestyle habits

4. Each of the following factors is typically associated with ethnicity, EXCEPT 4.____
   A. culture
   B. language
   C. economic status
   D. physical characteristics

5. Among the communication skills necessary for effective communication with people, the foundation upon which all others are based is considered to be 5.____
   A. confrontation
   B. authoritativeness
   C. attending behavior
   D. observation

6. Which of the following offers the BEST definition of the word "ethics"? 6.____
   A. An individual's means of obtaining what he wants from and for other people in a society
   B. Standards of conduct that express a society's concept of right and wrong

C. A formal code of conduct that delineates a strict set of rules and framework for punishment
D. Morality and the consequences of behaviors

7. Which of the following is a measurement of a rate? 7.____
A. The ratio of the number of new African-American arrestees for drug-related crimes in the 35-49 age bracket during a specific year, compared to the number of African-Americans in the same age group in the entire community
B. The number of white females, aged 18-25, who are arrested each year on child endangerment charges
C. The percentage change in the number of property crimes in a given year, compared to the previous year
D. The ratio of the number of persons currently under prosecution for violent crimes to the number of people, aged 14-55, in the entire community

8. In recent weeks, several patrons at a local restaurant have had their cars broken into by having a window smashed in, and then having valuable items taken from the car. Officer Jackson is patrolling the restaurant parking lot. 8.____
Which situation below should she regard as MOST suspicious?
A. A young man in a hooded sweatshirt walking around the parking lot at lunchtime, carrying a long, heavy flashlight
B. A car parked so as to partially block other cars from exiting the parking lot
C. A man's voice raised in anger coming from the parking lot
D. Several young men leaning against the outside of the parking lot fence in the early evening, bouncing a basketball and apparently waiting for the arrival of another person

9. Among the skills important to effective communication with people, the MOST complex and difficult to master are those that help to 9.____
A. encourage B. confront C. influence D. summarize

10. The FIRST step in dealing with an alcohol or drug addiction is to 10.____
A. admit there is a problem
B. talk to a counselor or close friend
C. stop taking the drug or drinking alcohol
D. join a support group or enter a rehabilitation center

11. Key elements of police professionalism include: 11.____
I. an advanced education
II. a clearly stated code of ethics
III. accountability through peer review
IV. demonstrated understanding of the field's core body of knowledge
The CORRECT answer is:
A. I, II B. I, III, IV C. II, III, IV D. I, II, III, IV

12. A factor that makes a police officer susceptible to corruption is that the officer 12.____
   A. is typically different from most members of society
   B. can be sure that if a suspect is arrested, the suspect will be prosecuted and punished
   C. is usually better off financially than most of the people she interacts with in carrying out her duties
   D. has the professional discretion not to enforce the law

13. In resolving an ethical dilemma, a police officer's FIRST step should generally be to 13.____
   A. identify the ethical issues that are in conflict
   B. identify the people and organizations likely to be affected by the decision
   C. consult with colleagues and appropriate experts
   D. examine the reasons in favor of and opposed to each possible course of action

14. During a lengthy interview with a witness, an officer decides to use "reflection of meaning" strategies in order to clarify the information he's being given. This strategy would involve each of the following EXCEPT 14.____
   A. trying to paraphrase longer statements offered by the witness
   B. closing with a check on the witness's words, such as "So do I understand this correctly?"
   C. beginning sentences with phrases such as "You mean....." or "Sounds as if you saw....."
   D. offering an interpretation of the witness's words

15. Officer McGee is meeting with several community members to determine a course of action for reducing gang-related activities in the area. Each of the following is a guideline to be used by an officer in building a constructive relationship with community members, EXCEPT 15.____
   A. viewing community members as equals
   B. adopting a completely neutral tone of voice when speaking with people
   C. using a shared vocabulary of easily understood, nonoffensive words
   D. asking for the input of community members before making any suggestions

16. In solving a complex problem, the FIRST step is always to 16.____
   A. develop a plan
   B. gather information
   C. define the problem
   D. envision contingencies

17. Role conflict can occur when an officer encounters two sets of expectations that are inconsistent with each other. Role strain can occur when an officer's role is limited by what he or she is authorized to do. The MAIN difference between these two is that role 17.____
   A. conflict is relatively rare among police officers
   B. conflict can be resolved; role strain cannot
   C. strain creates stressful situations for officers
   D. strain has a greater influence on the officer's exercise of discretion

18. Generally, police community relations differs from public relations in that they 18.____
   A. consider the needs of the community first
   B. are much more successful in reducing social problems
   C. are without inherent spheres of interest
   D. encourage two-way communications

19. Factors that place a man at risk as a potential batterer include each of the following, EXCEPT 19.____
   A. poverty
   B. drug or alcohol use
   C. 30-45 years of age
   D. witnessing spousal abuse between parents

20. The four major categories of commonly abused substances include 20.____
   A. stimulants B. alcohol C. nicotine D. caffeine

21. After receiving their monthly assistance payments from the local social services agency, some members of the homeless community immediately use the money to carry out drug transactions. 21.____
In his patrol of the area around the agency, which situation below should Officer Garcia regard as MOST suspicious?
   A. A group of several homeless people who meet every day in a local park, where they sit together for about three hours and then move on
   B. A homeless woman who walks up and down the entire length of a busy city street all day long, endlessly smoking cigarettes
   C. An abandoned car that sits on a privately-owned lot and is used as a sleeping place by several homeless people throughout the day
   D. A single man remaining in the same area for several hours at a time, during which many homeless people approach him and greet him with handshakes

22. The MOST significant factor that requires police to perform functions other than law enforcement is 22.____
   A. greater public trust relative to other agencies or institutions
   B. a broader resource base
   C. round-the-clock availability
   D. the level of police interaction with community members

23. A "minority" group is a group that is discriminated against on the basis of 23.____
   A. physical or cultural characteristics
   B. the size of the group relative to the majority
   C. race
   D. the group's degree of conformity to the norms of the majority

24. An officer is talking with a resident of a high-crime urban neighborhood about a recent increase in drug-related activities. Because of the active police presence in the area, some residents are suspicious of the police. 24.____
Each of the following nonverbal cues is a likely indicator of distrust on the part of a listener, EXCEPT

A. holding arms crossed over one's chest
B. steady eye contact
C. clenched jaw
D. shoulders angled away from speaker

25. Personality characteristics necessary for the successful performance of police duties include 25.____
I. dependent style in problem-solving
II. emotional expressiveness in interpersonal communication
III. cohesiveness in group performance
IV. emotional restraint
The CORRECT answer is:
A. I, III B. I, II, IV C. II, III, IV D. I, II, III, IV

KEY (CORRECT ANSWERS)

1.	B	11.	D
2.	B	12.	D
3.	C	13.	A
4.	C	14.	D
5.	C	15.	B
6.	B	16.	C
7.	B	17.	B
8.	A	18.	D
9.	C	19.	C
10.	A	20.	A

21. D
22. C
23. A
24. B
25. C

EXAMINATION SECTION

TEST 1

DIRECTIONS: Each question or incomplete statement is followed by several suggested answers or completions. Select the one that BEST answers the question or completes the statement. *PRINT THE LETTER OF THE CORRECT ANSWER IN THE SPACE AT THE RIGHT.*

1. Officer Hayes has arrived at the scene of an automobile accident to find the two drivers arguing heatedly in the middle of the intersection, where their two cars remain entangled by their front bumpers. Traffic has backed up on all four sides of the intersection. As Officer Hayes approaches, the two drivers each begin to tell their side of the story at the same time. As they grow more agitated and begin to call each other names, one of the drivers threatens the other with physical harm. 1.____
Officer Hayes' FIRST action should be to
   A. ask each driver to stand on an opposite corner of the intersection and wait for him to begin documenting the accident
   B. call a tow truck to clear the accident from the intersection
   C. arrest the driver who made the threat
   D. ask the drivers to pull their cars out of the intersection and off to the side of the road

2. Probably the MOST important thing a police officer can do to build and strengthen a trusting relationship with community members is to 2.____
   A. patrol the area often and conspicuously
   B. listen to them in a respectful and nonjudgmental way
   C. make sure people understand his background and qualifications
   D. establish clear, reachable goals for improving the community

3. Which of the following is NOT a factor that should influence an officer's exercise of discretion? 3.____
   A. Clear statutes and protocols
   B. Informal expectations of legislatures and the public
   C. Use of force
   D. Limited resources

4. The term for the policing style which emphasizes order maintenance is _____ style. 4.____
   A. service B. coercive C. watchman D. legalistic

5. Officer Torres, a community service law enforcement officer, approaches the home of recent Vietnamese immigrants to speak to several community members gathered there. He notices several pairs of shoes on the front porch. 5.____

It is reasonable for Officer Torres too assume that
A. the people in the home are superstitious
B. the house must have some religious significance
C. if he removes his own shoes before entering, it will be perceived as a sign of respect
D. the homeowners are having their carpets cleaned

6. Ethical issues are 6.____
A. usually a problem only in individual behaviors
B. relevant to all aspects of police work
C. usually referred to a board or committee for decision-making
D. the same as legal issues

7. In using the "reflection of meaning" technique in a client interview, a social worker should do each of the following, EXCEPT 7.____
A. begin with a sentence stem such as "You mean..." or "Sounds like you believe..."
B. offer an interpretation of the client's words
C. add paraphrasing of longer client statements
D. close with a "check-out" such as, "Am I hearing you right?"

8. A police officer is speaking with a victim who is hearing-impaired. The police officer should try to do each of the following, EXCEPT 8.____
A. speak slowly and clearly
B. gradually increase the volume of his voice
C. face the victim squarely
D. reduce or eliminate any background or ambient noise

9. An officer is interviewing a witness who is a recent immigrant from China. In general, the officer should avoid 9.____
A. verbal tracking or requests for clarification
B. open-ended questions
C. sustained eye contact
D. attentive body language

10. Which of the following statements about rape is FALSE? 10.____
A. The use of alcohol and drugs can reduce sexual inhibitions.
B. Rape is a crime of violence.
C. Rape is a crime that can only be committed against women.
D. It is not a sustainable legal charge if the partner has already consented to sex in the past.

11. A person's individual code of ethics is typically determined by each of the following factors, EXCEPT 11.____
A. reason B. religion C. emotion D. law

12. Officer Long, new to the urban precinct where he is assigned patrol, has received a pair of complaints from two customers about the owner of a local convenience store, who works the cash register on most days. According to one customer, the owner became angry and ordered her out of the store after she had asked the price of a certain item. The other customer claims that on another occasion, the owner pulled a handgun from behind the counter and trained it on him as he walked slowly out of the store with his hands up. Each of the customers has lived in the neighborhood for many years and has never before seen or heard of any strange behavior on the owner's part. 12.____
In investigating these complaints, Officer Long should suspect that
   A. the owner should be considered armed and dangerous and any entry into the store should be made with weapons drawn
   B. the cause of the problem is most likely the onset of a serious psychological disturbance
   C. the customers may have reasons to be untruthful about the convenience store owner
   D. the store owner has probably experienced a recent trauma, such as a robber attempt or a personal loss

13. Typical signs and symptoms of stress include 13.____
   I. weakened immune system
   II. prolonged, vivid daydreams
   III. insomnia
   IV. depression
   The CORRECT answer is:
   A. I only
   B. I, III, IV
   C. III, IV
   D. I, II, III, IV

14. Other than solid, ethical police work, an officer's BEST defense against a lawsuit or complaint is usually 14.____
   A. detailed case records
   B. a capable advocate
   C. a vigorous counterclaim against the plaintiff
   D. the testimony of professional character witnesses

15. Assertive people 15.____
   A. avoid stating feelings, opinions, or desires
   B. appear passive, but behave aggressively
   C. state their views and needs directly
   D. appear aggressive, but behave passively

16. In the non-verbal communication process, meaning is MOST commonly provided by 16.____
   A. body language
   B. touch
   C. tone of voice
   D. context

17. The MOST obvious practical benefit that deviance has on a society is the 17.____
   A. advancement of the status quo
   B. vindication of new laws
   C. inducement to reach cultural goals
   D. promotion of social unity

18. What is the term for policing that focuses on providing a wider and more thorough array of social services to defeat the social problems that cause crime? 18.____
    A. Reflecting policing
    B. Order maintenance
    C. Social engineering
    D. Holistic policing

19. The term "active listening" MOSTLY refers to a person's ability to 19.____
    A. both listen and accomplish other tasks at the same time
    B. take an active role in determining which information is provided by the speaker
    C. concentrate on what is being said
    D. indicate with numerous physical cues that he/she is listening

20. Police officers in any jurisdiction are MOST likely to receive calls about 20.____
    A. threats
    B. suspicious persons
    C. petty theft or property crime
    D. disturbances, such as family arguments

21. Which of the following is NOT a physiological explanation for rape? 21.____
    A. Uncontrollable sex drive
    B. Lack of available partners
    C. Reaction to repressed desires
    D. Consequence of the natural selection process

22. Which of the following is an element of self-discipline? 22.____
    A. Establishing and reaching short-term goals
    B. Establishing and reaching long-term goals
    C. Taking an honest look at one's lifestyle and making conscious changes toward improvement
    D. Taking an honest look at one's personality and revealing traits, both good and bad, to others

23. Most of the events in a person's life are the result of 23.____
    A. chance events
    B. a sense of intuition
    C. individual choices and decisions
    D. the decisions of one's parents or other authority figures

24. Which of the following is the MOST effective way for a department to limit the discretion exercised by police officers? 24.____
    A. Open and flexible departmental directives
    B. Close supervision by departmental management
    C. Broadening role definitions for officers
    D. Statutory protection from civil liability lawsuits

25. Police officers who demonstrate critical thinking skills are also more likely to demonstrate each of the following, EXCEPT 25.____
    A. the ability to empathize
    B. the tendency to criticize
    C. self-awareness
    D. reflective thinking

KEY (CORRECT ANSWERS)

1. A
2. B
3. A
4. C
5. C

6. B
7. B
8. B
9. C
10. D

11. D
12. D
13. B
14. A
15. C

16. A
17. D
18. D
19. C
20. D

21. C
22. C
23. C
24. B
25. B

TEST 2

DIRECTIONS: Each question or incomplete statement is followed by several suggested answers or completions. Select the one that BEST answers the question or completes the statement. *PRINT THE LETTER OF THE CORRECT ANSWER IN THE SPACE AT THE RIGHT.*

1. Officer Park responds to a domestic disturbance call to find a mother and her two young children huddled together in the living room, all of them crying. The mother explains that her husband is no longer there; he flew into a fit of rage and then stormed out to join his friends for a night of drinking. 1.____
Officer Park's FIRST action would MOST likely be to
   A. determine the location of the husband
   B. contact the appropriate social services agency to arrange a consultation
   C. try to calm the family down and ask the mother to explain what happened
   D. refer the mother to a local battered-spouse shelter

2. Most commonly, the reason for crimes involving stranger violence is 2.____
   A. anger B. retaliation C. hate D. robbery

3. For a police officer, "burst stress" is MOST likely to be caused by 3.____
   A. a shootout B. financial troubles
   C. departmental politics D. substance abuse

4. The MOST significant factor in whether a person achieves success in his/her personal life, school, and career is 4.____
   A. intelligence B. a positive attitude
   C. existing financial resources D. innate ability

5. Typically, a professional code of ethics 5.____
   A. embodies a broad picture of expected moral conduct
   B. is voluntary
   C. provides specific guidance for performance in situations
   D. are decided by objective ethicists outside of the profession

6. Components recognized by contemporary society as elements of sexual harassment include 6.____
   I. abuse of power II. immature behavior
   III. sexual desire IV. hormonal imbalance
The CORRECT answer is:
   A. I only B. I, III C. II, III D. I, II, III, IV

7. The phrase "substance abuse" is typically defined as 7.____
   A. an addiction to an illegal substance
   B. the continued use of a psychoactive substance even after it creates problems in a person's life
   C. the overuse of an illegal substance
   D. a situation in which a person craves a drug and organizes his or her life around obtaining it

8. The humanist perspective of behavior holds that people who commit crimes or otherwise act badly are 8.____
   A. willfully disregarding societal norms
   B. reacting to the deprivation of basic needs
   C. suffering from a psychological illness
   D. experiencing a moral lapse

9. Which of the following is NOT involved in the process of empathic listening? 9.____
   A. Actually hearing exactly what the other person is saying
   B. Searching for the “hidden meanings” behind statements
   C. Listening without judgment
   D. Communicating that you’re hearing what the other person is saying, both verbally and nonverbally

10. Which of the following is NOT a component in developing a stress-resistant lifestyle? 10.____
   A. Finding leisure time
   B. Eating nutritious foods
   C. Getting enough sleep
   D. Seeking financial independence

11. Which of the following was NOT a factor that led to the expansion of a community policing model? 11.____
   A. Information obtained at a crime scene during a preliminary investigation was the most important factor determining the probability of an arrest.
   B. Police response times typically had little to do with the probability of making an arrest.
   C. Traditional “preventive patrols” generally failed to reduce crime.
   D. People who knew police officers personally often tried to take advantage of them.

12. Most of the correspondence in a pyramid scheme that has defrauded several elderly victims has been traced to a post office box in a rural area. 12.____
   Probably the simplest and most efficient way of arresting the suspect(s) in this case would be to
   A. use an elderly man as a “victim” to lure the suspects into an attempt to defraud him
   B. address a letter to the post office box asking the user to come in for questioning
   C. check Postal Service records to see who is leasing the post office box
   D. physically observe the post office box for a while, to see who is using it

13. The process of hiring a police officer typically involves each of the following, EXCEPT 13.____
   A. technical preparation
   B. medical examination
   C. background checks
   D. physical ability test

14. The MOST common form of rape is _____ rape. 14.____
   A. stranger
   B. acquaintance
   C. sadistic
   D. spousal

15. Officer Stevens and his partner respond to a domestic disturbance call involving a father and his teenage daughter. As the officers arrive at their home, the two are still arguing heatedly, but when the officers enter, the daughter retreats to the kitchen, where she continues crying. The father explains that his wife, the daughter's mother, died last year, and the daughter's behavior and school performance have suffered as a result. The father is afraid that the daughter is falling in with the wrong crowd, and may be getting involved with drugs. He is afraid for her and doesn't know what to do. 15.____
Within the scope of his police role, the MOST appropriate action for Officer Stevens to take in this case would be to
   A. warn both the father and the daughter of the potential consequences of conviction on a charge of disturbing the peace
   B. refer the father and the daughter to a social services or counseling agency
   C. inform the daughter of the drug statutes that may apply in her case as a way to influence her choices
   D. question the daughter about her feelings surrounding the death of her mother

16. During an interview, a suspect confesses to the rape of a co-worker that occurred in the office after the rest of the employees had left for the day. The suspect says he was tormented by the seductive behavior of the co-worker until he could no longer stand it. He was himself a victim, he says. 16.____
In this case, the suspect is making use of the psychological defense mechanism known as
   A. projection B. regression C. denial D. sublimation

17. Which of the following is NOT a good stress-reduction strategy? 17.____
   A. Spend some time each day doing absolutely nothing
   B. Become more assertive
   C. Develop a hobby
   D. Have a sense of humor

18. The term for the policing style which emphasizes problem-solving is _____ style. 18.____
   A. watchman B. order maintenance
   C. service D. legalistic

19. According to current rules and statutes, any employer 19.____
   A. may inquire as to a job applicant's age or date of birth
   B. may keep on file information regarding an employee's race, color, religion, sex, or national origin
   C. may refuse employment to someone without a car
   D. must give a woman who has taken time off for maternity leave her same job and salary when she is read to return to work

20. During a conversation with the mother of a teenage boy who has been arrested twice for shoplifting, an officer attempts to be an active listener as the mother explains why she thinks the boy is having so much trouble. 20.____
Being an active listener includes each of the following strategies, EXCEPT
   A. putting the speaker at ease
   B. interrupting with questions to clarify meaning
   C. summarizing the speaker's major ideas and feelings
   D. withholding criticism

21. Which of the following is NOT a characteristic of the typical poverty-class family? 21.____
   A. Female-headed, single-parent families
   B. Unwed parents
   C. Isolated from neighbors and relatives
   D. High divorce rates

22. When speaking with community members about improving the quality of life in the neighborhood, an officer should look for signs of social desirability bias among the people with whom he's talking. 22.____
Social desirability bias often causes people to
   A. judge other people based on their social role rather than inner character
   B. attribute their successes to skill, while blaming external factors for failures
   C. modify their interactions or behaviors based on what they think is acceptable to others
   D. contend for leadership positions

23. For a number of reasons, Officer Stone thinks a fellow officer might have a drinking problem, and decides to talk to her about it. The officer says she doesn't have a drinking problem; she doesn't even take a drink until after it gets dark. 23.____
Her answer indicates that she
   A. doesn't have a drinking problem
   B. is probably a social drinker
   C. drinks more during the winter months
   D. is in denial

24. Factors which shape the police role include each of the following, EXCEPT 24.____
   A. individual goals
   B. role expectations
   C. role acquisition
   D. multiple-role phenomenon

25. "Deviance" is a social term denoting 25.____
   A. any violation of norms
   B. any serious violation of norms
   C. a type of nonconforming behavior recognizable in all cultures
   D. a specific set of crime statistics

KEY (CORRECT ANSWERS)

1. C
2. D
3. A
4. B
5. A

6. A
7. B
8. B
9. B
10. D

11. D
12. D
13. A
14. B
15. B

16. A
17. A
18. C
19. B
20. B

21. C
22. C
23. D
24. A
25. A

EXAMINATION SECTION

TEST 1

DIRECTIONS: This section contains descriptions of problem situations. Each problem situation has four alternative actions that might be taken to deal with the problem. You are to make two judgments for each problem.

First, decide which alternative you would MOST LIKELY choose in response to the problem. It might not be exactly what you would do in that situation, but it should be the alternative that comes closest to what you would actually do. Record your answers on the answer sheet by writing the appropriate letter next to the prompt for MOST LIKELY.

Second, decide which alternative you would be LEAST LIKELY to choose in that situation. Write the letter of that alternative next to the prompt for LEAST LIKELY.

1. You realize that an error has been made in the documentation of evidence for a case. The amount of the cash reported seized at the scene is now significantly less than when it was originally recorded. You would
   A. go back and talk to everyone who was involved in the chain of custody
   B. immediately tell a supervisor about the problem
   C. consider it a clerical error and try to conceal the discrepancy while you try to figure out how it happened but tell a supervisor if you cannot figure out what happened
   D. consider that the mistake was made when the evidence was seized, and alter the log to reflect the existing amount

   Most likely:______ Least likely:______

2. You are assigned to lead a search for evidence that may have been deposited somewhere within a large tract of woods. The recovery of this evidence is critical to the prosecution of the suspect in the crime. For this task, you are MOST likely to lead by
   A. blazing a trail for others to follow
   B. helping people choose the best course of action
   C. punishing mistakes
   D. appealing to shared goals and values

   Most likely:______ Least likely:______

3. Your partner, who has become your oldest and dearest friend, recently admitted to you that he removed something from the evidence room that might suggest the innocence of a suspect whom he knew without a doubt to be guilty. Your supervisor has discovered that the evidence is missing, and your partner asks you to say that you forgot to log the evidence in. You know that this would easily resolve the situation. You would
   A. not go along with the idea to say the mistake was yours, and tell the supervisor what happened
   B. not go along with the idea, but would say nothing about your partner's admission

C. not go along with the idea, and encourage your partner to own up to what he did
D. go along with your partner; he broke the rules but his intentions were good

Most likely:______ Least likely:______

4. You are having a telephone conversation with a supervisor who is leaving a confidential message to another agent in your office about facts pertaining to an important case. You are on your cellphone, in a public area, surrounded by many unfamiliar people. In order to verify that you have correctly taken the message, you
   A. read the message back to the supervisor
   B. ask the supervisor to call you back later
   C. explain that you will call back when you can find a more private location
   D. ask the supervisor to repeat the message

   Most likely:______ Least likely:______

5. You're in a conversation with someone who has difficulty finding the proper words to say. You
   A. wait for the person to finish, and then offer a restatement of what you think she was trying to say
   B. gladly interrupt and supply the words for her
   C. wait for her to finish, and then ask a series of clarifying questions
   D. interrupt and ask that she take some time to think about it before speaking

   Most likely:______ Least likely:______

6. You are meeting with several other law enforcement officials and community members to determine a course of action for reducing drug trafficking in the area. In order to build a constructive relationship with officials and community members, you
   A. assure the group that you are an expert who has a long record of experience in these matters, and tell them how the problem can be solved
   B. advise them that the solution to the problem can be solved
   C. ask for input from representatives from each group before making suggestions
   D. adopt a completely neutral tone of voice when addressing group members

   Most likely:______ Least likely:______

7. When working in a group, someone raises a question that you've already given a lot of thought. You're not sure, however, about how the question should best be answered. You decide to
   A. speak up, briefly explaining the different alternatives that occurred to you
   B. wait for somebody to mention something that has already occurred to you, and then voice your agreement
   C. advise the group that this is a thorny problem that probably can't be solved
   D. keep quiet and listen to the group's discussion, offering feedback when you think it's appropriate

   Most likely:______ Least likely:______

8. Completely by accident, you notice a significant error in a colleague's report. The report is about to be released to key decision-makers, and you have absolutely no responsibility for the report. You would MOST likely
   A. spread the word about the error to the colleague's co-workers, in the hope that the information makes its way to the report's author
   B. take a mental note of the error and mention it if anyone asks
   C. keep quiet—it's not your responsibility and you don't want to create friction
   D. find the person who wrote the report and point out the mistake

   Most likely:______ Least likely:______

9. A detective who is often nasty to you and your colleagues has compiled an impressive record of success in her investigations; nearly all have led to arrests, and every one of those arrests has ended in conviction. In going over one of the detective's reports, you notice that she has neglected to properly document the chain of custody for a piece of evidence. You aren't that familiar with the case, and don't know how important it is to the case. You have a feeling that the detective will be angry if you point out her mistake. You
   A. do nothing and let her deal with the consequences
   B. pull her aside and tell her about the mistake
   C. tell her you noticed a mistake in her report, and ask her if she is interested in knowing what it is
   D. inform her supervisor and her partner about the mistake

   Most likely:______ Least likely:______

10. A crime was recently committed. You believe that, among the following, the MOST useful interview subject would probably be a(n)
    A. informant B. victim C. suspect D. witness

    Most likely:______ Least likely:______

11. In order to complete a certain task, you need to ask a favor of a colleague whom you don't know very well. The BEST way to do this would be to
    A. ask the colleague briefly for assistance, stating your reasons for asking
    B. ask the colleague and offer to do something for him in return
    C. tell the colleague there will be many intangible rewards associated with his cooperation
    D. explain that one of the ways the colleague can gain favor with his superiors is to cooperate with you

    Most likely:______ Least likely:______

12. A team composed of you and your colleagues encounters a problem similar to one you have encountered when working within another team in the past. Together, you and your team come up with a solution that has the potential for success, even though it is significantly different from the one that worked for you in the past. Your reaction to this new solution is to

A. feel good about the team's originality and go along for the ride on this new plan
B. be concerned about the possibility of failure with the new solution, but accept that there may be more than one way to solve the problem
C. tell them there is a proven way to succeed in solving this problem, and insist that they adopt your solution
D. tell colleagues you're uneasy with the unknowns and variables involved in this new solution, and then urge them to go with your proven success

Most likely:______ Least likely:______

13. You have become so proficient at the documentation/paperwork part of your job that you actually now have some time to spare during work hours. With this extra time, you decide to
A. take initiative and propose a new project to the supervisor
B. see your supervisor and tell him or her you are ready for more work
C. take care of some personal errands that you have been unable to do because of work
D. take some of the pressure off existing work and take more time to complete existing tasks

Most likely:______ Least likely:______

14. Your investigative team is having a disagreement about strategy that has become a heated debate, with members divided nearly equally between two strategic choices. You think both choices have some merit, and don't feel strongly one way or the other about which is selected. You
A. take the side of the group that contains more of your friends and associates
B. calmly wait for them to work out their differences
C. try to figure out which side is more likely to win the argument before taking sides
D. calmly point out the benefits of both plans and suggest a compromise

Most likely:______ Least likely:______

15. You turn the corner at the office one day and spot an agent altering the evidence log, which has been left unattended. Later, you look and see that the entry was for an amount of an illicit substance, and the new entry appears to match the amount that exists in the evidence room. You are not sure how much of the substance was initially collected. You would
A. ask the agent to return the missing evidence and tell him/her that if you see it happen again you will tell your supervisor
B. tell the agent you saw him making the change, and ask him why it was necessary
C. let the matter drop; you don't know that anything untoward occurred, and bringing it up will only result in bad feelings
D. tell other colleagues and try to confront the agent as a group to try to deal with the problem on your own

Most likely:______ Least likely:______

16. In developing a plan for investigating a crime spree that has taken place on both sides of the state line, a team encounters problems in how to coordinate the input of federal and state resources. The FIRST step in solving this problem would be to
    A. gather information
    B. define the problem as completely as possible
    C. envision contingencies
    D. develop a plan for solving the problem

    Most likely:______ Least likely:______

17. Because your work unit has recently become severely understaffed, you are asked to perform a task that you believe is far beneath the skills and capabilities associated with your position. You respond to this request by
    A. performing the task slowly or inadequately before resuming your more important work, in order to insure that you won't be asked again
    B. doing what is asked, but asking a supervisor to make sure these tasks are evenly distributed among co-workers until the unit can be fully staffed
    C. refusing it on the grounds of professional integrity
    D. complying cheerfully and accepting the task as part of a new expanded job description

    Most likely:______ Least likely:______

18. Your supervisor has decided to transfer you to an unfamiliar department as part of an agency restructuring of your organization. The department is in the same building and there will be no changes in compensation or benefits. Your reaction is to be
    A. thrilled at the opportunity to push yourself and learn new skills
    B. not to mind the transfer, because it is likely to teach you something new
    C. entirely neutral, since you won't have to relocate or take a pay cut
    D. disappointed that you will have to change your regular routine

    Most likely:______ Least likely:______

19. Your investigative team has developed a plan for investigating a series of violent crimes that have occurred in the tri-state area. In developing the plan, your team must balance the need to conduct the investigation "by the book" meticulously gathering and documenting a body of evidence and testimony, with the need to catch the criminal before another person becomes a victim. The plan, in attempting to balance these concerns, includes a few procedures that involve certain risks. The team should attempt to minimize the consequences of risk-taking by
    A. keeping the focus on capturing the suspect as soon as possible, and dealing with the consequences as they come
    B. reworking the plan to avoid risk whenever possible
    C. setting aside emotional concerns about victims and assembling an airtight case
    D. planning ahead and preparing for each outcome

    Most likely:______ Least likely:______

20. An informant has come forward to offer information about a crime. You believe it is important to understand the informant's motivation for coming forward, so you ask him about this
    A. when he least expects it
    B. after he has given an account, but before you have asked any questions
    C. at the conclusion of the interview
    D. at the beginning of the interview

    Most likely:______ Least likely:______

21. You are faced with a problem that, try as you might, you're unable to solve. You
    A. ask your most trusted associate
    B. ask for input from several people who you know will have different viewpoints
    C. drop it, hope that it won't become a significant concern, and move on to another task
    D. shift your focus to another problem for a while before giving this problem a fresh look

    Most likely:______ Least likely:______

22. You are interviewing several witnesses to a particularly violent crime that was committed recently. One of the witnesses, an older woman, is so upset that she can barely speak coherently. Her testimony does not seem to make much sense, especially when compared to that of others. In continuing to interview her, you make a mental note to document her emotional state when you write up the interview, because strong emotional responses are likely to affect a person's
    A. prior knowledge
    B. intelligence
    C. perceptions of current reality
    D. reflexes

    Most likely:______ Least likely:______

23. An informant in an ongoing investigation tells you that he resents having to work with you because you have adopted a superior attitude with him and made work unpleasant. The informant is working on the investigation as a condition of a prior court plea. Your BEST response would be to
    A. tell the informant that you are not interested in his opinion of you; he is required to cooperate on the case
    B. try to find out why the offender cannot work with you and tell him that his work is important to the case
    C. consider the informant as rebellious, and inform the court that the terms of his sentencing have been violated
    D. apologize to the offender and tell him you have been under a lot of strain

    Most likely:______ Least likely:______

24. Within a few days, you will meet with supervisors for a scheduled work evaluation. For the review, you will
    A. take the evaluation as it comes and improvise your responses
    B. prepare a list of your accomplishments, skills, and ideas for how to contribute more to the organization

C. assume that your performance will be criticized, and prepare for the attack
D. undertake a little reflection on your failures and successes, but nothing elaborate

Most likely:______ Least likely:______

25. You and your partner are in the middle of a very heated argument about the conduct of an investigation. You normally like your partner and get along very well with her, but you are so furious that you are about to say something very nasty that you know will hurt her feelings. Your MOST likely reaction would be to
A. walk away immediately without saying a word
B. say what is on your mind and sort it out later
C. say that you are too angry to talk right now and give yourself time to calm down
D. leave the room while mumbling the comment in a low voice

Most likely:______ Least likely:______

26. In casual conversation, a person asks you for information about your work as an FBI agent. You should
A. explain that you are not supposed to talk about your responsibilities to outsiders
B. refer the person to the public relations department
C. speak vaguely and give out as few facts as possible
D. be frank and tell the person as much factual information as you can about your general responsibilities

Most likely:______ Least likely:______

27. In the field, you are in an isolated and rural area and find yourself in a situation with circumstances you have never encountered before. You would be MOST likely to use your own judgment
A. when existing policy and rules appear to be unfair in their application
B. when immediate action is necessary and the rules do not cover the situation
C. only if a superior is present
D. whenever a situation is not covered by established rules

Most likely:______ Least likely:______

28. One of your colleagues has gone on vacation and his mother, an elderly woman who lives in another state, has filed a complaint with your office; she thinks she may have been defrauded via an e-mail scam. The case has been assigned to Agent Broom, who works in your office. Your colleague phones you from his vacation and asks if you can find out more about her case. Your reaction is to
A. simply refuse to answer your colleague's questions
B. find the case file and tell the colleague what he wants to know
C. speak to your supervisor, explain the situation and ask for the information that your colleague wants
D. ask the mother if she gives permission for you to find out more from Agent Broom

Most likely:______ Least likely:______

29. When working with team members, you offer what you think is a well-reasoned solution to a problem. Your team members reject it out of hand, saying that it could never work. In a later meeting with mid-level administrators, your supervisor makes the same suggestion. You
    A. say nothing to the supervisor, but later make sure your team members understand that they should be more deferential to your judgment
    B. make sure the supervisor knows you suggested the same solution, but were ignored
    C. feel vindicated by the supervisor's concurrence, but don't feel the need to say anything
    D. demand an apology from your team members for being so closed-minded

    Most likely:______ Least likely:______

30. After your partner conducts an interview with an informant, the informant emerges from the interrogation room with some swelling around his right eye. You are pretty sure the swelling was not present when the informant entered the room. You
    A. do nothing; you can't be certain your partner did anything wrong
    B. immediately report the partner's abuse to a supervisor
    C. ask other agents in the office if anything like this has ever happened before
    D. confront your partner and ask what happened

    Most likely:______ Least likely:______

31. You and another agent in your unit do not get along, to put it mildly. The problem is, you and she have been assigned to direct an investigation together, and in order to have a good outcome, the two of you need to get along. You
    A. realize the destructive potential for run-ins with her, and quietly get yourself assigned to another case
    B. make an effort to be civil, but if she isn't returning the favor, try to keep a low profile and get the work done
    C. take this as a personal challenge and make it your mission to win her over
    D. try to get your supervisors to understand the seriousness of the friction between you, and ask that they reassign her to another case

    Most likely:______ Least likely:______

32. At the end of a busy day at work, you accidentally send an e-mail containing an attachment with some confidential case file information to the wrong person. Which of the following would be the BEST thing to do?
    A. Forget what happened and send the e-mail to the correct person
    B. Leave the office for the day and deal with it tomorrow
    C. Explain to your supervisor what has happened and let her handle the issue
    D. Immediately send another e-mail to the 'wrong' person explaining your mistake

    Most likely:______ Least likely:______

33. A crime has just been committed at a bank, and you arrive at the scene first, before any local law enforcement personnel. Before the police arrive, a handful of bank officials arrive and ask to enter the crime scene. You would
   A. request their cooperation in remaining outside the scene until the area can be properly secured
   B. keep them out by any means necessary
   C. tell them to take it up with the police when they arrive
   D. defer to their wishes

   Most likely:______ Least likely:______

34. You are interviewing the victim of a crime that was committed only about an hour ago. During the course of the interview you try to
   A. maintain a calm and steady demeanor
   B. make sure at least one other agent is present before beginning
   C. get the facts by any means necessary
   D. keep the victim away from others who are familiar to him/her

   Most likely:______ Least likely:______

35. You inherit a large sum of money, and your financial advisor suggests two types of investments. In the first, you invest a moderate, set amount each year, and receive a modest guaranteed payoff at the end of the investment period. The second choice includes a much larger investment (most of your inheritance), but also has a larger potential payoff, with the possibility of losing all your money in an economic downturn. Which type of investment would you choose?
   A. A combination of the two
   B. The first type of investment
   C. The second type of investment
   D. Neither. You wouldn't risk your savings on investments.

   Most likely:______ Least likely:______

36. You and your partner are working on a complex project that demands a great deal of effort from both of you. Your partner is frequently absent as a result of burnout and stress from his personal problems. You do not know much about the circumstances, nor have you known him for long. Your partner contributes very little to the project, and, as a result, you are putting in an excessive amount of overtime in order to keep the project moving ahead. You feel that your health may begin to suffer if you continue to work this many hours. You handle this situation by
   A. raising the issue with your supervisor and request additional help to ensure that the project is completed on schedule
   B. offering to help your partner deal with his personal problems
   C. continuing to put in overtime to keep the project moving ahead
   D. meeting with your partner to request that he does his share of the work

   Most likely:______ Least likely:______

37. For the first time, you are assigned the lead on a case. You oversee a team of about five people. Your supervisor has assigned you a fairly clear-cut case, and in the end, despite a few logistical and technical problems, you and your team wrap things up fairly quickly. After a speedy conviction, you meet with a group of three supervisors, who congratulate you on your success. They then launch a critique of your leadership of the case that, while pointing out your strengths as a leader, can only be interpreted as somewhat unfavorable, given the team's logistical and technical problems. Most likely, your reaction is to feel that
    A. it probably would not be a good idea for you to assume leadership of a more difficult case in the future
    B. you should keep this critique in mind the next time you take charge of a team
    C. the bottom line is that the case resulted in a conviction, and this is the only measure that really matters
    D. the members of your team really let you down with their mistakes

    Most likely:______ Least likely:______

38. You and another agent are conducting an investigation together. You have noticed that the other agent is taking some shortcuts as he collects evidence and obtains statements from the victims and witnesses. These shortcuts are reducing the quality of the investigation. You would MOST likely
    A. point out to the trooper the impact his shortcuts will have on the traffic investigation
    B. notify your supervisor of the shortcuts being taken by the other agent
    C. go back and redo those aspects of the investigation on which the agent has taken shortcuts
    D. ignore the agent's work performance, since it is not your responsibility to monitor his performance

    Most likely:______ Least likely:______

39. During a meeting, you and a group of supervisors are discussing your performance on a recently completed project. Using a list of objective criteria, the supervisors explain where you performed most successfully. They then shift their focus to areas in which your performance fell short of the standards. Your reaction is to
    A. launch a vigorous defense of your performance and explain why you think the standards are not appropriate in your case
    B. listen carefully, ask for clarification when necessary, and then discuss with them why these shortcomings occurred
    C. tell them you are very sorry and promise to do better in the future
    D. explain that you did your best and are skeptical that any of them could have done better, given the circumstances

    Most likely:______ Least likely:______

40. While you are conducting an investigation at a crime scene, a citizen walks past you and makes a demeaning and derogatory comment about your law enforcement responsibilities. You would MOST likely

A. ask the person to come back and explain why he made such a comment
B. ask the person to show you some identification, so that you can take his name down in case of further trouble
C. ignore the comment and continue with your work
D. confront the individual and demand an apology for the comment

Most likely:______ Least likely:______

41. You are working on a case under the direct supervision of a regional supervisor. In your opinion, she has her mind set on a plan that is mediocre, uninspired, and likely to meet only a minimal set of objectives. She is happy with having finally made a decision, wants to finalize, and makes a point of telling you not to try to talk her out of her plan. You think the plan is a waste of resources and perhaps even a mistake, even though most of your colleagues have already told you to let it go. How would you deal with the situation?
   A. Quietly work to get transferred to another project
   B. Tell the supervisor that she is making a mistake, and try to convince her to change her mind
   C. Resist the temptation to try changing her mind
   D. Ask if she is certain she doesn't want to think it over one last time

   Most likely:______ Least likely:______

42. When interviewing a potential witness, you notice that she has a tendency to wander off the subject and talk about herself and her family for expended intervals. When you ask her where she was at about noon the day before yesterday, she launches into a long description of her normal daily routine. You respond by
   A. telling her sternly that your time is limited and you would like her to stick to answering your questions
   B. waiting for a pauses in her speech during which you can politely steer the conversation back toward her whereabouts yesterday at noon
   C. cutting her off and repeating the question, as if she hadn't been speaking at all
   D. letting her "talk herself out" and then repeating the question, this time in a more closed-ended format

   Most likely:______ Least likely:______

43. You are the leader of an investigative team, and wonder about the role of praise in the team's success. As the leader, your philosophy about praise is that it
   A. can improve performance if it is given when it is most appropriate
   B. should almost always be withheld in order to make team members understand there is always room for improvement
   C. should be given sparely, and reserved for truly exceptional achievements
   D. should be given to team members even, and perhaps especially, when they perform poorly, in order to boost their self-esteem

   Most likely:______ Least likely:______

44. You are assigned to an investigation with Agent Stark, who is known to be somewhat inattentive to detail. His mistakes or omissions have resulted in at least one case dismissal that you know of. Throughout the course of the investigation, you
   A. make it a point to be involved in every aspect of the investigation, accompanying Agent Stark on every interview, and insisting on collaboration in written work
   B. leave Agent Stark mostly alone, and then go back and make corrections to his work and documentation when they are necessary
   C. work to block Agent Stark's access to important witnesses, evidence, and case files, thereby minimizing the harm he is likely to do
   D. document every one of Agent Stark's missteps and report them to your superiors as they occur, in order to avoid jeopardizing the case

   Most likely:______ Least likely:______

45. An interview has strayed far beyond what you had intended. To redirect the subject's response, you say
   A. "I'm interested in what you were saying a few minutes ago. Can you tell me more about it?"
   B. "Why are we talking about this?"
   C. "Let me ask the rest of the questions I need answered, then we can talk."
   D. "This is interesting, but it isn't related to the business of this interview."

   Most likely:______ Least likely:______

46. You have been asked to recruit a new detective to come work for your regional office. She is an up-and-coming star with a lot of potential, and you and your supervisor both feel she would be a good fit for your office. Unfortunately, despite your best efforts, she ends up seeking and receiving an assignment elsewhere. You later find out through your supervisor that you came off as seeming a little too aggressive and desperate. Your supervisor offers you some suggestions for how to handle this situation if it ever comes up again. Your reaction is to think that
   A. putting you in charge of the detective's recruitment was a terrible idea to begin with
   B. the detective's choice was her own loss; you made it clear that your office had the most to offer
   C. you wish there was some way you could make it up to your supervisor
   D. maybe you did come on too strong and should re-examine your methods

   Most likely:______ Least likely:______

47. You have become aware that a colleague, who is nearing retirement and now working only part-time for the bureau, has been using office phone and tax facilities to run his own private investigation business. You think that he may have been warned about this once before and that he promised to stop. You have just found a fax for his business placed in your mailbox by mistake. You would MOST likely
   A. Put the fax in your colleague's mailbox without saying anything to anyone
   B. Politely inform your colleague that you will tell your supervisor the next time you catch him using agency resources for his own private business.

C. Put the fax in your supervisor's mailbox without saying anything to anyone
D. Give the fax to your co-worker and remind her that office equipment is not supposed to be used for personal use.

48. You are working on a case with a detective in another regional office who has, once again, rescheduled your meeting appointment at the last minute. Apparently, he left a last-minute message for you this time, but you didn't get it because you were already on your way. This is not the first time you have canceled prior engagements to accommodate his schedule. Each time you have been inconvenienced and very irritated, but this is a very important case and he is a good detective when he is at work. How do you react to this person?
A. Tell the detective it is disrespectful and inconvenient when he makes last-minute changes to your schedule
B Don't let on that you are irritated, but ask the detective to give you longer notice the next time he has to cancel.
C. Maintain a cold professionalism when rescheduling the appointment
D. Don't let on that you are irritated, but make a point to subject the detective to a few last-minute cancellations of his own, so he'll know how it feels

Most likely:______ Least likely:______

49. A pharmacist has complained to the police department that several drug addicts in his neighborhood have been attempting to obtain drugs illegally, often by passing fake prescriptions. Based only on this information during a stakeout of the prescription counter, you would be MOST likely to find suspicious
A. a young African-American male in a hooded sweatshirt on a hot day
B. a woman in her thirties who glances around furtively and brings a large amount of nonprescription items to the counter for purchase
C. a middle-aged man who appears homeless and is poorly groomed
D. none of the above should be regarded as suspicious on the basis of their appearance alone

Most likely:______ Least likely:______

50. At a work meeting, your supervisor mentions an interesting new assignment that has not been assigned yet. It sounds like something you could handle, though it would be demanding. You
A. grow increasingly nervous about the possibility that you would be assigned the job
B. immediately volunteer to handle the project yourself
C. tell the supervisor that you would be willing to take it on, but ask if it might be possible to delegate some of your current workload
D. tell the supervisor that you would be willing to take it on, but only if you receive a raise in pay

Most likely:______ Least likely:______

SITUATIONAL JUDGMENT
KEY TO EXERCISES

NOTE: While a few situations in the examination have one choice that is clearly better or worse than the others, some have two or even three choices that would be equally as good or bad as the rest. The key that follows should be taken as a rough guideline and not a definitive formula for success on the test. The answers below reflect the fact that the situational judgment test is designed to measure your:

- Ability to Organize, Plan, and Prioritize
- Ability to Relate Effectively with Others
- Ability to Maintain a Positive Image
- Ability to Evaluate Information and Make Judgment Decisions
- Ability to Adapt to Changing Situations Integrity

1. Most Likely: B; Least Likely: D
2. Most Likely: D, Least Likely: C
3. Most Likely: A or C; Least Likely: D
4. Most Likely: D; Least Likely: A
5. Most Likely: A or C; Least Likely: D

6. Most Likely: C; Least Likely; A or B
7. Most Likely: A; Least Likely: C
8. Most Likely: D; Least Likely: C
9. Most Likely: B; Least Likely: A
10. Most Likely: D; Least Likely: C

11. Most Likely: A; Least Likely: D
12. Most Likely: B; Least Likely: C
13. Most Likely: B; Least Likely: C or D
14. Most Likely: D; Least Likely: A, B, or C
15. Most Likely: B; Least Likely: A

16. Most Likely: B; Least Likely: A, C, or D
17. Most Likely: B; Least Likely: C
18. Most Likely: B; Least Likely: D
19. Most Likely: D; Least Likely: A, B, or C
20. Most Likely: C; Least Likely: A, B, or D

21. Most Likely: B; Least Likely: C
22. Most Likely: C; Least Likely: A, B, or D
23. Most Likely: B; Least Likely: C
24. Most Likely: B; Least Likely: C
25. Most Likely: C; Least Likely: B

26. Most Likely: D; Least Likely: A
27. Most Likely: B; Least Likely: D
28. Most Likely: C; Least Likely: A
29. Most Likely: C; Least Likely: D
30. Most Likely: D; Least Likely: A

31. Most Likely: C; Least Likely: A or D
32. Most Likely: C; Least Likely: A
33. Most Likely: A; Least Likely: B, C, or D
34. Most Likely: A; Least Likely: C or D
35. Most Likely: A; Least Likely: D

36. Most Likely: A; Least Likely: C
37. Most Likely: B; Least Likely: A, C, or D
38. Most Likely: A; Least Likely: D
39. Most Likely: B; Least Likely: C or D
40. Most Likely: C; Least Likely: A, B, or D

41. Most Likely: D; Least Likely: A
42. Most Likely: B; Least Likely: A
43. Most Likely: A; Least Likely: B or D
44. Most Likely: A; Least Likely: C
45. Most Likely: A; Least Likely: B

46. Most Likely: D; Least Likely: A or B
47. Most Likely: D; Least Likely: A
48. Most Likely: B; Least Likely: D
49. Most Likely: D; Least Likely: A, B, or C
50. Most Likely: C; Least Likely: A or D

EXAMINATION SECTION

TEST 1

DIRECTIONS: Each question or incomplete statement is followed by several suggested answers or completions. Select the one that BEST answers the question or completes the statement. *PRINT THE LETTER OF THE CORRECT ANSWER IN THE SPACE AT THE RIGHT.*

1. While a police officer is on his way to report for an urgent assignment at a fire in a school during school hours, he sees several teenage boys fighting. Under these circumstances, the BEST procedure for him to follow at this time is to 1.____
   A. find the police officer assigned to duty in the area and let him handle the situation
   B. telephone the station house to send someone to stop the fight
   C. ignore the fight
   D. stop the fight since it is his duty as a police officer to see that order is preserved on a public thoroughfare

2. There has been a series of burglaries on a street containing many small stores. A police officer has been assigned to select a store on this street in which to wait in hiding for an attempt to burglarize the store and thereby trap the burglars in the act. Of the following, the BEST store to be selected for this purpose would be the one 2.____
   A. which is operated by an elderly widower who keeps it open long past usual business hours
   B. which is larger and more expensive looking than the others
   C. whose owner reports that suspicious-looking people have been loitering nearby
   D. which was recently burglarized and from which $2,000 worth of clothing was taken

3. While investigating the theft of a new bicycle from a retail store, a police officer discovers that the bicycle is in the possession of a boy who appears heartbroken at the prospect of losing it. The FIRST action for the police officer to take is to 3.____
   A. return the bicycle to the storekeeper and asks him to withdraw the charge
   B. tell the boy he can keep the bicycle until it is needed as evidence
   C. arrest the boy since he probably stole the bicycle
   D. ask the boy how he got the bicycle

4. While on patrol of his post, a police officer discovers a man wandering about in a dazed manner, talking to himself, and making peculiar gestures. He seems to be mentally ill and is unable to answer any questions in a sensible manner. The station house is nearby. 4.____

For the police officer to take him to the station house would be
A. *undesirable*; it is always quicker to summon an ambulance
B. *desirable*; at the station house he may be kept from harm or harming others until he can be taken to a hospital
C. *undesirable*; the man has committed no crime
D. *desirable*; the police officer can question the man in private to determine his sanity

5. There is an old abandoned house in a run-down area on one of the streets of your patrol post. Late at night, you notice several suspicious-looking people entering the house from the rear. 5.____
Of the following, the BEST course of action for you to take FIRST is to
A. inquire of the neighbors as to any suspicious occurrences
B. get to the nearest telephone and call your superior officer at once for assistance
C. continue on patrol since you do not know that a crime has been committed
D. attempt to observe what is going on in the house

6. Police officers are instructed to give particular attention at night to all automobiles in business districts moving at a slow rate through the streets or parking with the motor running. 6.____
Of the following, the MOST likely reason for this order is that
A. the ownership of suspicious cars can be confirmed
B. some store robberies may be prevented
C. dangerous weapons may be discovered
D. traffic accidents may be averted

7. The police often follow the practice of returning a suspect to the scene of the crime. 7.____
Of the following, the LEAST valid reason for this action is that the
A. suspect may more readily be able to remember certain events
B. psychological effect on the suspect may produce additional valuable evidence
C. suspect may be more readily confronted by witnesses to the crime
D. statements made by the suspect may be clarified

8. When assigned to keep crowds in order at the scene of a fire, police officers are instructed to be alert for persons showing extreme interest in the progress of the fire. 8.____
Of the following, the MOST probable purpose of this instruction is to
A. make certain that another fire is not started
B. detect the person who may have caused the fire
C. obtain the services of experts who can assist in stopping the fire
D. enroll interested persons in the Civil Defense volunteer fire organization

9. While patrolling his regular post, a police officer observes a storekeeper sweeping the sidewalk in front of his store and pushing the refuse into the roadway. This is the first time it has happened. This practice is forbidden by law. 9.____
Of the following, the BEST course of action for the police officer to follow is to
   A. warn the shopkeeper that he is violating the law
   B. ignore the storekeeper's action since this is a relatively minor offense
   C. arrest the storekeeper
   D. report the storekeeper to the Department of Sanitation

10. A man who has a history of several previous convictions for burglary is a suspect in a recent case of burglary. 10.____
In examining a file on this person, the one of the following items which would be of LEAST value as an indication as to whether this suspect is likely to have committed this particular crime is a
   A. description of his usual method of breaking into a building
   B. list of members of the suspect's family who have criminal records
   C. statement of the time of the day or night during which he generally operates
   D. listing of the tools he favors using

11. Investigation of a reported theft from a private house reveals that part of the missing property consisted of some very heavy articles. 11.____
Of the following, the MOST valid conclusion that may be made from this fact is that
   A. the stolen property was most likely carried away in a truck
   B. footprints will surely be found on the walk leading to the front or back door
   C. the stolen merchandise is probably nearby
   D. more than one person was probably involved

12. Police officers assigned to foot patrol shall proceed directly to their own posts so as to arrive there at the time designated. The practice of congregating in one area of the precinct preparatory to going to their posts shall cease. 12.____
Of the following, the BEST reason for this order is to
   A. aid the supervisors in checking attendance at assigned posts
   B. avoid having too many men cover nearby posts while distant posts are neglected
   C. have the police officers on duty at their posts without undue delay
   D. have police officers while on the way to their posts observe conditions in the precinct

13. It is sometimes necessary for police officers to be assigned in the vicinity of a factory where employees are on strike. These assignments are in addition to police assignments at the factory itself. 13.____
Of the following, the MOST valid reason for this precaution is that
   A. picket lines are illegal
   B. factory employees may meet and conduct their union activity on the street

C. disorder may occur between strikers and non-strikers at other places in the neighborhood
D. the employees probably live in the neighborhood of the factory

14. A fugitive from the police in a serious crime is known to be suffering from an illness which requires constant treatment and medication. 14.____
Of the following, the BEST means of utilizing this fact in attempting to find the fugitive would be to
A. check drugstores in the business sections of the city where he is thought to be living
B. contact hospitals, clinics, and doctors in the city where he is thought to be living
C. search the homes of relatives and friends for poisonous drugs
D. station a police officer directly outside of each drugstore, hospital, clinic, and doctor's office in the city where he is thought to be living

15. It is customary for the police to keep records of lost or stolen automobile license plates. 15.____
Of the following, the BEST reason for this practice is to
A. permit the prompt issuance of new plates
B. keep a record of all outstanding license plates in use
C. prevent cars from being stolen
D. capture or detain any person found using or attempting to use any of these plates

16. A police officer on duty observes a blind man going through the cars of a subway train playing a saxophone and soliciting money in violation of the law. 16.____
Of the following, the BEST course of action for the police officer to take is to
A. permit the blind man to continue since it is his means of livelihood
B. warn the blind man that he is not permitted to solicit on the transit system
C. inform the blind man that he must register with a recognized social agency caring for blind persons
D. escort the blind man to his home and leave him there

17. While a police officer is on duty in a crowded subway station, a woman runs up to him and complains that a man, still standing nearby on the station, has just pushed her so that she fell down and was injured. 17.____
Of the following, the FIRST thing for the police officer to do is to
A. ask the man to produce some form of identification
B. urge the woman to overlook the incident since the subways are so crowded
C. question the woman to determine if the pushing was deliberate
D. arrest the man

18. While a police officer is on post in a busy subway station, the clerk in the change booth calls him to eject two disorderly teenagers from the area near the change booth. These teenagers use this station every day, and this is one of a series of undesirable activities on their part. 18.____

Of the following, the MOST important concern of the police officer in such a situation is to

A. administer sufficient punishment to make sure they will not do the same thing again
B. record the identity of the teenagers so that preventive action may be taken
C. avoid damaging transit system property
D. be certain not to cause any injury to the teenagers

19. While on duty on a subway platform, a police officer is stopped by a passenger who asks for some travel directions. The man is drunk and has caused a few people to gather. 19.____
Of the following, the BEST action for the police officer to take is to

A. give the directions to one of the bystanders so that the bystander may help the man get the proper train and then continue with his duties
B. ignore the man since he is incapable of understanding directions
C. arrest the man since he may create a disturbance
D. place the man on the proper train in the same car as the conductor if possible

20. It is the practice in the transit system to place lost property in bags provided for this purpose and also to give a receipt to the employee or other person who has turned in the property. 20.____
Of the following, the BEST reason for this procedure is to

A. prevent breakage of glass items and check on employee honesty
B. keep the items in good condition and protect the claim of the finder if the owner does not appear
C. safeguard valuables from being stolen and prevent any accidental damage
D. record the names of employees who may be rewarded for their honesty

21. Generally, before making an arrest for a serious crime, the police officer must have facts to provide a reasonable basis for believing the person to be guilty. 21.____
The BEST reason for this rule is to

A. reduce the number of arrests
B. protect himself against being charged with false arrest
C. safeguard the rights of citizens against improper arrest
D. place the burden of disproving the charges upon the accused

22. A police officer is on patrol in an area on a weekday evening and hears many small explosions of firecrackers coming from various directions. The sale, storage, or use of firecrackers is forbidden. 22.____
Under these circumstances, the BEST course of action for the police officer to take is to

A. attempt to find out where the firecrackers are sold
B. arrest the first boy seen lighting firecracker since he has violated the law
C. make no note in his memo book until he actually sees firecrackers being exploded
D. investigate all reports of injuries to see if any were caused by firecrackers

23. As a police officer, you are taking a person under arrest to the station house. While so doing, an influential friend of the prisoner stops you and asks you to release the prisoner. 23.____
Of the following, the MOST desirable course of action for you to take is to
A. ask the friend if he will be personally responsible for the conduct of the prisoner and, if so, let the prisoner go with his friend
B. explain the reason for the arrest so that the friend can realize it is warranted
C. arrest the friend of the prisoner for interfering with the performance of a police officer's duty
D. inform the friend that this is a police matter and proceed with your duty

24. During a riot, it is the practice of the police to take the leaders into custody as soon as possible. 24.____
Of the following, the MOST valid reason for this practice is that it will
A. arrest suspects in order of their importance
B. remove the leaders from the scene so that the rioting may cease sooner
C. punish the leaders more than other rioters which is fair since they started the riot
D. obtain valuable information from the leaders

25. While you are on patrol duty, a woman excitedly complains to you that her purse has been snatched by three boys wearing black leather jackets and dungarees. Later you observe three boys in such clothing. As you approach them, one boy runs away. 25.____
Of the following, the BEST course of action for you to take is to
A. shoot at the fleeing boy since flight indicates he is probably guilty of snatching the purse
B. fire a warning shot to try to halt the fleeing boy; and if this fails, chase after him
C. question the two boys who remained
D. run after the fleeing boy and attempt to overtake him

26. While on patrol of his post, a police officer receives a report that a car has suddenly backed onto a sidewalk and seriously injured an elderly man. Upon arriving at the scene, he finds that a large crowd has gathered. The driver of the car is slumped over the wheel in a state of shock. An ambulance has been summoned for the injured man. 26.____
Of the following, the BEST action for the police officer to take next is to
A. order the crowd to disperse
B. ask someone to assist him in moving the injured elderly man into a nearby store
C. ask the driver about the accident
D. move the car off the sidewalk into the roadway

27. A police officer on duty observes that a window of one of the stores is defaced with indecent and anti-religious remarks written on it. A group of teenage youths is standing nearby. 27.____

Of the following, the BEST course of action for the police officer to take is to

A. explain to the youths the need for tolerance and understanding among the various groups in the community
B. arrest the leader of the group for defacing property
C. question the youths to determine if they did it or if they saw anyone do it
D. ask a fellow officer to assist in bringing all the youths to the station house

28. Many authorities in the field of juvenile delinquency accept youth gangs as a natural development in the community. 28.____
If this is correct, the one of the following which is MOST desirable is to attempt to

A. encourage younger members of gangs to break away
B. set up an interesting lecture course on the evils of gang warfare
C. channel gang activity into worthwhile areas
D. secure legislation making gang activity illegal

29. An officer conducting an investigation usually avoids expressing his personal opinions on politics or morals when he is interviewing anyone in connection with the investigation. 29.____
The BEST reason for this policy is that

A. discussions of politics frequently lead to argument
B. the officer's opinions may influence the information offered by the person being interviewed
C. the interviews will take less time since the officer will be more likely to stick to the facts
D. public employees should have no opinions on politics or morals

30. The MOST important factor for you to consider in using information which you have received from a certain person as a basis for further investigation is the 30.____

A. availability of the person for further questioning
B. expense involved in finding the person
C. arrest record of the person
D. value of the information as related to the case in question

31. An important feature of the modern concept of patrol is to have available an officer whose general location is known to the residents of the area. 31.____
The one of the following which is likely to be an IMPORTANT reason for this feature of patrol is to

A. be able to summon an officer quickly in case of emergency
B. rotate assignments so that each officer will become familiar with the police problems of the post
C. prevent undesirable incidents from developing and occurring
D. insure that all areas in and about the precinct are adequately protected

32. A police officer has arrested a man for attempted robbery. 32.____
Before taking him to the nearest police station, the FIRST precaution for the police officer to take is to
   A. check the man's identification
   B. return any stolen articles found in the man's possession
   C. determine if the man has a criminal record
   D. see that the man is unarmed

33. A police officer, off duty and going home from work at night, observes three suspicious men loitering near a supermarket that is closed. He stops for a while to watch, unseen by them. Two of the men enter the store and open the wall safe. 33.____
Of the following, the BEST course of action for the police officer to take is to
   A. draw his gun, enter the store, and fire at the two men
   B. ignore the incident since he is off duty
   C. wait until the two men come out, draw his gun, and prepare to arrest all three
   D. ask the man who remained outside if any of them is an employee of the store

34. A police officer is investigating a complaint that a man is brandishing a gun in the rear of a restaurant at a time when customers are present. 34.____
Of the following, the BEST reason for the police officer to exercise caution as he enters is that
   A. the man may open fire without warning and injure others
   B. a police officer should not expose himself to risk which endangers him
   C. the man may injure himself
   D there may be a second exit from the room

35. Police officers have been ordered to be on the alert for a man who has recently committed a series of robberies. The victims have described the man as being white, of medium height and weight, wearing a black leather jacket and a cap, and having the lower part of his face covered. While on patrol, you observe a man of medium height, wearing a black leather jacket. 35.____
Of the following, the one which is the BEST reason for questioning this man is that he
   A. has his hands in his pockets
   B. is fat
   C. has a scar on the lower part of his cheek
   D. has just driven up in a new car

36. The officer who investigates accidents is always required to make a complete and accurate rate report. 36.____
Of the following, the BEST reason for this procedure is to
   A. protect the operating agency against possible false claims
   B. provide a file of incidents which can be used as basic material for an accident prevention campaign

C. provide the management with concrete evidence of violations of the rules by employees
D. indicate what repairs need to be made

37. It is suggested that an officer keep all persons away from the area of an accident until an investigation has been completed. 37.____
This suggested procedure is
A. *good*; witnesses will be more likely to agree on a single story
B. *bad*; such action blocks traffic flow and causes congestion
C. *good*; objects of possible use as evidence will be protected from damage or loss
D. *bad*; the flow of normal pedestrian traffic provides an opportunity for an investigator to determine the cause of the accident

38. An officer receives instructions from his supervisor which he does not fully understand. 38.____
For the officer to ask for a further explanation would be
A. *good*, chiefly because his supervisor will be impressed with his interest in his work
B. *poor*, chiefly because the time of the supervisor will be needlessly wasted
C. *good*, chiefly because proper performance depends on full understanding of the work to be done
D. *poor*, chiefly because officers should be able to think for themselves

39. A person is making a complaint to an officer which seems unreasonable and of little importance. 39.____
Of the following, the BEST action for the officer to take is to
A. criticize the person making the complaint for taking up his valuable time
B. laugh over the matter to show that the complaint is minor and silly
C. tell the person that anyone responsible for his grievance will be prosecuted
D. listen to the person making the complaint and tell him that the matter will be investigated

40. A member of the department shall not indulge in intoxicating liquor while in uniform. A member of the department not required to wear a uniform and a uniformed member while out of uniform shall not indulge in intoxicants to an extent unfitting him for duty. 40.____
Of the following, the MOST correct interpretation of this rule is that a
A. member, off duty, not in uniform, may drink intoxicating liquor
B. member, not on duty, but in uniform, may drink intoxicating liquor
C. member, on duty, in uniform, may drink intoxicants
D. uniformed member, in civilian clothes, may not drink intoxicants

Questions 41-65.

DIRECTIONS: In each of Questions 41 through 65, select the lettered word or phrase which means MOST NEARLY the same as the word in capital letters. Place the letter which corresponds to your choice in the space at the right.

41. INTERROGATE 41.____
A. question B. arrest C. search D. rebuff

42. PERVERSE 42.____
A. manageable B. poetic C. contrary D. patient

43. ADVOCATE 43.____
A. champion B. employ C. select D. advise

44. APPARENT 44.____
A. desirable B. clear C. partial D. possible

45. INSINUATE 45.____
A. survey B. strengthen C. suggest D. insist

46. MOMENTOUS 46.____
A. important B. immediate C. delayed D. short

47. AUXILIARY 47.____
A. exciting B. assisting C. upsetting D. available

48. ADMONISH 48.____
A. praise B. increase C. warn D. polish

49. ANTICIPATE 49.____
A. agree B. expect C. conceal D. approve

50. APPREHEND 50.____
A. confuse B. sentence C. release D. seize

51. CLEMENCY 51.____
A. silence B. freedom C. mercy D. severity

52. THWART 52.____
A. enrage B. strike C. choke D. block

53. RELINQUISH 53.____
A. stretch B. give up C. weaken D. flee from

54. CURTAIL 54.____
A. stop B. reduce C. repair D. insult

55. INACCESSIBLE 55.____
A. obstinate B. unreachable
C. unreasonable D. puzzling

56. PERTINENT 56.____
A. related B. saucy C. durable D. impatient

57. INTIMIDATE 57.____
A. encourage B. hunt C. beat D. frighten

58. INTEGRITY 58.____
A. honesty B. wisdom
C. understanding D. persistence

59. UTILIZE 59.____
A. use B. manufacture
C. help D. include

60. SUPPLEMENT 60.____
A. regulate B. demand C. add D. answer

61. INDISPENSABLE 61.____
A. essential B. neglected C. truthful D. unnecessary

62. ATTAIN 62.____
A. introduce B. spoil C. achieve D. study

63. PRECEDE 63.____
A. break away B. go ahead C. begin D. come before

64. HAZARD 64.____
A. penalty B. adventure C. handicap D. danger

65. DETRIMENTAL 65.____
A. uncertain B. harmful C fierce D. horrible

Questions 66-70.

DIRECTIONS: Questions 66 through 70 are to be answered on the basis of the information given in the table below. The numbers which have been omitted can be calculated from the other numbers which are given.

NUMBER OF VEHICLE ACCIDENTS IN GREAT CITY
FOR THE PERIOD 2015 TO 2020

COUNTY	2015	2016	2017	2018	2019	2020	TOTAL
A	8,141	8,680	8,554	8,213	8,822	8,753	?
B	3,301	3,836	3,623	4,108	4,172	3,735	22,775
C	6,480	7,562	7,275	7,872	8,554	8,341	46,084
D	3,366	3,801	3,715	3,740	4,473	4,390	23,485
E	259	272	9	252	255	457	1,741
TOTAL	21,547	24,151	23,413	24,185	26,276	25,676	145,248

66. For the total period covered by the table, the average number of vehicle accidents per year in County A exceeded the average number per year in County D by approximately 66.____
   A. 4,550 B. 5,450 C. 8,520 D. 27,000

67. In comparing the years 2019 and 2020, the one of the following statements which is MOST accurate is that the 67.____
   A. number of accidents in County E and County B combined increased
   B. number of accidents decreased in each of the five counties
   C. number of accidents in County D and County E combined increased
   D. decrease in the number of accidents in County C amounted to more than one-half of the decrease in the total number of accidents for the entire city

68. The percentage increase in 2020 over 2015 in vehicle accidents was LARGEST in County 68.____
   A. A B. B C. C D. E

69. If the counties are ranked for each year according to the number of accidents (largest number to rank first), a county which will NOT have the same rank each year is County 69.____
   A. A B. D C. C D. E

70. The LARGEST increase in the number of vehicle accidents from any one year to the next was in County 70.____
   A. C B. B C. A D. D

71. During the first nine months of 2020, an officer spent an average of $270 a month. In October and November, he spent an average of $315 a month. In December, he spent $385. 71.____
   His average monthly spending during the year was MOST NEARLY
   A. $254 B. $287 C. $323 D. $3,000

72. In 2018 there were 8,270 arrests in a certain city. In 2019 the number of arrests increased by 12½%. In 2020 the number of arrests decreased 5% from the 2019 figures. 72.____
   The number of arrests in 2020 was MOST NEARLY
   A. 8,840 B. 9,770 C. 6,870 D. 7,600

73. Assume that parking space is to be provided for 25% of the tenants in a new housing development. The project will have five 6-story buildings, having seven tenants on each floor, and eight 11-story buildings, having eight tenants on each floor. 73.____
   The number of parking spaces needed is MOST NEARLY
   A. 215 B. 230 C. 700 D. 895

74. A stolen vehicle traveling at 60 miles per hour passes by a police car, which is standing still with the engine running. The police car immediately starts out in pursuit, and one minute later, having covered a distance of half a mile, it reaches a speed of 90 miles per hour and continues at this speed. 74.____

In how many minutes after the stolen vehicle passes the police car will the police car overtake it? _____ minute(s)

A. 1 B. 1½ C. 2 D. 3

75. A police officer found his 42-hour work week was divided as follows: 1/6 of his time in investigating incidents on his patrol post, 1/2 of his time patrolling his post, and 1/8 of his time in special traffic duty. The rest of his time was devoted to assignments at precinct headquarters. 75._____
The percentage of his work week which was spent at precinct headquarters is MOST NEARLY

A 10% B. 15% C. 20% D. 25%

76. In 2020, the Department of Sanitation towed away 8,430 cars which were abandoned or illegally parked on city streets. 76._____
If the value of the abandoned cars was $1,038,200 and that of the illegally parked cars was $6,234,800, then the average value of one of the towed away cars was MOST NEARLY

A. $400 B. $720 C. $860 D. $1,100

77. Two percent of all school children are problem children. Some 80% of these problem children become delinquents, and about 80% of the delinquent children become criminals. 77._____
If the school population is 1,000,000 children, the number of this group who will eventually become criminals, according to this analysis, is

A. 12,800 B. 1,280 C. 640 D. 128

78. A patrol car began a trip with 12 gallons of gasoline in the tank and ended with 7½ gallons. The car traveled 17.3 miles for each gallon of gasoline. During the trip, gasoline was bought for $23.20 at a cost of $2.90 per gallon. 78._____
The total number of miles traveled during this trip was MOST NEARLY

A. 9 B. 196 C. 216 D. 229

Questions 79-81.

DIRECTIONS: Questions 79 through 81 are to be answered SOLELY on the basis of the following paragraph.

Foot patrol has some advantages over all other methods of patrol. Maximum opportunity is provided for observation within range of the senses and for close contact with people and things that enable the police officer to provide a maximum service as an information source and counselor to the public and as the eyes and ears of the police department. A foot police officer loses no time in alighting from a vehicle, and the performance of police tasks is not hampered by responsibility for his vehicle while afoot. Foot patrol, however, does not have many of the advantages of a patrol car. Lack of both mobility and immediate communication with headquarters lessens the officer's value in an emergency. The area that he can cover effectively is limited and, therefore, this method of patrol is costly.

79. According to this paragraph, the foot police officer is the eyes and ears of the police department because he is 79.____
   A. in direct contact with the station house
   B. not responsible for a patrol vehicle
   C. able to observe closely conditions on his patrol post
   D. a readily available information source to the public

80. The MOST accurate of the following statements concerning the various methods of patrol, according to this paragraph, is that 80.____
   A. foot patrol should sometimes be combined with motor patrol
   B. foot patrol is better than motor patrol
   C. helicopter patrol has the same advantages as motor patrol
   D. motor patrol is more readily able to communicate with superior officers in an emergency

81. According to this paragraph, it is CORRECT to state that foot patrol is 81.____
   A. economical since increased mobility makes more rapid action possible
   B. expensive since the area that can be patrolled is relatively small
   C. economical since vehicle costs need not be considered
   D. expensive since giving information to the public is time-consuming

Questions 82-84.

DIRECTIONS: Questions 82 through 84 are to be answered SOLELY on the basis of the following paragraph.

All applicants for an original license to operate a catering establishment shall be finger-printed. This shall include the officers, employees, and stockholders of the company and the members of a partnership. In case of a change, by addition or substitution, occurring during the existence of a license, the person added or substituted shall be fingerprinted. However, in the case of a hotel containing more than 200 rooms, only the officer or manager filing the application is required to be fingerprinted. The police commissioner may also at his discretion exempt the employees and stockholders of any company. The fingerprints shall be taken on one copy of Form C.E. 20 and on two copies of C.E. 21. One copy of Form C.E. 21 shall accompany the application. Fingerprints are not required with a renewal application.

82. According to this paragraph, an employee added to the payroll of a licensed catering establishment which is not in a hotel must 82.____
   A. always be fingerprinted
   B. be fingerprinted unless he has been previously fingerprinted for another license
   C. be fingerprinted unless exempted by the police commissioner
   D. be fingerprinted only if he is the manager or an officer of the company

83. According to this paragraph, it would be MOST accurate to state that 83.____
   A. Form C.E. 20 must accompany a renewal application
   B. Form C.E. 21 must accompany all applications
   C. Form C.E. 21 must accompany an original application
   D. both Forms C.E. 20 and C.E. 21 must accompany all applications

84. A hotel of 270 rooms has applied for a license to operate a catering establishment on the premises. 84.____
According to the instructions for fingerprinting given in his paragraph, the _____ shall be fingerprinted.
A. officers, employees, and stockholders
B. officers and the manager
C. employees
D. officer filing the application

Questions 85-86.

DIRECTIONS: Questions 85 through 87 are to be answered SOLELY on the basis of the following paragraph.

It is difficult to instill in young people inner controls on aggressive behavior in a world marked by aggression. The slum child's environment, full of hostility, stimulates him to delinquency; he does that which he sees about him. The time to act against delinquency is before it is committed. It is clear that juvenile delinquency, especially when it is committed in groups of gangs, leads almost inevitably to an adult criminal life unless it is checked at once. The first signs of vandalism and disregard for the comfort, health, and property of the community should be considered as storm warnings which cannot be ignored. The delinquent's first crime has the underlying element of testing the law and its ability to hit back.

85. A suitable title for this entire paragraph based on the material it contains is 85.____
A. The Need for Early Prevention of Juvenile Delinquency
B. Juvenile Delinquency as a Cause of Slums
C. How Aggressive Behavior Prevents Juvenile Delinquency
D. The Role of Gangs in Crime

86. According to this paragraph, an initial act of juvenile crime usually involves a(n) 86.____
A. group or gang activity
B. theft of valuable property
C. test of the strength of legal authority
D. act of physical violence

87. According to this paragraph, acts of juvenile delinquency are MOST likely to a criminal career when they are 87.____
A. acts of vandalism
B. carried out by groups or gangs
C. committed in a slum environment
D. such as to impair the health of the neighborhood

Questions 88-90.

DIRECTIONS: Questions 88 through 90 are to be answered SOLELY on the basis of the following paragraph.

The police laboratory performs a valuable service in crime investigation by assisting in the reconstruction of criminal action and by aiding in the identification of persons and things. When studied by a technician, physical things found at crime scenes often reveal facts useful in identifying the criminal and in determining what has occurred. The nature of substances to be examined and the character of the examinations are to be made so widely that the services of a large variety of skilled scientific persons are needed in crime investigations. To employ such a complete staff and to provide them with equipment and standards needed for all possible analyses and comparisons is beyond the means and the needs of any but the largest police departments. The search of crime scenes for physical evidence also calls for the services of specialists supplied with essential equipment and assigned to each tour of duty so as to provide service at any hour.

88. If a police department employs a large staff of technicians of various types in its laboratory, it will affect crime investigation to the extent that 88.____
   A. most crimes will be speedily solved
   B. identification of criminals will be aided
   C. search of crime scenes for physical evidence will become of less importance
   D. investigation by police officers will not usually be required

89. According to his paragraph, the MOST complete study of objects found at the scenes of crimes is 89.____
   A. always done in all large police departments
   B. based on assigning one technician to each tour of duty
   C. probably done only in large police departments
   D. probably done in police departments of communities with low crime rates

90. According to this paragraph, a large variety of skilled technicians is useful in criminal investigations because 90.____
   A. crimes cannot be solved without their assistance as a part of the police team
   B. large police departments need large staffs
   C. many different kinds of tests on various substances can be made
   D. the police cannot predict what methods may be tried by wily criminals

Questions 91-92.

DIRECTIONS: Questions 91 and 92 are to be answered SOLELY on the basis of the following paragraph.

The emotionally unstable person is always potentially a dangerous criminal, who causes untold misery to other persons and is a source of considerable trouble and annoyance to law enforcement officials. Like his fellow criminals, he will be a menace to society as long as he is permitted to be at large. Police activities against him serve to sharpen his wits and imprisonment gives him the opportunity to learn from others how to commit more serious crimes when he is released. This criminal's mental structure makes it impossible for him to profit by his experience with the police officials, by punishment of any kind or by sympathetic understanding and treatment by well-intentioned persons, professional and otherwise.

91. According to the above paragraph, the MOST accurate of the following statements concerning the relationship between emotional instability and crime is that 91.____
   A. emotional instability is proof of criminal activities
   B. the emotionally unstable person can become a criminal
   C. all dangerous criminals are emotionally unstable
   D. sympathetic understanding will prevent the emotionally unstable person from becoming a criminal

92. According to the above paragraph, the effect of police activities on the emotionally unstable criminal is that 92.____
   A. police activities aid this type of criminal to reform
   B. imprisonment tends to deter this type of criminal from committing future crimes
   C. contact with the police serves to assist sympathetic understanding and medical treatment
   D. police methods against this type of criminal develop him for further unlawful acts

Questions 93-95.

DIRECTIONS: Questions 93 through 95 are to be answered SOLELY on the basis of the following paragraph.

Proposals to license gambling operations are based on the belief that the human desire to gamble cannot be suppressed and, therefore, it should be licensed and legalized with the people sharing in the profits, instead of allowing the underworld to benefit. If these proposals are sincere, then it is clear that only one is worthwhile at all. Legalized gambling should be completely controlled and operated by the state with all the profits used for its citizens. A state agency should be set up to operate and control the gambling business. It should be as completely removed from politics as possible. In view of the inherent nature of the gambling business with its close relationship to lawlessness and crime, only a man of the highest integrity should be eligible to become head of this agency. However, state gambling would encourage mass gambling with its attending social and economic evils in the same manner as other forms of legal gambling; but there is no justification whatever for the business of gambling to be legalized and then permitted to operate for private profit or for the benefit of any political organization.

93. The central thought of this paragraph may be correctly expressed as the 93.____
   A. need to legalize gambling in the state
   B. state operation of gambling for the benefit of the people
   C. need to license private gambling establishments
   D. evils of gambling

94. According to this paragraph, a problem of legalized gambling which will still occur if the state operates the gambling business is 94.____
   A. the diversion of profits from gambling to private use
   B. that the amount of gambling will tend to diminish

C. the evil effects of any form of mass gambling
D. the use of gambling revenues for illegal purposes

95. According to this paragraph, to legalize the business of gambling would be 95.____
A. *justified*, because gambling would be operated only by a man of the highest integrity
B. *justified*, because this would eliminate politics
C. *unjustified* under any conditions because the human desire to gamble cannot be suppressed
D. *unjustified* if operated for private or political profit

Questions 96-97.

DIRECTIONS: Questions 96 and 97 are to be answered SOLELY on the basis of the following paragraph.

For many years, slums had been recognized as breeding disease, juvenile delinquency, and crime which not only threatened the health and welfare of the people who lived there, but also weakened the structure of society as a whole. As far back as 1834, a sanitary inspection report in New York City pointed out the connection between insanitary, overcrowded housing, and the spread of epidemics. Down through the years, evidence of slum-produced evils accumulated as the slums themselves continued to spread. This spread of slums was nationwide. Its symptoms and its ill effects were peculiar to no locality, but were characteristic of the country as a whole and imperiled the national welfare.

96. According to this paragraph, people who live in slum dwellings 96.____
A. cause slums to become worse
B. are threatened by disease and crime
C. create bad housing
D. are the chief source of crime in the country

97. According to this paragraph, the effects of juvenile delinquency and crime in slum areas were 97.____
A. to destroy the structure of society
B. noticeable in all parts of the country
C. a chief cause of the spread of slums
D. to spread unsanitary conditions in New York City

Questions 98-100.

DIRECTIONS: Questions 98 through 100 are to be answered SOLELY on the basis of the following paragraph.

Whenever, in the course of the performance of their duties in an emergency, members of the force operate the emergency power switch at any location on the transit system and thereby remove power from portions of the track, or they are on the scene where this has been done, they will bear in mind that, although power is removed, further dangers exist; namely, that a train may coast into the area even though the power is off, or that the rails may be energized by a train which may be in a position to transfer electricity from a live portion of the third rail through its shoe beams. Employees must look in each direction before stepping upon, crossing or standing close to tracks, being particularly careful not to come into contact with the third rail.

98. According to this paragraph, whenever an emergency occurs which has resulted in operating the emergency switch, it is MOST accurate to state that 98.____
   A. power is shut off and employees may perform their duties in complete safety
   B. there may still be power in a portion of the third rail
   C. the switch will not operate if a portion of the track has been broken
   D. trains are not permitted to stop in the area of the emergency

99. An important precaution which this paragraph urges employees to follow after operating the emergency power switch is to 99.____
   A. look carefully in both directions before stepping near the rails
   B. inspect the nearest train which has stopped to see if the power is on
   C. examine the third rail to see if the power is on
   D. check the emergency power switch to make sure it has operated properly

100. A trackman reports to you, the police officer, that a dead body is lying on the road bed. You operate the emergency power switch. A train which has been approaching comes to a stop near the scene. 100.____
In order to act in accordance with the instructions in the above paragraph, you should
   A. climb down to the road bed and remove the body
   B. direct the train motorman to back up to the point where his train will not be in position to transfer electricity through its shoe beams
   C. carefully cross over the road bed to the body, avoiding the third rail and watching for train movements
   D. have the train motorman check to see if power is on before crossing to the tracks

---

KEY (CORRECT ANSWERS)

1.	C	21.	C	41.	A	61.	A	81.	B
2.	C	22.	A	42.	C	62.	C	82.	C
3.	D	23.	D	43.	A	63.	D	83.	C
4.	B	24.	B	44.	B	64.	D	84.	D
5.	D	25.	C	45.	C	65.	B	85.	A
6.	B	26.	A	46.	A	66.	A	86.	C
7.	C	27.	C	47.	B	67.	C	87.	B
8.	B	28.	C	48.	C	68.	D	88.	B
9.	A	29.	B	49.	B	69.	B	89.	C
10.	B	30.	D	50.	D	70.	A	90.	C
11.	D	31.	A	51.	C	71.	B	91.	B
12.	C	32.	D	52.	D	72.	A	92.	D
13.	C	33.	C	53.	B	73.	B	93.	B
14.	B	34.	A	54.	B	74.	C	94.	C
15.	D	35.	C	55.	B	75.	C	95.	D
16.	B	36.	A	56.	A	76.	C	96.	B
17.	C	37.	C	57.	D	77.	A	97.	B
18.	B	38.	C	58.	A	78.	C	98.	B
19.	D	39.	D	59.	A	79.	C	99.	A
20.	B	40.	A	60.	C	80.	D	100.	C

EXAMINATION SECTION

TEST 1

DIRECTIONS: Each question or incomplete statement is followed by several suggested answers or completions. Select the one that BEST answers the question or completes the statement. *PRINT THE LETTER OF THE CORRECT ANSWER IN THE SPACE AT THE RIGHT.*

1. A sergeant tells an officer to perform a certain duty. 1.____
If the officer does not completely understand the order, she should
   A. carry out the order to the best of her ability and then request further information if necessary
   B. carry out the order to the best of her ability so that she does not give the appearance of being unable to follow orders
   C. inform the sergeant that she does not understand the order
   D. request clarification from a more experienced officer

2. While on patrol, you are informed by the manager of a supermarket that an object which appears to be a homemade bomb has been discovered in his market. 2.____
Your FIRST action should be to
   A. go to the market and make sure that everyone leaves it immediately
   B. go to the market, examine the bomb, and then decide what action is to be taken
   C. question the manager in detail in an effort to determine whether this is really a bomb
   D. telephone the Bomb Squad for instructions as to how the bomb should be rendered harmless

3. An officer on post would be MOST likely to make a regular hourly signal-box call to his precinct, rather than an immediate call, when he 3.____
   A. discovers a traffic signal light which is not functioning properly
   B. discovers what appears to be an abandoned car on his post
   C. notices a street name sign which has been damaged
   D. overhears a conversation relation to a possible disturbance between two groups of teenagers

4. An officer is on post, and a citizen sees him *ringing in* on a street police call box to the station house. The citizen asks him what the purpose of the box is. 4.____
Of the following, the BEST course of action for the officer to follow in this situation is to
   A. speak to the desk officer over the call box phone and get his permission to answer the question
   B. suggest that he write to the Community Relations Office of the Police Department for complete information
   C. tactfully suggest to the man it is a police matter and hence confidential
   D. tell the man what the call box is and what it is used for

5. The MOST reasonable advice that an officer can give to a merchant who asks what he should do if he receive a telephone call from a person he doesn't recognize regarding an alleged emergency at his store after ordinary business hours is that the merchant should go to the store and, if police officers are not at the scene, he should 5.____
   A. continue past the store and call the police for assistance
   B. continue past the store and return and enter it if there doesn't appear to be an emergency
   C. enter the store and ascertain whether the alleged emergency exists
   D. enter the store only if there is no one apparently loitering in the vicinity

6. An officer is asked by a citizen the location of a candy store which the officer knows is under observation for suspected bookmaking activity. 6.____
   In such a situation, the officer should
   A. give the proper directions to the citizen
   B. give the proper directions to the citizen, but tell him the store is under observation
   C. state that he does not know the location of the store
   D. tell the citizen that he may be arrested if the store is raided

7. *Whenever a crime has been committed, the criminal has disturbed the surroundings in one way or another by his presence.* 7.____
   The LEAST valid deduction for the police to make from this statement is that
   A. clues are thus present at all crime scenes
   B. even the slightest search at crime scenes will turn up conclusive evidence
   C. the greater the number of criminals involved in a crime, the greater the number of clues likely to be available
   D. the completely clueless crime is rarely encountered in police work

8. It is suggested that a suspect should not be permitted to walk in or about the scene of a crime where fingerprints may be present until a thorough search has been made for such evidence. 8.____
   This suggested procedure is
   A. *good*; the suspect would, if permitted to walk about the scene, smear all fingerprints that might be found by police investigators
   B. *bad*; the return of a suspect to the scene of a crime provides an opportunity to obtain additional fingerprints from the suspect
   C. *good*; if the suspect handled any objects at the scene, the value of any original fingerprints, as evidence, might be seriously impaired
   D. *bad*; the return of a suspect to the scene of a crime provides an opportunity to identify objects that had been handled during the commission of the crime

9. Of the following, the one which is the purpose of the police fingerprinting procedure is the 9.____
   A. identification of deceased persons
   B. identification of the guilty
   C. protection of the innocent
   D. recognition of first offenders

10. An officer is the first one to arrive at the scene of a murder. A suspect offers to make a statement to him concerning the crime. The officer refuses to accept the statement. 10.____
The officer's action was
   A. *good*; interrogation of suspects should be performed by experienced detectives
   B. *poor*; the suspect may later change his mind and refuse to make any statement
   C. *good*; the officer will be too busy maintaining order at the scene to be able to accept the statement
   D. *poor*; a statement made by the suspect would quickly solve the crime

11. The scene of a crime is the area within the immediate vicinity of the specific location of the crime in which evidence might be found. 11.____
This definition serves as an acceptable working guide for the discovery of evidence by the police because
   A. evidence found outside the crime scene can be just as valuable as evidence found nearly
   B. it assigns the finding of evidence to those responsible for its discovery
   C. it is likely that the most important evidence will be found within the area of the crime scene
   D. evidence found within the area of the crime scene is more readily accepted

12. It is important that the police give proper attention to the investigation of apparently minor, as well as major, complaints made by citizens. 12.____
Of the following, the one which is the MOST valid reason for doing so is that
   A. minor complaints are frequently of great importance to the complainant
   B. minor complaints are more readily disposed of
   C. minor complaints may be an indication of a serious police problem
   D. police efficiency is determined by their attitude towards citizen complaints

13. Hearsay evidence may be defined as testimony by one person that another person told him about a criminal act which that other person had witnessed. 13.____
Hearsay evidence is usually NOT admissible in a criminal trial MAINLY because
   A. hearsay evidence is consistently biased and deliberately distorted
   B. hearsay evidence is usually not relevant to the issues of the case
   C. such evidence is usually distorted by both the original witness and the person to whom he stated his observations
   D. the witness to the criminal act is not being cross-examined under oath

14. Arrests should not be given too much weight in the appraisal of a police officer's performance since a large number of arrests does not necessarily indicate that an officer is doing a good police job. 14.____
This statement is
   A. *true*; factors other than the total of arrests must also be considered in judging police effectiveness
   B. *false*; the basic job of the police is to suppress crime and the surest measure of this is the number of arrests made

C. *true*; arrest figures are not indicative in any way of an officer's efficiency
D. *false*; although some officers are in a better position to make arrests than others, the law of averages should operate to even this out

15. Arson is a particularly troublesome crime for the police. 15.____
Of the following statements, the one which is the MOST important reason why this is so is that
A. arsonists usually seek the protection of darkness for their crimes
B. arsons occur so frequently that the police lack a definite approach
C. important evidence is frequently destroyed by the fire itself
D. witnesses find it difficult to distinguish arsonists from other criminals

16. Undoubtedly, the police have an important contribution to make to the welfare of youth. 16.____
Of the following, the PRINCIPAL reason for this is that
A. effectiveness is a result of experience and the police have had the longest experience in youth work
B. no other agency can make use of the criminal aspects of the law as effectively as the police
C. the police are in a strategic position to observe children actually or potentially delinquent and the condition contributing thereto
D. welfare agencies lack an understanding of the problems of youth

17. Adolescents, whether delinquent or not, are especially sensitive to the attitudes attitudes of their own small group and are more responsive to the judgments of their companions than to those of their own family. 17.____
According to this statement, it would be MOST accurate to conclude that
A. adolescents are concerned more with their gang's opinion of them than with their own families' reaction to their behavior
B. adolescents are more personal sensitive to criticism of their conduct than adults
C. adolescent misbehavior can best be approached through the family
D. adolescent misbehavior is often caused by the lack of parental interest

18. It is safe to say that the significant patterns of behavior conveyed by movies, press or radio must reach individuals whose behavior resistance is low, in order to be influential. 18.____
It follows from the above statement that it would be MOST desirable to
A. consider the public press a negative factor in the developmental pattern of individuals
B. encourage youth to imitate significant patterns of behavior which they observe
C. exclude all children from attending movies which portray patterns of behavior of an anti-social nature
D. prevent exposure of potentially delinquent children to unfavorable influences

19. The suggestion has been made that the police department issue identification cards to be used by juveniles over 21 who wish to drink alcoholic beverages in bars. 19.____
The one of the following which is NOT a valid criticism of this proposal is that it might
   A. appear to bestow positive social approval on the consumption of alcoholic beverages by youths
   B. induce more youngsters to congregate in bars
   C. lead to a *black market* in counterfeit identification cards
   D. shield youths from exposure to unwholesome situations

20. An apparently senile man informs a patrolman that he is returning from a visit to his daughter and that he is unable to find his way back home because he has forgotten his address. 20.____
Of the following courses of action, the FIRST one that should be taken by the patrolman is to
   A. question the man in an effort to establish his identity
   B. request the police missing persons section to describe to you any person recently reported as missing
   C. suggest that the man return to his daughter for travel directions to his home
   D. telephone a description of the man to the precinct station house

21. Of the following facts about a criminal, the one which would be of MOST value in apprehending and identifying the criminal would be that he 21.____
   A. drives a black Cadillac 2019 sedan with chrome license plate holders
   B. invariably uses a .38 caliber Colt blue-steel revolver with walnut stock and regulation front sight
   C talks with a French accent and frequently stutters
   D. usually wears 3-button single-breasted Ivy League suits and white oxford cloth button-down shirts

22. A pawnshop dealer has submitted to the police an accurate and complete description of a wristwatch which he recently purchased from a customer. 22.____
The one of the following factors that would be MOST important in determining whether this wristwatch was stolen is the
   A. degree of investigative perseverance demonstrated by the police
   B. exactness of police records describing stolen property
   C. honesty and neighborhood reputation of the pawnbroker
   D. time interval between the purchase of the wristwatch by the pawnbroker and his report to the police

23. An officer noticed a man fumbling at the controls of an automobile, starting with a lurch, grinding the gear, and then driving on the wrong side of the street. The officer signaled the car to stop, warned the driver about his driving and permitted him to depart. 23.____

This procedure was

A. *right*; it is good public relations for the police to caution rather than punish inadvertent violations of law
B. *wrong*; the officer should have arrested the driver for driving while in an intoxicated condition
C. *right*; the bad driving probably was due to nervousness caused by the presence of the officer
D. *wrong*; the officer should have investigated the possibility that this was a stolen car

24. An officer at the scene of a serious vehicular accident requests two witnesses to the accident not to speak to each other until he has received from each of them a statement concerning the accident. 24.____
The MOST likely reason for this request by the officer is that if the witnesses were allowed to speak to each other at this time, they might
A. become involved in a violent quarrel over what actually occurred
B. change their opinion so that identical statements to the police would result
C. discuss the possibility of a bribe offer to either of them by one of the operators involved in the accident
D. have their original views of the accident somewhat altered by hearing each other's view of the accident

25. Officer Z is directing traffic when he observes a car approaching him which appears to meet the description of a car stolen several days previously. Officer Z signals the driver of this car to stop. The car does not stop or slacken its speed and proceeds past Officer Z. In an effort to stop the car, Officer Z fires several shots at the car. 25.____
The action of Officer Z was
A. *improper*; Officer Z should know that pistol marksmanship is not always accurate, even at relatively close ranges
B. *proper*; it is legally justifiable to fire at an escaping felon
C. *improper*; it is possible that the driver misunderstood the officer's signal to stop
D. *proper*; Officer Z was on foot duty and there was no other immediately available means of halting the car

26. Assume that a recent study showed a 2% increase in highway fatalities in the first six months of 2019 over the last six months of 2018. 26.____
Of the following factors, generally the LEAST important one to include in a report evaluating this study is the
A. age and sex distribution of drivers
B. total number of automobiles in use
C. total number of miles automobiles were driven
D. total population

27. Tests have shown that sound waves set up by a siren have a greater intensity ahead than at either side or at the rear of a police car. 27.____
On the basis of this statement, it would be MOST reasonable for the operator of a police car, when responding to the scene of an emergency and using the siren, to expect that a motorist approaching an intersection from
   A. a side street may not stop his vehicle as soon as a more distant motorist directly ahead of the police car
   B. directly ahead may not stop his vehicle as soon as a more distant motorist approaching from the rear of the police car
   C. directly ahead may not stop his vehicle as soon as a more distant motorist approaching from the side of the police car
   D. the rear of the police car may stop his vehicle before the less distant motorist approaching from the street

28. An alarm broadcast for criminals escaping by car directs police officers to observe occupants of all cars, even occupants in cars not meeting the description of the fleeing car. 28.____
The MOST likely reason for this is that
   A. cars of the same make are not distinctive enough to be of any recognition value
   B. the car's appearance may have been greatly altered after the crime was committed
   C. the criminals may have disguised themselves after the commission of the crime
   D. the escaping criminal may change to a different car after leaving the scene

29. Five minutes after receiving an alarm for a blue 2010 Buick four-door sedan which had been used as a get-away car by bank robbers, a radio patrol team spots and stops a car which seems to fit the description. 29.____
The one of the following which is MOST likely to indicate the need for further careful investigation is that the
   A. car has a cracked rear side window
   B. driver does not have a registration certificate for this car
   C. rear license plate is rusted
   D. occupants of the car consist of three poorly dressed men

30. A foot patrol officer who is several blocks away observes a woman being dragged into a car, which drives off very rapidly. 30.____
Of the following, his FIRST action should be to
   A. call headquarters from the nearest call box or public telephone
   B. commandeer a bus and pursue the other car
   C. shoot in the direction of the scene as a warning
   D. step into a hallway and await the approach of the car

31. A citizen requests police assistance in locating his adult son who has not been home for a period of twenty-four hours. Questioning of the citizen reveals no reason for the son's absence. 31.____

The MOST appropriate of the following actions that the police should take is to
A. advise the citizen to contact all nearly hospitals and then contact the police again if this is not successful
B. conduct a thorough investigation in an attempt to locate the missing son
C. politely inform the citizen that no police action will be taken since the son is an adult
D. suggest that the citizen wait several days; and if his son has not then returned home, they will accept the complaint

32. An officer is guarding the entrance of an apartment in which a homicide occurred. While awaiting the arrival of the detectives assigned to the case, he is approached by a newspaper reporter who asks to be admitted. The officer refuses to admit him. 32.____
The officer's action was
A. *wrong*; the police should cooperate with the press
B. *right*; the reporter might unintentionally destroy evidence if admitted
C. *wrong*; experienced police reporters can be trusted to act intelligently in this situation
D. *right*; this reporter should not be given an advantage over other newspaper men

33. A police officer investigating a reported store hold-up, which occurred shortly before his arrival, enters the store. The salesclerk who witnessed the hold-up starts telling the officer, in a confused and excited manner, what had happened. 33.____
The BEST course for the officer to follow initially is to
A. ask the clerk to write out an account of what had happened
B. let the clerk tell her story without interruption
C. try to confine the clerk to answering relevant questions
D. wait until the clerk calms down before taking her statement

34. A phone call is received at police headquarters indicating that a burglary is now taking place in a large loft building. Several radio motor patrol teams are dispatched to the scene. 34.____
In order to prevent the escape of the burglars, the two patrolmen arriving first at the building, knowing that there is at least one entrance on each of the four side of the building, should FIRST
A. station themselves at diagonally opposite corners, outside of the building
B. enter the building and proceed to search for the criminals
C. station themselves at the most likely exit from the building
D. enter the building and remain on the ground floor, attempting to keep all stairways under observation

Questions 36-45.

DIRECTIONS: In each of Questions 36 through 45, select the lettered word which means MOST NEARLY the same as the capitalized word. Place the letter which corresponds to your choice in the space at the right.

35. AVARICE 35.____
A. flight B. greed C. pride D. thrift

36. PREDATORY 36.____
A. offensive B. plundering C. previous D. timeless

37. VINDICATE 37.____
A. clear B. conquer C. correct D. illustrate

38. INVETERATE 38.____
A. backward B. erect C. habitual D. lucky

39. DISCERN 39.____
A. describe B. fabricate C. recognize D. seek

40. COMPLACENT 40.____
A. indulgent B. listless C. overjoyed D. satisfied

41. ILLICIT 41.____
A. insecure B. unclear C. unlawful D. unlimited

42. PROCRASTINATE 42.____
A. declare B. multiply C. postpone D. steal

43. IMPASSIVE 43.____
A. calm B. frustrated C. thoughtful D. unhappy

44. AMICABLE 44.____
A. cheerful B. flexible C. friendly D. poised

45. FEASIBLE 45.____
A. breakable B. easy C. likeable D. practicable

KEY (CORRECT ANSWERS)

1.	C	11.	C	21.	C	31.	B	41.	C
2.	A	12.	C	22.	B	32.	B	42.	C
3.	C	13.	D	23.	D	33.	C	43.	A
4.	D	14.	A	24.	D	34.	A	44.	C
5.	A	15.	C	25.	C	35.	B	45.	D
6.	A	16.	C	26.	D	36.	B		
7.	B	17.	A	27.	A	37.	A		
8.	C	18.	D	28.	B	38.	C		
9.	B	19.	D	29.	B	39.	C		
10.	B	20.	A	30.	A	40.	D		

TEST 2

DIRECTIONS: Each question or incomplete statement is followed by several suggested answers or completions. Select the one that BEST answers the question or completes the statement. *PRINT THE LETTER OF THE CORRECT ANSWER IN THE SPACE AT THE RIGHT.*

Questions 1-11.

DIRECTIONS: In each of Questions 1 through 11, select the lettered word which means MOST NEARLY the same as the capitalized word. Place the letter which corresponds to your choice in the space at the right.

1. INNOCUOUS 1.____
   A. harmless B. insecure C. insincere D. unfavorable

2. OSTENSIBLE 2.____
   A. apparent B. hesitant C. reluctant D. showy

3. INDOMITABLE 3.____
   A. excessive B. unconquerable
   C. unreasonable D. unthinkable

4. CRAVEN 4.____
   A. cowardly B. hidden C. miserly D. needed

5. ALLAY 5.____
   A. discuss B. quiet C. refine D. remove

6. ALLUDE 6.____
   A. denounce B. refer C. state D. support

7. NEGLIGENCE 7.____
   A. carelessness B. denial C. objection D. refusal

8. AMEND 8.____
   A. correct B. destroy C. end D. list

9. RELEVANT 9.____
   A. conclusive B. careful C. obvious D. related

10. VERIFY 10.____
    A. challenge B. change C. confirm D. reveal

11. INSIGNIFICANT 11.____
    A. incorrect B. limited C. unimportant D. undesirable

Questions 12-16.

DIRECTIONS: Questions 12 through16 are to be answered on the basis of the graphs shown below.

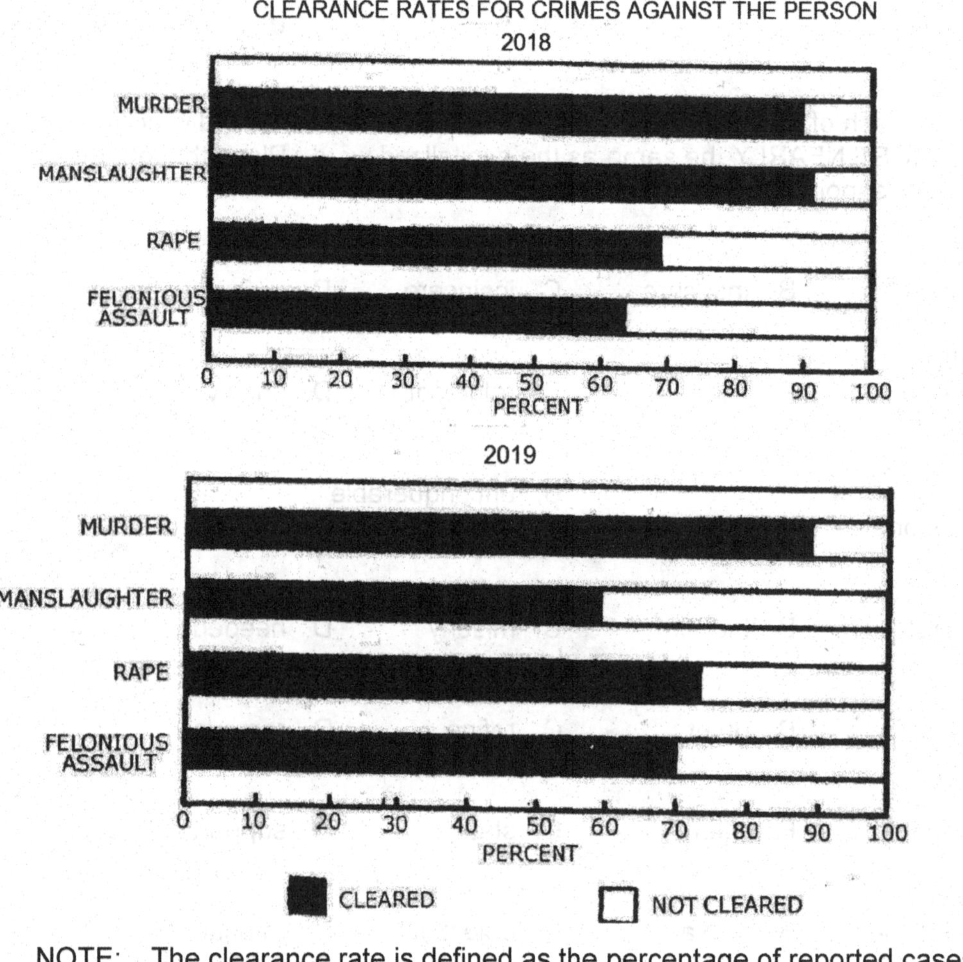

NOTE: The clearance rate is defined as the percentage of reported cases which were closed by the police through arrests or other means.

12. According to the above graphs, the AVERAGE clearance rate for all four crimes for 2019 12._____
    A. was greater than in 2018
    B. was less than in 2018
    C. was the same as in 2018
    D. cannot properly be compared to the 2018 figures

13. According to the above graphs, the crimes which did NOT show an increasing clearance rate from 2018 to 2019 were 13._____
    A. manslaughter and murder
    B. rape and felonious assault
    C. manslaughter and felonious assault
    D. rape and murder

14. According to the above graphs, the average clearance rate for the two-year period 2018-2019 was SMALLEST for the crime of 14.____
   A murder
   B. manslaughter
   C. rape
   D. felonious assault

15. If, in 2019, 63 cases of reported felonious assault remained *not cleared*, then the total number of felonious assault cases reported that year was MOST NEARLY 15.____
   A. 90
   B. 150
   C. 210
   D. 900

16. In comparing the graphs for 2018 and 2019, it would be MOST accurate to state that 16.____
   A. it is not possible to compare the total number of crimes cleared in 2018 with the total number cleared in 2019
   B. the total number of crimes reported in 2018 is greater than the number in 2019
   C. there were fewer manslaughter cases cleared during 2018 than in 2019
   D. there were more rape cases cleared during 2019 than manslaughter cases cleared in the same year

17. A radio motor patrol car finds it necessary to travel at 90 miles per hour for a period of 1 minute and 40 seconds. 17.____
   The number of miles which the car travels during this period is
   A. $1^5/_6$
   B. 2
   C. 2½
   D. 3¾

18. A radio motor patrol car has to travel a distance of 15 miles in an emergency. If it does the first two-thirds of the distance at 40 m.p.h. and the last third at 60 m.p.h., the total number of minutes required for the entire run is MOST NEARLY 18.____
   A. 15
   B. 20
   C. 22½
   D. 25

19. A patrol car had 11½ gallons of gasoline at the beginning of a trip of 196 miles and 5½ gallons at the end of the trip. During the trip, gasoline was bought for $21.70 at a cost of $3.10 per gallon. 19.____
   The average number of miles driven per gallon of gasoline is MOST NEARLY
   A. 14
   B. 14.5
   C. 15
   D. 15.5

20. There are 15 police officers assigned to a certain operation. One-third earn $42,000 per year, three earn $44,100 per year, one earns $49,350 per year, and the rest earn $55,810 per year. 20.____
   The average annual salary of these officers is MOST NEARLY
   A. $47,500
   B. $48,000
   C. $48,500
   D. $49,000

21. In 2022, the cost of patrol car maintenance and repair was $2,500 more than in 2021, representing an increase of 10%. 21.____
   The cost of patrol car maintenance and repair in 2022 was MOST NEARLY
   A. $2,750
   B. $22,500
   C. $25,000
   D. $27,500

22. A police precinct has an assigned strength of 180 officers. Of this number, 25% are not available for duty due to illness, vacation, and other reasons. Of those who are available for duty, 1/3 are assigned outside of the precinct for special emergency duty. 22.____
The ACTUAL available strength of the precinct, in terms of officers immediately available for precinct duty, is
A. 45 B. 60 C. 90 D. 135

23. Five police officers are taking target practice. The number of rounds fired by each and the percentage of perfect shots is as follows: 23.____

Officer	Rounds Fired	Perfect Shots
R	80	30%
S	70	40%
T	75	60%
U	92	25%
V	96	66 2/3%

The average number of perfect shots fired by them is MOST NEARLY
A. 30 B. 36 C. 42 D. 80

24. A dozen 5-gallon cans of paint weigh 494 pounds. Each can, when empty weighs 3 pounds. 24.____
The weight of one gallon of paint is MOST NEARLY _____ lbs.
A. 5 B. 6½ C. 7½ D. 8

Questions 25-26.

DIRECTIONS: Questions 25 and 26 are to be answered SOLELY on the basis of the following paragraph.

The medical examiner may contribute valuable data to the investigator of fires which cause fatalities. By careful examination of the bodies of any victims, he not only establishes cause of death, but may also furnish, in many instances, answers to questions relating to the identity of the victim and the source and origin of the fire. The medical examiner is of greatest value to law enforcement agencies because he is able to determine the exact cause of death through an examination of tissue of apparent arson victims. Thorough study of a burned body of even of parts of a burned body will frequently yield information which illuminates the problems confronting the arson investigator and the police.

25. According to the above paragraph, the MOST important task of the medical examiner in the investigation of arson is to obtain information concerning the 25.____
A. identity of arsonists
B. cause of death
C. identity of victims
C. source and origin of fires

26. The CENTRAL thought of the above paragraph is that the medical examiner aids in the solution of crimes of arson when 26.____
   A. a person is burnt to death
   B. identity of the arsonist is unknown
   C. the cause of the fire is known
   D. trained investigators are not available

Questions 27-30.

DIRECTIONS: Questions 27 through 30 are to be answered SOLELY on the basis of the following paragraph.

A foundling is an abandoned child whose identity is unknown. Desk officers shall direct the delivery, by a policewoman if available, of foundlings actually or apparently under two years of age to the American Foundling Hospital, or if actually or apparently two years of age or over, to the Children's Center. In all other cases of dependent or neglected children, other than foundlings, requiring shelter, desk officers shall provide for obtaining such shelter as follows: between 9 A.M. and 5 P.M., Monday through Friday, by telephone direct to the Bureau of Child Welfare, in order to ascertain the shelter to which the child shall be sent; at all other times, direct the delivery of a child actually or apparently under two years of age to the American Foundling Hospital, of if the child is actually or apparently two years of age or over to the Children's Center.

27. According to the above paragraph, it would be MOST correct to state that 27.____
   A. a foundling as well as a neglected child may be delivered to the American Foundling Hospital
   B. a foundling but not a neglected child may be delivered to the Children's Center
   C. a neglected child requiring shelter, regardless of age, may be delivered to the Bureau of Child Welfare
   D. the Bureau of Child Welfare may determine the shelter to which a foundling may be delivered

28. According to the above paragraph, the desk officer shall provide for obtaining shelter for a neglected child, apparently under two years of age, by 28.____
   A. directing its delivery to Children's Center if occurrence is on a Monday between 9 A.M. and 5 P.M.
   B. telephoning the Bureau of Child Welfare if occurrence is on a Sunday
   C. directing its delivery to the American Foundling Hospital if occurrence is on a Wednesday at 4 P.M.
   D. telephoning the Bureau of Child Welfare if occurrence is a 10 A.M. on a Friday

29. According to the above paragraph, the desk officer should direct delivery to the American Foundling Hospital of any child who is 29.____
   A. actually under two years of age and requires shelter
   B. apparently under two years of age and is neglected or dependent
   C. actually two years of age and is a foundling
   D. apparently under two years of age and has been abandoned

30. A 12-year-old neglected child requiring shelter is brought to a police station on Thursday at 2 P.M. 30.____
Such a child should be sent to
   A. a shelter selected by the Bureau of Child Welfare
   B. a shelter selected by the desk office
   C. the Children's Center
   D. the American Foundling Hospital when a brother or sister, under 2 years of age, also requires shelter

Questions 31-33.

DIRECTIONS: Questions 31 through 33 are to be answered SOLELY on the basis of the following paragraph.

In addition to making the preliminary investigation of crimes, police officers should serve as eyes, ears, and legs for the detective division. The patrol division may be used for surveillance, to serve warrants, and bring in suspects and witnesses, and to perform a number of routine tasks for the detectives which will increase the time available for tasks that require their special skills and facilities. It is to the advantage of individual detective, as well as of the detective division, to have officers working in this manner; more cases are cleared by arrest and a greater proportion of stolen property is recovered when, in addition to the detective regularly assigned, a number of officers also work on the case. Detectives may stimulate the interest and participation of officers by keeping them currently informed of the presence, identity, or description, hangouts, associates, vehicles and method of operation of each criminal known to be in the community.

31. According to the above paragraph, an officer should 31.____
   A. assist the detective in certain of his routine functions
   B. be considered for assignment as a detective on the basis of his patrol performance
   C. leave the scene once a detective arrives
   D. perform as much of the detective's duties as time permits

32. According to the above paragraph, officers should aid detectives by 32.____
   A. accepting assignments from detectives which give promise of recovering stolen property
   B. making arrests of witnesses for the detective's interrogation
   C. performing all special investigative work for detectives
   D. producing for questioning individuals who may aid the detective in his investigation

33. According to the above paragraph, detectives can keep officers interested by 33.____
   A. ascertaining that officers are doing investigative work properly
   B. having officers directly under his supervision during an investigation
   C. informing officers of the value of their efforts in crime prevention
   D. supplying the officers with information regarding known criminals in the community

Questions 34-35.

DIRECTIONS: Questions 34 and 35 are to be answered SOLELY on the basis of the following paragraph.

State motor vehicle registration departments should and do play a vital role in the prevention and detection of automobile thefts. The combatting of theft is, in fact, one of the primary purposes of the registration of motor vehicles. In 2018, there were approximately 61,309,000 motor vehicles registered in the United States. That same year, some 200,000 of them were stolen. All but 6 percent have been or will be recovered. This is a very high recovery ratio compared to the percentage of recovery of other stolen personal property. The reason for this is that automobiles are carefully identified by the manufacturers and carefully registered by many of the states

34. The CENTRAL thought of the above paragraph is that there is a close relationship between the 34.____
   A. number of automobiles registered in the United States and the number stolen
   B. prevention of automobile thefts and the effectiveness of police departments in the United States
   C. recovery of stolen automobiles and automobile registration
   D. recovery of stolen automobiles and of other stolen property

35. According to the above paragraph, the high recovery ratio for stolen automobiles is due to 35.____
   A. state registration and manufacturer identification of motor vehicles
   B. successful prevention of automobile thefts by state motor vehicle departments
   C. the fact that only 6% of stolen vehicles are not properly registered
   D. the high number of motor vehicles registered in the United States

Questions 36-39.

DIRECTIONS: Questions 36 through 39 are to be answered SOLELY on the basis of the following paragraph.

It is not always understood that the term *physical evidence* embraces any and all objects, living or inanimate. A knife, gun, signature, or burglar tool is immediately recognized as physical evidence. Less often is it considered that dust, microscopic fragments of all types, even an odor, may equally be physical evidence and often the most important of all. It is well established that the most useful types of physical evidence are generally microscopic in dimensions, that is, not noticeable by the eye and, therefore, most likely to be overlooked by the criminal and by the investigator. For this reason, microscopic evidence persists for months or years after all other evidence has been removed and found inconclusive. Naturally, there are limitations to the time of collecting microscopic evidence as it may be lost or decayed. The exercise of judgment as to the possibility or profit of delayed action in collecting the evidence is a field in which the expert investigator should judge.

36. The one of the following which the above paragraph does NOT consider to be physical evidence is a 36.____
    A. criminal thought
    B. minute speck of dust
    C. raw onion smell
    D. typewritten note

37. According to the above paragraph, the rechecking of the scene of a crime 37.____
    A. is useless when performed years after the occurrence of the crime
    B. is advisable chiefly in crimes involving physical violence
    C. may turn up microscopic evidence of value
    D. should be delayed if the microscopic evidence is not subject to decay or loss

38. According to the above paragraph, the criminal investigator should 38.____
    A. give most of his attention to weapons used in the commission of the crime
    B. ignore microscopic evidence until a request is received from the laboratory
    C. immediately search for microscopic evidence and ignore the more visible objects
    D. realize that microscopic evidence can be easily overlooked

39. According to the above paragraph, 39.____
    A. a delay in collecting evidence must definitely diminish its value to the investigator
    B. microscopic evidence exists for longer periods of time than other physical evidence
    C. microscopic evidence is generally the most useful type of physical evidence
    D. physical evidence is likely to be overlooked by the criminal and by the investigator

Questions 40-42.

DIRECTIONS: Questions 40 through 42 are to be answered SOLELY on the basis of the following paragraph.

Sometimes, but not always, firing a gun leaves a residue of nitrate particles on the hands. This fact is utilized in the paraffin test which consists of applying melted paraffin and gauze to the fingers, hands, and wrists of a suspect until a cast of approximately 1/8 of an inch is built up. The heat of the paraffin causes the pores of the skin to open and release any particles embedded in them. The paraffin cast is then removed and tested chemically for nitrate particles. In addition to gunpowder, fertilizers, tobacco ashes, matches, and soot are also common sources of nitrates on the hands.

40. Assume that the paraffin test has been given to a person suspected of firing a gun and that nitrate particles have been found. 40.____
    It would be CORRECT to conclude that the suspect
    A. is guilty
    B. is innocent
    C. may be guilty or innocent
    D. is probably guilty

41. In testing for the presence of gunpowder particles on human hands, the characteristic of paraffin which makes it MOST serviceable is that it 41.____
    A. causes the nitrate residue left by a fired gun to adhere to the gauze
    B. is waterproof
    C. melts at a high temperature
    D. helps to distinguish between gunpowder nitrates and other types

42. According to the above paragraph, in the paraffin test, the nitrate particles are removed from the pores because the paraffin 42.____
    A. enlarges the pores
    B. contracts the pores
    C. reacts chemically with nitrates
    D. dissolves the particles

Questions 43-45.

DIRECTIONS: Questions 43 through 45 are to be answered SOLELY on the basis of the following paragraph.

Pickpockets operate most effectively when there are prospective victims in either heavily congested areas or in lonely places. In heavily populated areas, the large number of people about them covers the activities of these thieves. In lonely spots, they have the advantage of working unobserved. The main factor in the pickpocket's success is the selection of the *right* victim. A pickpocket's victim must, at the time of the crime, be inattentive, distracted, or unconscious. If any of these conditions exist, and if the pickpocket is skilled in his operations, the stage is set for a successful larceny. With the coming of winter, the crowds move southward and so do most of the pickpockets. However, some pickpockets will remain in certain areas all year around. They will concentrate on theater districts, bus and railroad terminals, hotels, or large shopping centers. A complete knowledge of the methods of this type of criminal and the ability to recognize them come only from long years of experience in performing patient surveillance and trailing of them. This knowledge is essential for the effective control and apprehension of this type of thief.

43. According to this paragraph, the pickpocket is LEAST likely to operate in a 43.____
    A. baseball park with a full capacity attendance
    B. subway station in an outlying area late at night
    C. moderately crowded dance hall
    D. over-crowded department store

44. According to the above paragraph, the one of the following factors which is NOT necessary for the successful operation of the pickpocket is that 44.____
    A. he be proficient in the operations required to pickpockets
    B. the *right* potential victims be those who have been subject of such a theft previously
    C. his operations be hidden from the view of others
    D. the potential victim be unaware of the actions of the pickpocket

45. According to the above paragraph, it would be MOST correct to conclude that police officers who are successful in apprehending pickpockets 45.____
   A. are generally those who have had lengthy experience in recognizing all types of criminals
   B. must, by intuition, be able to recognize potential *right* victims
   C. must follow the pickpocket in their southward movement
   D. must have acquired specific knowledge and skills in this field

---

KEY (CORRECT ANSWERS)

1.	A	11.	C	21.	D	31.	A	41.	A
2.	A	12.	B	22.	C	32.	D	42.	A
3.	B	13.	A	23.	B	33.	D	43.	C
4.	A	14.	D	24.	C	34.	C	44.	B
5.	B	15.	C	25.	B	35.	A	45.	D
6.	B	16.	A	26.	A	36.	A		
7.	A	17.	C	27.	A	37.	C		
8.	A	18.	B	28.	D	38.	D		
9.	D	19.	C	29.	D	39.	C		
10.	C	20.	C	30.	A	40.	C		

EXAMINATION SECTION

TEST 1

DIRECTIONS: Each question or incomplete statement is followed by several suggested answers or completions. Select the one that BEST answers the question or completes the statement. *PRINT THE LETTER OF THE CORRECT ANSWER IN THE SPACE AT THE RIGHT.*

1. The basic purpose of patrol is to create a public impression of police presence everywhere so that potential offenders will think there is no opportunity for successful misconduct. 1.____
   In the assignment of police personnel, the type of police activity that MOST NEARLY realizes this purpose is
   A. traffic summons duty
   B. traffic duty
   C. patrol of all licensed premises
   D. patrol by the detective force
   E. radio motor patrol

2. A patrolman, who is asked by a civilian about a legal matter, directs him to the appropriate court. 2.____
   Of the following information given by the patrolman, the item which is LEAST likely to be useful to the civilian is
   A. hours during which the court is in session
   B. location of the court
   C. name of the Magistrate sitting in this court
   D. location of the complaint clerk within the court building
   E. transportation directions necessary to get to the court

3. An officer discovers two teenaged gangs, numbering about 50 boys, engaged in a free-for-all fight. 3.____
   The BEST immediate course for the officer to adopt is to
   A. call the station house for reinforcements
   B. fire over the heads of the boys and order them to disperse
   C. arrest the ringleaders
   D. call upon adult bystanders to assist him in restoring order
   E. attempt to stop the fight by using his club

4. A radio motor patrol team arrives on the scene a few minutes after a pedestrian has been killed on a busy street by a hit-and-run driver. 4.____
   After obtaining a description of the car, the FIRST action the officer should take is to
   A. radio a description of the fleeing car to precinct headquarters
   B. try to overtake the fleeing car
   C. obtain complete statements from everyone at the scene
   D. call for an ambulance
   E. inspect the site of the accident for clues

5. A police officer is approached by an obviously upset woman who reports that her husband is missing. 5.____
The FIRST thing the officer should do is to
   A. check with the hospitals and the police station
   B. tell the woman to wait a few hours and call the police station if her husband has not returned by then
   C. obtain a description of the missing man so that an alarm can be broadcast
   D. ask the woman why she thinks her husband is missing
   E. make certain that the woman lives in his precinct

6. A violin is reported as missing from the home of Mrs. Brown. 6.____
It would be LEAST important to the police, before making a routine check of pawnshops, to know that this violin
   A. is of a certain unusual shade of red
   B. has dimensions which are different from those of most violins
   C. has a well-known manufacturer's label stamped inside the violin
   D. has a hidden number given to the police by the owner
   E. has one tuning key with a chip mark on it in the shape of a triangle

7. In making his rounds, an officer should following the same route and schedule each time. 7.____
The suggested procedure is
   A. *good*; a fixed routine enables the officer to proceed methodically and systematically
   B. *poor*; criminals can avoid observation by studying the officer's routine
   C. *good*; without a fixed routine, an officer may overlook some of his many duties
   D. *poor*; a fixed routine reduces an officer's alertness and initiative
   E. *good*; residents in the area covered will have more confidence in police efficiency

8. Police officers should call for ambulances to transport injured people to the hospital rather than use patrol cars for this purpose. 8.____
Of the following, the MOST valid reason for this policy is that
   A. there is less danger of aggravating injuries
   B. patrol cars cannot be spared from police duty
   C. patrol cars are usually not equipped for giving emergency first aid
   D. medical assistance reaches the injured person sooner
   E. responsibility for treating injured people lies with the Department of Hospitals

9. A businessman requests advice concerning good practice in the use of a safe in his business office. 9.____
The one of the following points which should be stressed MOST in the use of safes is that
   A. a safe should not be placed where it can be seen from the street
   B. the combination should be written down and carefully hidden in the office

C. a safe located in a dark place is more tempting to a burglar than one which is located in a well-lighted place
D. factors of size and weight alone determine the protection offered by a safe
E. the names of the manufacturer and the owner should be painted on the front of the safe

10. During a quarrel on a crowded city street, one man stabs another and flees. An officer arriving at the scene a short time later finds the victim unconscious, calls for an ambulance, and orders the crowd to leave. 10.____
His action was
A. *bad*; there may have witnesses to the assault among the crowd
B. *good*; it is proper first aid procedure to give an injured person room and air
C. *bad*; the assailant is probably among the crowd
D. *good*; a crowd may destroy needed evidence
E. *bad*; it is poor public relations for the police to order people about needlessly

11. An officer walking his post at 3 A.M. notices heavy smoke coming out of a top floor window of a large apartment house. 11.____
Of the following, the action he should take FIRST is to
A. make certain that there really is a fire
B. enter the building and warn all the occupants of the apartment house
C. attempt to extinguish the fire before it gets out of control
D. call the Fire Department
E. call precinct headquarters for Fire Department help

12. Two rival youth gangs have been involved in several minor classes. The youth officer working in their area believes that a serious clash will occur if steps are not taken to prevent it. 12.____
Of the following, the LEAST desirable action for the officer to take in his effort to head of trouble is to
A. arrest the leaders of both groups as a warning
B. warn the parents of the dangerous situation
C. obtain the cooperation of religious and civic leaders in the community
D. alert all social agencies working in that neighborhood
E. report the situation to his superior

13. Police officers are instructed to pay particular attention to anyone apparently making repairs on an auto parked on a street. 13.____
The MOST important reason for this rule is that
A. the auto may be parked illegally
B. the person making the repairs may be obstructing traffic
C. working on autos is prohibited on certain streets
D. many people injure themselves while working on autos
E. the person making the repairs may be stealing the auto

14. After making an arrest of a criminal, the officer is LEAST likely to request some kind of transportation if the 14.____
    A. prisoner is apparently a violent mental patient
    B. distance to be traveled is considerable
    C. prisoner is injured
    D. prisoner is in an alcoholic stupor
    E. prisoner talks of escaping

15. The Police Department, in an effort to prevent losses due to worthless checks, suggests to merchants that they place near the cash register a card stating that the merchant reserves the right to require positive identification and fingerprint from all persons who cash checks. 15.____
    This procedure is
    A. *poor*; the merchant's regular customers may be offended by compulsory fingerprinting
    B. *poor*; the taking of fingerprints would not deter the professional criminal
    C. *good*; the police criminal files may be enlarged by the addition of all fingerprints taken
    D. *poor*; this system could not work unless the fingerprinting was made mandatory
    E. *good*; the card might serve to discourage persons from attempting to cash worthless checks

16. A factory manager asks an officer to escort his payroll clerk to and from the local bank when payroll money is withdrawn. The officer knows that it is against departmental policy to provide payroll escort service. 16.____
    The officer should
    A. refuse and explain why he cannot do what is requested
    B. refer the manager to his precinct commander
    C. tell the manager that police officers have more important tasks
    D. advise the manager that he will provide this service if other duties do not interfere
    E. suggest that paychecks be issued to employees

17. A motorist who has been stopped by a motorcycle police officer for speeding acts rudely. He hints about his personal connections with high officials in the city government and demands the officer's name and shield number. 17.____
    The officer should
    A. arrest the motorist for threatening an officer in the performance of his duty
    B. give his name and shield number without comment
    C. ignore the question since his name and shield number will be on the summons he is about to issue
    D. give his name and shield number but add to the charges against the motorist
    E. ask the motorist why he wants the information and give it only if the answer is satisfactory

18. Tire skidmarks provide valuable information to policemen investigating automobile accidents. 18.____
The MOST important information obtained from this source is the
   A. condition of the road at the time of the accident
   B. effectiveness of the automobile's brakes
   C. condition of the tires
   D. point at which the driver first saw the danger
   E. speed of the automobile at the time of the accident

19. An officer observes several youths in the act of looting a peanut-vending machine. The youths flee in several directions as he approaches, ignoring his order to halt. The officer then shoots at them, and they halt and are captured 19.____
The officer's action was
   A. *right*; it was the most effective way of capturing the criminals
   B. *wrong*; extreme measures should not be taken in apprehending petty offenders
   C. *right*; provided that there was no danger of shooting innocent bystanders
   D. *wrong*; this is usually ineffective when more than one offender is involved
   E. *right*; it is particularly important to teach juvenile delinquents respect for the law

20. Before permitting automobiles involved in an accident to depart, an officer should take certain measures. 20.____
Of the following, it is LEAST important that the officer make certain that
   A. both drivers are properly licensed
   B. the automobiles are in safe operating condition
   C. the drivers have exchanged names and license numbers
   D. the drivers are physically fit to drive
   E. he obtains the names and addresses of drivers and witnesses

21. A detective, following a tip that a notorious bank robber is to meet a woman in a certain restaurant, is seated in a booth from which he can observe people entering and leaving. While waiting, he notices a flashily dressed woman get up from a table and slip by the cashier without paying her check. The detective ignored the incident and continued watching for the wanted man. 21.____
This course of action was
   A. *correct*; the woman probably forgot to pay her bill
   B. *incorrect*; he should have arrested the woman since a *bird in the hand is worth two in the bush*
   C. *correct*; it is not the duty of the police department to protect businessmen from loss due to their own negligence
   D. *incorrect*; he should have followed the woman since she may lead to the bank robber
   E. *correct*; the detective should not risk losing the bank robber by checking on this incident

22. All officers are required to maintain a record of their daily police activity in a memorandum book. 22.____
The LEAST likely reason for this requirement is to
    A. make it unnecessary for the officer to remember police incidents
    B. give supervisors information concerning the officer's daily work
    C. serve as a possible basis to refute unjustified complaints against the officer
    D. make a record of information that may have a bearing on a court action
    E. record any action which may later require an explanation

23. Police officers have a duty to take into custody any person who is actually or apparently mentally ill. 23.____
Of the following cases, the one LEAST likely to fall under this provision of the law is the
    A. quarrelsome person who makes unjustifiable accusations
    B. elderly man who appears confused and unable to dress or feed himself
    C. young man who sits on the sidewalk curb staring into space and, when questioned, gives meaningless answers
    D. man who shouts obscenities at strangers in the streets
    E. woman who accuses waiters of attempting to poison her

24. An officer should not take notes while first questioning a suspect. 24.____
Of the following, the MOST important reason for this procedure is that
    A. information obtained at this time will probably not be truthful
    B. unessential facts can be eliminated if statements are written late
    C. the physical reactions of the suspect during interrogation can be better observed
    D. the exact wording is of no importance
    E. the statement will be better organized if written later

25. An officer should know the occupations and habits of the people on his beat. In heavily populated districts, however, it is too much to ask that the officer know all the people on his beat. 25.____
If this statement is correct, the one of the following which would be the MOST practical course for an officer to follow is to
    A. concentrate on becoming acquainted with the oldest residents of the beat
    B. limit his attention to people who work as well as live in the district
    C. limit his attention to people with criminal records
    D. concentrate on becoming acquainted with key people such as janitors, bartenders, and local merchants
    E. concentrate on becoming acquainted with the newest residents of the beat

26. An officer off-duty but in uniform recognizes a stolen car parked outside of a tavern. He notices that the radiator of the car is warm, indicating recent use. 26.____
Of the following, the MOST practical course for the officer to follow is to
    A. enter the tavern and ask aloud for the driver of the car
    B. stand in a nearby doorway and watch the car

C. search for the officer on the beat and report the facts to him
D. telephone the station house as soon as he arrives home
E. enter the tavern and privately ask the bartender if he knows who owns the car

27. When a person is arrested, he is always asked whether he uses narcotics, regardless of the charge against him. 27.____
Of the following, the MOST important reason for asking this question is that
A. drug addicts can be induced to confess by withholding narcotics from them
B. the theft of narcotics is becoming a serious police problem
C. criminals are usually drug addicts
D. many drug addicts commit crimes in order to obtain money for the purchase of narcotics
E. it may be possible to convict the suspect of violation of the narcotics law

28. Of the following types of crimes, increased police vigilance would probably be LEAST successful in preventing 28.____
A. murder B. burglary C. prostitution
D. automobile thefts E. robbery

29. The Police Department has been hiring civilian women to direct traffic at school crossings. 29.____
The MOST important reason for this policy is
A. to stimulate civic interest in police problems
B. to dramatize the traffic safety problem
C. that women are more careful of the safety of children
D. that young school children have more confidence in women who are mothers of their playmates
E. to free policemen for regular patrol duty

30. Of the following, the fact that makes it MOST difficult to identify stolen cars is that 30.____
A. thieves frequently damage stolen cars
B. many cars are similar in appearance
C. thieves frequently disguise stolen cars
D. owners frequently don't report stolen cars which are covered by insurance
E. owners frequently delay reporting the theft

31. When testifying in a criminal case, it is MOST important that a policeman endeavor to 31.____
A. avoid technical terms which may be unfamiliar to the jury
B. lean over backwards in order to be fair to the defendant
C. assist the prosecutor even if some exaggeration is necessary
D. avoid contradicting other prosecution witnesses
E. confine his answers to the questions asked

32. When investigating a burglary, a policeman should obtain as complete descriptions as possible of articles of value which were stolen, but should list, without describing, stolen articles which are relatively valueless. 32.____
This suggested procedure is
   A. *poor*; what is valueless to one person may be of great value to another
   B. *good*; it enables the police to concentrate on recovering the most valuable articles
   C. *poor*; articles of little value frequently provide the only evidence connecting the suspect to the crime
   D. *good*; the listing of the inexpensive items is probably incomplete
   E. *poor*; the police should make the same effort to recover all stolen property, regardless of value

33. At 10 A.M. on a regular school day, an officer notices a boy about11 years old wandering in the street. When asked the reason he is not in school, he replies that he attends school in the neighborhood, but that he felt sick that morning. The officer then took the boy to the principal of the school. 33.____
This method of handling the situation was
   A. *bad*; the officer should have obtained verification of the boy's illness
   B. *good*; the school authorities are best equipped to deal with the problem
   C. *bad*; the officer should have obtained the boy's name and address and reported the incident to the attendance officer
   D. *good*; seeing the truant boy escorted by an officer will deter other children from truancy
   E. *bad*; the principal of a school should not be saddled with a truancy problem

34. During an investigation of a robbery, an officer caught one of the witnesses contradicting himself on one point. Upon questioning, the witness readily admitted the contradiction. 34.____
The officer should conclude that
   A. the witness was truthful but emotionally disturbed by the experience
   B. all of the statements of the witness should be disregarded as untrustworthy
   C. the statements of the witness should be investigated carefully
   D. the witness was trying to protect the guilty person
   E. contradictions of this sort are inevitable

35. A woman was found dead by her estranged husband in the kitchen of a ground floor apartment. The husband stated that, although the apartment was full of gas and tightly closed, all the burners of the kitchen range were shut. The husband had gone to the apartment to get some clothes. When an officer arrived, the apartment was still heavy with gas fumes. 35.____
Of the following, the MOST likely explanation for these circumstances is that
   A. gas seeped into the apartment under the door from a defective gas furnace in the basement
   B. the husband has given false information to mislead the police

C. the woman changed her mind about committing suicide and shut off the jets just before she collapsed
D. a leak in the kitchen range had developed
E. the woman had died from some other cause than asphyxiation

36. An officer on post hears a cry for help from a woman in a car with two men. He approaches the car and is told by the woman that the men are kidnapping her. The men claim to be the woman's husband and doctor and state that they are taking her to a private mental hospital. 36.____
Of the following, the BEST course for the officer is to
A. take all of them to the station house for further questioning
B. permit the woman to depart and arrest the men
C. call for an ambulance to take the woman to the nearest city mental hospital
D. accompany the car to the private mental hospital
E. permit the car to depart on the basis of the explanation

37. Social security cards are not acceptable proof of identification for police purposes. 37.____
Of the following, the MOST important reason for this rule is that the social security card
A. is easily obtained
B. states on its face *for social security purposes—not for identification*
C. is frequently lost
D. does not contain the address of the person
E. does not contain a photograph, description, or fingerprints of the person

38. Many well-meaning people have proposed that officers in uniform not be permitted to arrest juveniles. 38.____
This proposal is
A. *good*; the police are not equipped to handle juvenile offenders
B. *bad*; juvenile offenders would lose respect for all law enforcement agencies
C. *good*; offending juveniles should be segregated from hardened criminals
D. *bad*; frequently it is the uniformed officer who first comes upon the youthful offender
E. *good*; contact with the police would prevent any rehabilitative measures from being taken

39. An off-duty police officer was seated in a restaurant when two men entered, drew guns, and robbed the cashier. The officer made no effort to prevent the robbery or apprehend the criminals. Later he justified his conduct by stating that an officer when off-duty is a private citizen with the same duties and rights of all private citizens. 39.____
The officer's conduct was
A. *wrong*; an officer must act to prevent crimes and apprehend criminals at all times
B. *right*; he was out of uniform at the time of the robbery
C. *wrong*; he had his gun with him at the time of the robbery

D. *right*; it would have been foolhardy for him to intervene when outnumbered by armed robbers
E. *wrong*; he should have obtained the necessary information and descriptions after the robbers left

40. Drivers with many convictions for traffic law violations sometimes try to conceal this record by cutting off the lower part of the operator's license and attaching to it clean section from a blank application form. 40.____
An officer who stops a driver and notices that his operator's license is torn and held together by transparent tape should FIRST
A. verify the driver's explanation of the torn license
B. examine both parts of the license to see if they match
C. request additional proof of identity
D. check the records of the Bureau of Motor Vehicles for unanswered summonses

Question 41-60.

DIRECTIONS: In answering Questions 41 through 60 select the lettered word or phrase which means MOST NEARLY the same as the word in capitals.

41. IMPLY 41.____
A. agree to B. hint at C. laugh at
D. mimic E. reduce

42. APPRAISAL 42.____
A. allowance B. composition C. prohibition
D. quantity E. valuation

43. DISBURSE 43.____
A. approve B. expend C. prevent
D. relay E. restrict

44. POSTERITY 44.____
A. back payment B. current procedure C. final effort
D. future generations E. rare specimen

45. PUNCTUAL 45.____
A. clear B. honest C. polite
D. prompt E. prudent

46. PRECARIOUS 46.____
A. abundant B. alarmed C. cautious
D. insecure E. placid

47. FOSTER 47.____
A. delegate B. demote C. encourage
D. plead E. surround

48. PINNACLE 48.____
A. center B. crisis C. outcome
D. peak E. personificaton

49. COMPONENT 49.____
A. flattery B. opposite C. part
D. revision E. trend

50. SOLICIT 50.____
A. ask B. prohibit C. promise
D. revoke E. surprise

51. LIAISON 51.____
A. asset B. coordination C. difference
D. policy E. procedure

52. ALLEGE 52.____
A. assert B. break C. irritate
D. reduce E. wait

53. INFILTRATION 53.____
A. consumption B. disposal C. enforcement
D. penetration E. seizure

54. SALVAGE 54.____
A. announce B. combine C. prolong
D. save E. try

55. MOTIVE 55.____
A. attack B. favor C. incentive
D. patience E. tribute

56. PROVOKE 56.____
A. adjust B. incite C. leave
D. obtain E. practice

57. SURGE 57.____
A. branch B. contract C. revenge
D. rush E. want

58. MAGNIFY 58.____
A. attract B. demand C. generate
D. increase E. puzzle

59. PREPONDERANCE 59.____
A. decision B. judgment C. outweighing
D. submission E. warning

60. ABATE 60.____
   A. assist
   B. coerce
   C. diminish
   D. indulge
   E. trade

Question 61-65.

DIRECTIONS: Questions 61 through 65 are to be answered on the basis of the table which appears below.

VALUE OF PROPERTY STOLEN – 2019 AND 2020
LARCENY

Category	2019 Number of Offenses	2019 Value of Stolen Property	2020 Number of Offenses	2020 Value of Stolen Property
Pocket-picking	20	$1,950	10	$950
Purse-snatching	175	5,750	20	12,500
Shoplifting	155	7,950	225	17,350
Automobile thefts	1,040	127,050	860	108,000
Thefts of auto accessories	1,135	34,950	970	24,400
Bicycle thefts	355	8,250	240	6,350
All other thefts	1,375	187,150	1,300	153,150

61. Of the total number of larcenies reported for 2019, automobile thefts accounted for MOST NEARLY 61.____
   A. 5%
   B. 15%
   C. 25%
   D. 50%
   E. 75%

62. The LARGEST percentage decrease in the value of the stolen property from 2019 to 2020 was in the category of 62.____
   A. pocket-picking
   B. automobile thefts
   C. thefts of auto accessories
   D. bicycle thefts
   E. all other thefts

63. In 2020, the average amount of each theft was LOWEST for the category of 63.____
   A. pocket-picking
   B. purse-snatching
   C. shoplifting
   D. thefts of auto accessories

64. The category which had the LARGEST numerical reduction in the number of offenses from 2019 to 2020 was 64.____
   A. pocket-picking
   B. automobile thefts
   C. thefts of auto accessories
   D. bicycle thefts
   E. all other thefts

65. When the categories are ranked for each year, according to the number of offenses committed in each category (largest number to rank first), the number of categories which will have the same rank in 2019 as in 2020 is 65.____
   A. 3
   B. 4
   C. 5
   D. 6
   E. 7

66. A parade is marching up an avenue for 60 city blocks. A sample count of the number of people watching the parade on one side of the street in the block is taken, first, in a block near the end of the parade, and then in a block at the middle; the former count is 4,000 and the latter is 6,000. 66.____
If the average for the entire parade is assumed to be the average of the two samples, then the estimated number of persons watching the entire parade is MOST NEARLY
A. 240,000 B. 300,000 C. 480,000 D. 600,000 E. 720,000

67. Suppose that the revenue from parking meters in a city was 5% greater in 2019 than in 2018, and 2% less in 2020 than in 2019. 67.____
If the revenue in 2018 was $1,500,000, then the revenue in 2020 was
A. $1,541,500 B. $1,542,000 C. $1,542,500
D. $1,543,000 E. $1,543,500

68. A radio motor patrol car completes a ten mile trip in twenty minutes. 68.____
If it does one-half the distance at a speed of twenty miles an hour, its speed, in miles per hour, for the remainder of the distance must be
A. 30 B. 40 C. 50 D. 60 E. 70

69. A public beach has two parking areas. Their capacities are in the ratio of two to one and, on a certain day, are filled to 60% and 40% of capacity, respectfully. 69.____
The entire parking facilities of the beach on that day are MOST NEARLY _____ filled.
A. 38% B. 43% C. 48% D. 53% E. 58%

70. While on foot patrol, an officer walks north for eleven blocks, turns around and walks south for six blocks, turns around and walks north for two blocks, then makes a right turn and walks one block. 70.____
In relation to his starting point, he is now _____ blocks away and facing _____.
A. twenty; east B. eight; east C. seven; west
D. nine; north E. seven; north

Question 71-73.

DIRECTIONS: Questions 71 through 73 are to be answered on the basis of the following paragraph.

When police officers search for a stolen car, they first check for the color of the car, then for make, model, year, body damage, and finally license number. The first five can be detected from almost any angle, while the recognition of the license number is often not immediately apparent. The serial number and motor number, though less likely to be changed than the easily substituted license number, cannot be observed in initial detection of the stolen car.

71. According to the above paragraph, the one of the following features which is LEAST readily observed in checking for a stolen car in moving traffic is 71.____
A. license number B. serial number C. model
D. make E. color

72. The feature of a car that cannot be determined from most angles of observation is the 72.____
    A. make B. model C. year
    D. license number E. color

73. Of the following, the feature of a stolen car that is MOST likely to be altered by a car thief shortly after the car is stolen is the 73.____
    A. license number B. motor number C. color
    D. model E. minor body damage

Question 74-75.

DIRECTIONS: Questions 74 and 75 are to be answered on the basis of the following paragraph.

The racketeer is primarily concerned with business affairs, legitimate or otherwise, and preferably those which are close to the margin of legitimacy. He gets his best opportunities from business organizations which meet the need of large sections of the public for goods or services which are defined as illegitimate by the same public, such as prostitution, gambling, illicit drugs or liquor. In contrast to the thief, the racketeer and the establishments he controls deliver goods and services for money received.

74. From the above paragraph, it can be deduced that suppression of racketeers is difficult because 74.____
    A. victims of racketeers are not guilty of violating the law
    B. racketeers are generally engaged in fully legitimate enterprises
    C. many people want services which are not obtainable through legitimate sources
    D. the racketeers are well organized
    E. laws prohibiting gambling and prostitution are unenforceable

75. According to the above paragraph, racketeering, unlike theft, involves 75.____
    A. objects of value B. payment for goods received
    C. organized gangs D. public approval
    E. unlawful activities

Question 76-78.

DIRECTIONS: Questions 76 through 78 are to be answered on the basis of the following paragraph.

A number of crimes, such as robbery, assault, rape, certain forms of theft and burglary, are highly visible crimes in that it is apparent to all concerned that they are criminal acts prior to or at the time they are committed. In contrast to these, check forgeries, especially those committed by first offenders, have low visibility. There is little in the criminal act or in the interaction between the check passer and the person cashing the check to identify it as a crime. Closely related to this special quality of the forgery crime is the fact that, while it is formally defined and treated as a felonious or infamous crime, it is informally held by the legally untrained public to be a relatively harmless form of crime.

76. According to the above paragraph, crimes of high visibility 76.____
   A. are immediately recognized as crimes by the victims
   B. take place in public view
   C. always involve violence or the threat of violence
   D. usually are committed after dark
   E. can be observed from a distance

77. According to the above paragraph, 77.____
   A. the public regards check forgery as a minor crime
   B. the law regards check forgery as a minor crime
   C. the law distinguishes between check forgery and other forgery
   D. it is easier to spot inexperienced check forgers than other criminals
   E. it is more difficult to identify check forgers than other criminals

78. As used in the above paragraph, an *infamous* crime is 78.____
   A. a crime attracting great attention from the public
   B. more serious than a felony
   C. less serious than a felony
   D. more or less serious than a felony, depending upon the surrounding circumstances
   E. the same as a felony

Question 79-81.

DIRECTIONS: Questions 79 through 81 are to be answered on the basis of the following paragraph.

Criminal science is largely the science of identification. Progress in this field has been marked and sometimes very spectacular because new techniques, instruments, and facts flow continuously from the scientist. But the crime laboratories are undermanned, trade secrets still prevail, and inaccurate conclusions are often the result. However, modern gadgets cannot substitute for the skilled intelligent investigator; he must be their master.

79. According to the above paragraph, criminal science 79.____
   A. excludes the field of investigation
   B. is primarily interested in establishing identity
   C. is based on the equipment used in crime laboratories
   D. uses techniques different from those used in other sciences
   E. is essentially secret in nature

80. Advances in criminal science have been, according to the above paragraph, 80.____
   A. extremely limited
   B. slow but steady
   C. unusually reliable
   D. outstanding
   E. infrequently worthwhile

81. A problem that has not been overcome completely in crime work is, according to the above paragraph, 81.____
   A. unskilled investigators
   B. the expense of new equipment and techniques
   C. an insufficient number of personnel in crime laboratories
   D. inaccurate equipment used in laboratories
   E. conclusions of the public about the value of this field

Question 82-84.

DIRECTIONS: Questions 82 through 84 are to be answered on the basis of the following paragraph.

The New York City Police Department will accept for investigation no report of a person missing from his residence if such residence is located outside of New York City. The person reporting same will be advised to report such fact to the police department of the locality where the missing person lives, which will, if necessary, communicate officially with the New York City Police Department. However, a report will be accepted of a person who is missing from a temporary residence in New York City, but the person making the report will be instructed to make a report also to the police department of the locality where the missing person lives.

82. According to the above paragraph, a report to the New York City Police Department of a missing person whose permanent residence is outside of New York City will 82.____
   A. always be investigated provided that a report is also made to his local police authorities
   B. never be investigated unless requested officially by his local police authorities
   C. be investigated in cases of temporary New York City residence, but a report should always be made to his local police authorities
   D. be investigated if the person making the report is a New York City resident
   E. always be investigated and a report will be made to the local police authorities by the New York City Police Department

83. Of the following, the MOST likely reason for the procedure described in the above paragraph is that 83.____
   A. non-residents are not entitled to free police service from New York City
   B. local police authorities would resent interference in their jurisdiction
   C. local police authorities sometimes try to unload their problems on the New York City Police
   D. local police authorities may be better able to conduct an investigation
   E. few persons are erroneously reported as missing

84. Mr. Smith, who lives in Jersey City, and Mr. Jones, who lives in Newark, arrange to meet in New York City, but Mr. Jones does not keep the appointment. Mr. Smith telephones Mr. Jones several times the next day and gets no answer. Mr. Smith believes that something has happened to Mr. Jones. 84.____

According to the above paragraph, Mr. Smith should apply to the police authorities of

A. Jersey City
B. Newark
C. Newark and New York City
D. Jersey City and New York City
E. Newark, Jersey City, and New York City

Question 85-87.

DIRECTIONS: Questions 85 through 87 are to be answered on the basis of the following paragraph.

Some early psychologists believed that the basic characteristic of the criminal type was inferiority of intelligence, if not outright feeblemindedness. They were misled by the fact that they had measurements for all kinds of criminals but, until World War I gave them a draft army sample, they had no information on a comparable group of non-criminal adults. As soon as acceptable measurements could be taken of criminals and a comparable group of non-criminals, concern with feeblemindedness or with low intelligence as a type took on less and less significance in research in criminology.

85. According to the above paragraph, some early psychologists were in error because they did not 85.____

A. distinguish among the various types of criminals
B. devise a suitable method of measuring intelligence
C. measure the intelligence of non-criminals as a basis for comparison
D. distinguish between feeblemindedness and inferiority of intelligence
E. clearly define the term *intelligence*

86. The above paragraph implies that studies of the intelligence of criminals and non-criminals 86.____

A. are useless because it is impossible to obtain comparable groups
B. are not meaningful because only the less intelligent criminals are detected
C. indicate that criminals are more intelligent than non-criminals
D. indicate that criminals are less intelligent than non-criminals
E. do not indicate that there are any differences between the two groups

87. According to the above paragraph, studies of World War I draft gave psychologists vital information concerning 87.____

A. adaptability to army life of criminals and non-criminals
B. criminal tendencies among draftees
C. the intelligence scores of large numbers of men
D. differences between intelligence scores of draftees and volunteers
E. the behavior of men under abnormal conditions

Question 88-90.

DIRECTIONS: Questions 88 through 90 are to be answered on the basis of the following paragraph.

The use of a roadblock is simply an adaptation to police practices of the military concept of encirclement. Successful operation of a roadblock plan depends almost entirely on the amount of advance study and planning given to such operations. A thorough and detailed examination of the roads and terrain under the jurisdiction of a given police agency should be made with the locations of the roadblocks pinpointed in advance The first principle to be borne in mind in the location of each roadblock is the time element. Its location must be at a point beyond which the fugitive could not have possibly traveled in the time elapsed from the commission of the crime to the arrival of the officers at the roadblock.

88. According to the above paragraph, 88.____
   A. military operations have made extensive use of roadblocks
   B. the military concept of encirclement is an adaptation of police use of roadblocks
   C. the technique of encirclement has been widely used by military forces
   D. a roadblock is generally more effective than encirclement
   E. police use of roadblocks is based on the idea of military encirclement

89. According to the above paragraph, 89.____
   A. the factor of time is the sole consideration in the location of a roadblock
   B. the maximum speed possible in the method of escape is of major importance in roadblock location
   C. the time of arrival of officers at the site of a proposed roadblock is of little importance
   D. if the method of escape is not known, it should be assumed that the escape is by automobile
   E. a roadblock should be sited as close to the scene of the crime as the terrain will permit

90. According to the above paragraph, 90.____
   A. advance study and planning are of minor importance in the success of roadblock operations
   B. a thorough and detailed examination of all roads within a radius of fifty miles should precede the determination of a roadblock location
   C. consideration of terrain features is important in planning the location of roadblocks
   D. the pinpointing of roadblocks should be performed before any advance study is made
   E. a roadblock operation can seldom be successfully undertaken by a single police agency

---

KEY (CORRECT ANSWERS)

1. E
2. C
3. A
4. A
5. D

6. C
7. B
8. A
9. C
10. A

11. D
12. A
13. E
14. E
15. E

16. A
17. B
18. E
19. B
20. C

21. E
22. A
23. A
24. C
25. D

26. B
27. D
28. A
29. E
30. C

31. E
32. C
33. B
34. C
35. B

36. A
37. E
38. D
39. A
40. B

41. B
42. E
43. B
44. D
45. D

46. D
47. C
48. D
49. C
50. A

51. B
52. A
53. D
54. D
55. C

56. B
57. D
58. D
59. C
60. C

61. C
62. A
63. D
64. B
65. C

66. D
67. E
68. D
69. D
70. B

71. B
72. D
73. A
74. C
75. B

76. A
77. A
78. E
79. B
80. D

81. C
82. C
83. D
84. B
85. C

86. E
87. C
88. E
89. B
90. C

EXAMINATION SECTION

TEST 1

DIRECTIONS: Each question or incomplete statement is followed by several suggested answers or completions. Select the one that BEST answers the question or completes the statement. *PRINT THE LETTER OF THE CORRECT ANSWER IN THE SPACE AT THE RIGHT.*

1. Many officers working in the field of juvenile delinquency accept youth gangs as a natural development in community life. 1.____
   If this assumption is correct, the one of the following which would be the MOST practical course of action with respect to youth gangs is to
   A. utilize the activity of the gang, diverting it from the criminal to the constructive
   B. change the structure of community life so that gangs will no longer be a natural development
   C. ignore youth gangs and concentrate on youthful offenders
   D. encourage younger members of gangs to break away from the gang leaders
   E. set up an interesting lecture and demonstration course pointing out the evils of gang warfare

2. An officer who is called to the scene of an automobile accident questions two witnesses concerning the accident. The officer knows that the two witnesses are outstanding and upright members of the community. The two witnesses give contradictory testimony. 2.____
   He should conclude that the MOST likely reason for the contradiction is that
   A. honest, upright people do not always make the best witnesses
   B. at least one of the witnesses has been upset by the questioning
   C. people do not always observe accurately
   D. at least one of the witnesses is lying
   E. contradictions in cases of this sort are inevitable

3. An officer, making his rounds, notices that one storekeeper has not cleared the snow from the sidewalk in front of his store. After reminding the storekeeper that he is breaking the law if the sidewalk is not cleared, the officer also points out that a dangerous situation may arise if ice forms. 3.____
   This method of handling the situation by the officer is USUALLY
   A. *bad*; the storekeeper broke the law and should be punished
   B. *good*; the storekeeper will clear the sidewalk and no one will be hurt
   C. *bad*; the patrolman should have forced the storekeeper to clear the sidewalk of snow immediately
   D. *good*; threatening severe punishment is the most desirable method to achieve compliance with the law
   E. *bad*; the patrolman should not have mentioned the law but asked the storekeeper to clear the walk as a personal favor to him

4. About 9:00 P.M., an officer observes two men loitering near a neighborhood movie theatre. He has not seen either of these two men in the neighborhood before. The agent for the theatre generally deposits the night receipts in the local bank's night deposit vault between 9:00 P.M. an 9:15 P.M. 4.____
Of the following, the MOST appropriate action for the officer to take is to
   A. approach the two men and tell them that no loitering is allowed near the theatre
   B. demand that they tell him their place of residence and the reason for their presence near the theatre
   C. pay no further attention since they are obviously waiting for some friend or relative who is in the theatre
   D. enter the theatre by the side entrance and warn the manager to be prepared for a possible attempt at robbery
   E. station himself so that he can observe their further actions until the theatre's money has been deposited

5. An officer stationed along the route of a parade has been ordered by his superior to allow no cars to cross the route while the parade is in progress. An ambulance driver on an emergency run attempts to drive his ambulance across the route while the parade is passing. 5.____
Under these circumstances, the officer should
   A. ask the driver to wait while the officer contacts his superior and obtains a decision
   B. stop the parade long enough to permit the ambulance to cross the street
   C. direct the ambulance driver to the shortest detour available which will add at least ten minutes to run
   D. hold up the ambulance in accordance with the superior's order
   E. advise the driver to telephone the hospital and notify his superior that he is being delayed by the parade

6. A woman has her husband arrested for severely beating his five-year-old son. A crowd of angry neighbors has gathered around the husband. 6.____
In making the arrest, the arresting officer should
   A. treat the husband like any other person accused of breaking the law
   B. deal with the husband sympathetically since the man may be mentally ill
   C. handle him harshly since his crime is a despicable one
   D. treat him roughly only if he shows no remorse for his actions
   E. let him be *roughed up* a bit by neighbors so long as he is not injured severely

7. An officer notices two students engaged in a fistfight in front of a high school. Three or four students have gathered around the fighting youngsters. 7.____
Of the following actions, the one the officer should take FIRST is to
   A. summon assistance before attending to the fight
   B. forcibly disperse the onlooking students and then attend to the belligerents
   C. try to separate the two belligerents without hurting either
   D. fire a shot into the air to warn the onlookers and the belligerents to disperse
   E. use his nightstick on the two belligerents to stop the fight

8. An officer who responded at 2 A.M. to a radio call that a burglary had been committed in an apartment heard the sound of clashing tools coming from the adjoining apartment. 8.____
For the officer to investigate the noise would be
   A. *undesirable*; he may not search without a warrant
   B. *desirable*; the thief may be found
   C. *undesirable*; unusual noises in apartments are common
   D. *desirable*; the victim would tend to be impressed by the concern shown
   E. *undesirable*; the thief may be armed

9. An off-duty officer in civilian clothes is riding in the rear of a bus. He notices two teenage boys tampering with the rear emergency door. 9.____
The MOST appropriate action for him to take is to
   A. watch the boys closely but take no action unless they actually open the emergency door
   B. report the boys' actions to the bus operator and let the bus operator take whatever action he deems best
   C. signal the bus operator to stop, show the boys his badge, and then order them off the bus
   D. show the boys his badge, order them to stop their actions, and take down their names and addresses
   E. tell the boys to discontinue their tampering, pointing out the dangers to life that their actions may create

10. At 3:00 A.M., while on his tour of duty, an officer notices a traffic light at an intersection is not operating. There is little traffic at this intersection. 10.____
Under these circumstances, the MOST appropriate action for the officer to take is to
   A. report this matter to his superior at the end of his tour of duty
   B. station himself at the intersection to direct traffic until the appearance of daylight reduces the hazard of a collision
   C. report this matter immediately to his precinct
   D. post a sign at the intersection stating that the traffic light is not operating
   E. ignore the situation since nothing can be done at this time and the patrolman on the day shift can make the necessary report

Questions 11-15.

DIRECTIONS: Questions 11 through 15 are to be answered on the basis of the following Police Department rule.

A description of persons or property wanted by the Police Department, which is to be given to the police force through the medium of a general alarm, if not distinctive, is of no value.

11. Mrs. R. Jones reported the theft of a valuable brooch from her apartment. The brooch was of gold and consisted of a very large emerald surrounded by 50 small diamonds. 11.____
The one of the following additional pieces of information which would be MOST helpful to you in identifying the brooch is that

A. the value of the brooch is $50,000
B. there are 48 small diamonds and 2 slightly larger diamonds
C. the emerald is carved in the form of a woman's head
D. the brooch is made of gold with a slightly green cast
E. the brooch is circular with the emerald in the center and the diamond around it

12. Assume that you have stopped a 2017 Dodge four-door sedan which you suspect is a car which had been reported as stolen the day before. 12.____
The one of the following items of information which would be of GREATEST value in determining whether this is the stolen car is that the
A. stolen car's license number was QA 2356; this car's license number is U21375
B. stolen car's engine number was AB 6231; this car's engine number is CS2315
C. windshield of the stolen car was not cracked; this car's windshield is cracked
D. stolen car had no dents; this car has numerous dents
E. stolen car had white-walled tires; this car does not have white-walled tires

13. Assume that you are questioning a woman who, you suspect, is wanted by the Department. 13.____
Of the characteristics listed below, the one which would be of GREATEST value in determining whether this is the wanted person is:
A. Age: about 30; Height: 5'8"; Weight: 160 lbs.
B. Eyes: blue; Hair: blonde; Complexion: fair
C. that she frequently drinks to excess
D. Scars: two thin, half-moon scars just on right cheek bone and below eye
E. that when last seen she was wearing a dark, grey wool dress and was accompanied by the prizefighter John Day

14. You are watching a great number of people leave the sports arena after a boxing match. 14.____
Of the characteristics listed below, the one which would be of GREATEST value to you in spotting a man wanted by the Department is
A. Height: 5'3"; Weight: 200 lbs.
B. Eyes: brown; Hair: black wavy; Complexion: sallow
C. that he frequents bars and grills and customarily associates with females
D. Scars: thin ½" scar on left upper lip; Tattoos: on right forearm – *Pinto*
E. Mustache: when last seen August 2020, he wore a small black mustache

15. Assume that on a hot summer day you are stationed on the grass of the south bank of a busy parkway looking at eastbound traffic for a light blue 2015 Ford two-door sedan. 15.____
If traffic is very heavy, the one of the following additional pieces of information which would be MOST helpful to you in identifying the car is that
A. all chrome is missing from the left side of the car
B. there is a bullethole in the left front window

C. motor number is 22674 AH
D. the front bumper is missing
E. the paint on the right side of the car is somewhat faded

16. While you are on patrol, you notice that the lone occupant of a car parked at the top of a long, steep hill is a boy about 7 years old. The boy is playing with the steering wheel and other controls. 16.____
The FIRST action for you to take is to
A. make sure that the car is safely parked
B. test the car's emergency brake to make sure it will hold
C. drive the car to the bottom of the hill and park it there
D. test the car's controls to make sure that the boy has not changed anything
E. order the boy to leave the car for his own safety

17. The proprietor of a tavern summons an officer and turns over to him a loaded revolver that was found in one of the tavern's booths. 17.____
Of the following, the LEAST appropriate action for the officer to take is to
A. close off the booth from use by other patrons
B. determine exactly when the revolver was found
C. obtain the names or descriptions of the persons who occupied the both before the revolver was found
D. question the proprietor very closely concerning the matter
E. unload the gun and place it in an inside pocket

18. The traditional method of training an officer—equipping him and putting him on the street with an experienced man—is no longer adequate. 18.____
The one of the following which is the MOST probable reason for this change in viewpoint is that
A. officers are no longer simply guardians of the peace but each one is a specialist
B. the kind of recruit that the Police Department gets has changed
C. the former belief that *the best way to learn is to do* is no longer accepted
D. there has been a great change in police problems and methods
E. more money has been made available for training purposes

19. An officer overhears a businessman complain that his sales of tires had fallen off sharply because a new competitor has suddenly appeared in his territory and is underselling him at unbelievably low prices. The officer recalls that a large shipment of tires had been reported stolen a short time ago. 19.____
It is ADVISABLE for the officer to
A. forget the matter as it is probably a coincidence
B. tell the businessman to report the new competitor to the Better Business Bureau for unfair practices
C. check to see if there is any connection between the two sets of circumstances
D. inform the businessman about the robbery and ask him if he thinks that there is a connection
E. arrest the owner of the new store as he is obviously involved in the robbery

20. While patrolling his post in a section of the county late Saturday night, an officer notices a well-dressed man break a car window with a rock, open a front door, and enter. He is followed into the car by a woman companion. 20.____
Of the following, the MOST essential action for the officer to take is to
   A. point his gun at the man, enter the car, and order the man to drive to the station house to explain his action
   B. approach the car and ask the man why it was necessary to break the car window
   C. take down the license number of the car and note the description of both the man and the woman in the event that the car is later reported as stolen
   D. *bawl the man out* for endangering himself by breaking the window
   E. request proof of ownership of the car from the man

21. Juveniles who rob do not usually use the money they obtain in this manner for essentials but rather to indulge in spending to impress others. 21.____
This observation indicates that clues leading to the apprehension of juvenile delinquents may be found by noting
   A. family requirements and needs
   B. the recreation habits of young people
   C. which young people have a tendency to commit robbery
   D. the relationships which exist in criminal gangs between criminals who commit crimes to satisfy essential needs and those who do not
   E. what objects are taken in robberies

22. A storekeeper complains to an officer that his store window has been broken by a gang of neighborhood hoodlums. The officer tells the storekeeper to notify headquarters. 22.____
This action is
   A. *desirable*; the storekeeper will be able to tell the proper official his story firsthand
   B. *undesirable*; the problem is so minor that there is no need to bother headquarters
   C. *desirable*; the storekeeper will be more confidant if his case is handled by a sergeant or lieutenant
   D. *undesirable*; buckpassing of this type makes for inefficiency and poor public relations
   E. *desirable*; investigation of the case would take the officer away from his post for too long a period

23. In order to reduce the amount of contradictory testimony, the witnesses to a crime should be allowed to discuss, as a group what had happened before they are questioned. 23.____
The procedure suggested is
   A. *bad*; a witness is less likely to commit himself if other witnesses to the event are present
   B. *good*; the need to sift stories will be considerably reduced

C. *bad*; a witness is less likely to blurt out the truth if other witnesses are present to give him moral backing
D. *good*; witnesses will be more apt to recall exactly what happened
E. *bad*; the views of the strongest personalities may be obtained rather than the truth

24. An officer positively recognizes a man on a busy street as one wanted for passing worthless checks. 24.____
Of the following, the MOST appropriate action for the officer to take is to
A. approach and then arrest the man
B. follow the man until a place is reached where there are few people; then take out his gun and arrest the man
C. immediately take out his gun, stop the man, and search him
D. follow the man until he stops long enough for the patrolman to summon aid from his precinct
E. follow the man as he may lead the way to associates

25. It is generally agreed that criminal tendencies are present in every person. 25.____
A basic difference, however, between the normal person and the criminal is that the
A. normal person, sometimes, commits trivial crimes but the criminal commits crimes of a major nature
B. criminal is unable to understand the possible results of antisocial acts he commits
C. normal person is able to control his antisocial tendencies and direct his activity in socially approved channels
D. criminal believes that he is not different from the person who does not commit crimes
E. normal person believes that he is not different from the person who commits crimes

26. It has been claimed that a person who commits a crime sometimes has an unconscious wish to be punished, which is caused by strong unconscious feelings of guilt. 26.____
The one of the following actions by a criminal which may be partly due to an unconscious desire for punishment is
A. claiming that he doesn't know anything about the crime when he is questioned by the police
B. running away from the state where he committed the crime
C. revisiting the place where he committed the crime
D. his care not to leave any clues at the scene of the crime
E. accusing someone else when he is captured by the police

27. Experience has shown that many crimes have been planned in prison. 27.____
From this finding, it is REASONABLE to assume that
A. the principal motive for the commission of first crimes is the wish to take revenge on society
B. some criminals may be influenced to continue their careers of crime because they associate with other criminals

C. the real motives for the commission of most crimes originate in punishment for criminal acts
D. fear or imprisonment will make a criminal who has been in jail plan his second crime more carefully
E. the criminal mind is sharpened by maturity

28. Any change in insurance coverage immediately prior to a fire should be considered. Strange as it may seem, most such changes made by convicted arsonists are made to a smaller amount. 28.____
The MOST probable reason for such changes is that the arsonist
A. usually is not a rational person
B. decided to set the fire after the change was made
C. did not have enough money to pay for the full amount
D. reduced the insurance to the amount he expected to be lost in the fire
E. was trying to divert suspicion

29. Suppose that you are an officer whose tour of duty extends from 12 Midnight to 8:00 A.M. While on the first round of your tour, you notice that the nightlight in the front of a small candy store is out. In the past, the proprietor has always left the light on. The door to the store is locked. 29.____
Of the following, the MOST appropriate action for you to take FIRST is to
A. use your flashlight to light the store interior so that you may inspect it for unusual conditions
B. continue on your beat since the light probably burned out
C. break open the door lock so that you may conduct a thorough search of the store
D. call the storekeeper to notify him that the nightlight is out
E. call your precinct and report this unusual condition

30. A criminal becomes either a thief, an assailant, or a sexual offender, never an all-around criminal. 30.____
Of the following, an IMPORTANT reason for these basic differences in criminal behavior is probably that
A. to be an all-around criminal requires more intelligence than the average criminal has
B. crime syndicates have gained control over certain branches of crime and have made it difficult for a beginner to break in
C. criminal acts are an expression of the criminal's whole personality
D. all-around crime is not as profitable as specialization in crime
E. most crimes are committed on the spur of the moment and without previous thought

31. A young man who was arrested for smashing a store window and stealing a portable radio was asked why he did it. He answered, *Well, I wanted a radio and I just took it.* 31.____
If this answer is characteristic of the behavior of the young criminal, it is MOST reasonable to believe that

A. the young criminal has a well-organized personality
B. he sizes up each new situation in terms of his past experiences
C. his decision to commit a crime is made after careful consideration of its possible effect on his future
D. his temptation to commit a crime is an isolated situation, having, in his mind, little relation to his life as a whole
E. he hesitates to commit a crime unless he thinks he can get away with it

32. When the bodies of two women were found stabbed in an inner room of an apartment, it was first believed that it was a case of mutual homicide. 32.____
Of the following clues found at the scene, the one which indicates that it was more likely a case of murder by a third party is the fact that
A. the door to the apartment was found locked
B. there were bloodstains on the outer door of the apartment
C. there was a switchblade knife in each body
D. no money could be found in the room where the bodies were
E. both women were fully clothed

33. A radio crime program dramatizing a different police case every week showed the capture or death of the criminal and ended with the slogan *Crime Does Not Pay*. It was found that a gang of teenage boys listened to this program every week in order to see what mistake was made by the criminal, and then duplicated the crime, trying to avoid the same mistake. 33.____
This case illustrates that
A. all criminal minds work the same way
B. attempts to keep young people out of crime by frightening them into obeying the law are not always successful
C. it is not possible to commit the perfect crime unless care is taken
D. radio crime programs should not be permitted as they lead to an increase in the number of unsolved crimes
E. most criminals learn from their own mistakes

34. While on patrol at 2 A.M., you notice a man and a woman walking down the street talking together in low tones. They do not see you as you are standing in the shadow. The pair stop in front of a large apartment house. The man takes a bunch of keys from his pocket and tries several before he finds one which will open the door. While he is doing this, the woman taps her foot impatiently. 34.____
At this point, as the two are entering the apartment house, you should
A. notify precinct headquarters of the incident
B. permit them to enter but follow close behind them to see what they do
C. ignore the incident and continue on your patrol
D. force them to show their identification papers
E. arrest them on suspicion of illegal entry

35. The one of the following which is the probable reason for restricting parking to alternate sides of some streets on successive days is that, without this restriction, the parked cars make it difficult for the 35.____
A. Police Department to direct traffic
B. Department of Water Supply, Gas and Electricity to service hydrants

C. Traffic Department to plan the flow of traffic
D. Sanitation Department to clear the streets
E. Fire Department to put out fires

36. Looking through the window of a jewelry store, an officer sees a man take a watch from the counter and drop it into his pocket while the jeweler is busy talking to someone else. The man looks around the store and then walks out. The officer should 36.____
A. follow the man to see what he does with the watch as thieves of this type usually work in pairs
B. ignore the incident; if the man were performing an illegal act, the jeweler would have called for help
C. arrest the man, take him to the station house, and then return to obtain the jeweler's statement
D. ignore the incident; if the man were a thief, the jeweler would not have left the watches unattended
E. stop the man and bring him back into the shop so that both he and the jeweler can be questioned

37. It is quite possible to set up a general procedure which will result in the rehabilitation of all juvenile delinquents. 37.____
This statement is, in general
A. *correct*; the major causes of all juvenile delinquency are improper home life and a general lack of morals; cure these and there will be no problem of juvenile delinquency
B. *not correct*; juvenile delinquency results from the generally lower moral climate; therefore, rehabilitation is not possible until the world climate changes
C. *correct*; if juvenile delinquents are severely punished, rehabilitation will follow
D. *not correct*; each case of juvenile delinquency is different and for most effective treatment must be hand on an individual basis
E. *correct*: if the proper general procedure is set up, it always can be applied

38. An officer observes a young man who is obviously very excited, walking unusually fast, and repeatedly halting to look behind him. Upon stopping the young man, the officer finds that he is carrying a gun and has just held up a liquor store a few blocks away. 38.____
This incidence illustrates that
A. circumstances that are not suspicious in themselves frequently provide clues for the solution of crimes
B. an experienced officer can pick the criminal type out of a crowd by alert observation
C. action is always to be preferred to thought
D. an officer should investigate suspicious circumstances
E. an officer who stops to think may sometimes fail to get his man

39. When making arrests, the officer should treat all suspects in the same manner. This suggested rule is 39.____
   A. *undesirable*; the specific problems presented should govern the officer's actions
   B. *desirable*; this is the only democratic solution to the problem
   C. *undesirable*; officers should not be expected to abide by rules as criminals do not
   D. *desirable*; only by setting up fixed and rigid rules can patrolmen know what is expected of them
   E. *undesirable*; persons who are only suspected are not criminals and should not be treated as such

40. One of the most difficult questions in a crime prevention program is to decide how many men are needed to police a particular area. There have been a number of attempts to invent a simple formula, but none has so far been successful. 40.____
   Of the following reasons for this, the MOST probable is that
   A. men, not formulas, patrol beats
   B. many factors are involved whose relative importance has not been determined
   C. there is no information on which to base such a formula
   D. such a formula, even if it were accurate, would be of little use as it would be theoretical
   E. police problems in no two areas in the city are alike in any way

Questions 41-43.

DIRECTIONS: Questions 41 through 43 are to be answered on the basis of the following paragraph.

Modern police science may be said to have three phases. The first phase embraces the identification of living and dead persons. The second embraces the field work carried out by specially trained detectives at the scene of the crime. The third embraces methods used in the police laboratory to examine and analyze clues and traces discovered in the course of the investigation. While modern police science has had a striking influence on detective work and will surely further enhance its effectiveness, the time-honored methods, that is, knowledge of methods used by criminals, patience, tact, industry, thoroughness and imagination, will always be requisites for successful detective work.

41. According to the above paragraph, we may expect modern police science to 41.____
   A. help detective work more and more
   B. become more and more scientific
   C. depend less and less on the time-honored methods
   D. bring together the many different approaches to detective work
   E. play a less important role in detective work

42. According to the above paragraph, a knowledge of the procedures used by criminals is 42.____
    A. solely an element of the modern police science approach to detective work
    B. related to the identification of persons
    C. not related to detective field work
    D. related to methods used in the police laboratory
    E. an element of the traditional approach to detective work

43. Modern police science and practical detective work, according to the above paragraph, 43.____
    A. when used together can only lead to confusion
    B. are based on distinctly different theories of detective work
    C. have had strikingly different influences on detective work
    D. should both be used for successful detective work
    E. lead usually to similar results

Questions 44-47.

DIRECTIONS: Questions 44 through 47 are to be answered on the basis of the following paragraph.

A member of the force shall render reasonable aid to a sick or injured person. He shall summon an ambulance, if necessary, by telephoning the communications bureau of the borough, who shall notify the precinct concerned. If possible, he shall wait in full view of the arriving ambulance and take necessary action to direct the responding doctor or attendant to the patient without delay. If the ambulance does not arrive in twenty minutes, he shall send in a second call. However, if the sick person is in his or her home, a member of the force, before summoning an ambulance, will ascertain whether such person is willing to be taken to a hospital for treatment.

44. According to the above paragraph, if an officer wants to get an ambulance for a sick person, he should telephone 44.____
    A. the precinct concerned
    B. only if the sick person is in his home
    C. the nearest hospital
    D. only if the sick person is not in his home
    E. the borough communications bureau

45. According to the above paragraph, if an officer telephones for an ambulance and none arrives within twenty minutes, he should 45.____
    A. ask the injured person if he is willing to be taken to a hospital
    B. call the borough communications bureau
    C. call the precinct concerned
    D. attempt to give the injured person such assistance as he may need
    E. call the nearest hospital

46. An officer is called to help a woman who has fallen in her own home and has apparently broken her leg. 46.____
According to the above paragraph, he should
   A. ask her if she wants to go to a hospital
   B. try to set her leg if it is necessary
   C. call for an ambulance at once
   D. attempt to get a doctor as quickly as possible
   E. not attempt to help the woman in any way before competent medical aid arrives

47. A man falls from a window into the backyard of an apartment house. Assume that you are an officer and that you are called to assist this man. 47.____
According to the above paragraph, after you have called for an ambulance and comforted the injured man as much as you can, you should
   A. wait in front of the house for the ambulance
   B. ask the injured man if he wishes to go to the hospital for treatment
   C. remain with the injured man until the ambulance arrives
   D. send a bystander to direct the nearest doctor to the patient
   E. not ask the man to explain how the accident happened

Questions 48-50.

DIRECTIONS: Questions 48 through 50 are to be answered on the basis of the following paragraph.

What is required is a program that will protect our citizens and their property from criminal and anti-social acts, will effectively restrain and reform juvenile delinquents, and will prevent the further development of anti-social behavior. Discipline and punishment of offenders must necessarily play an important part in any such program. Serious offenders cannot be mollycoddled merely because they are under twenty-one. Restraint and punishment necessarily follow serious anti-social acts. But punishment, if it is to be effective, must be a planned part of a more comprehensive program of treating delinquency.

48. The one of the following goals NOT included among those listed above is to 48.____
   A. stop young people from defacing public property
   B. keep homes from being broken into
   C. develop an intra-city boys' baseball league
   D. change juvenile delinquents into useful citizens
   E. prevent young people from developing anti-social behavior patterns

49. According to the above paragraph, punishment is 49.____
   A. not satisfactory in any program dealing with juvenile delinquents
   B. the most effective means by which young vandals and hooligans can be reformed
   C. not used sufficiently when dealing with serious offenders who are under twenty-one
   D. of value in reducing juvenile delinquency only if it is part of a complete program
   E. most effective when it does not relate to specific anti-social acts

50. With respect to serious offenders who are under twenty-one, the above paragraph suggests that they 50.____
   A. be mollycoddled
   B. be dealt with as part of a comprehensive program to punish mature criminals
   C. should be punished
   D. be prevented, by brute force if necessary, from performing anti-social acts
   E. be treated as delinquent children who require more love than punishment

Questions 51-54.

DIRECTIONS: Questions 51 through 54 are to be answered on the basis of the following paragraph.

In all cases of homicide, members of the police department who investigate will make every effort to obtain statements from dying persons. Such statements are of the greatest importance to the District Attorney. In many cases, there may be a failure to solve the crime if they are not taken. The principal element to be considered in taking the declaration of a dying person is his mental attitude. In order to be admissible in evidence, the person must have no hope of recovery. The patient will be fully interrogated on that point before a statement is taken.

51. In cases of homicide, according to the above paragraph, members of the police force will 51.____
   A. try to change the mental attitude of the dying person
   B. attempt to obtain a statement from the dying person
   C. not give the information they obtain directly to the District Attorney
   D. be careful not to injure the dying person unnecessarily
   E. prevent unauthorized persons from taking dying declarations

52. The mental attitude of the person making the dying statement is of great importance because it can determine, according to the above paragraph, whether the 52.____
   A. victim should be interrogated in the presence of witnesses
   B. victim will be willing to make a statement of any kind
   C. victim has been forced to make the statement
   D. statement will tell the District Attorney who committed the crime
   E. statement can be used as evidence

53. District Attorneys find that statements of a dying person are important, according to the above paragraph, because 53.____
   A. it may be that the victim will recover and then refuse to testify
   B. they are important elements in determining the mental attitude of the victim
   C. they present a point of view
   D. it may be impossible to punish the criminal without such a statement
   E. dead men tell no tales

54. A well-known gangster is found dying from a bullet wound. The officer first on the scene, in the presence of witnesses, tells the man that he is going to die and asks, *Who shot you?* The gangster says, *Jones shot me, but he hasn't killed me. I'll live to get him.* He then falls back dead. 54.____
According to the above paragraph, this statement is
   A. *admissible* in evidence; the man was obviously speaking the truth
   B. *not admissible* in evidence; the man obviously did not believe that he was dying
   C. *admissible* in evidence; there were witnesses to the statement
   D. *not admissible* in evidence; the victim did not sign any statement and the evidence is merely hearsay
   E. *admissible* in evidence; there was no time to interrogate the victim

Questions 55-57.

DIRECTIONS: Questions 55 through 57 are to be answered on the basis of the following paragraph.

The factors contributing to crime and delinquency are varied and complex. The home and its immediate environment have been found to be crucial in determining the behavior patterns of the individual, and criminality can frequently be traced to faulty family relationships and a bad neighborhood. But in the search for a clearer understanding of the underlying causes of delinquent and criminal behavior, the total environment must be taken into consideration.

55. According to the above paragraph, family relationships 55.____
   A. tend to become faulty in bad neighborhoods
   B. are important in determining the actions of honest people as well as criminals
   C. are the only important element in the understanding of causes of delinquency
   D. are determined by the total environment
   E. of criminals are understandable only in terms of the behavior patterns of the individuals concerned

56. According to the above paragraph, the causes of crime and delinquency are 56.____
   A. not simple
   B. not meaningless
   C. meaningless
   D. simple
   E. always understandable

57. According to the above paragraph, faulty family relationships frequently are 57.____
   A. responsible for varied and complex results
   B. caused by differences
   C. caused when one or both parents have a criminal behavior pattern
   D. independent of the total environment
   E. the cause of criminal acts

Questions 58-60.

DIRECTIONS: Questions 58 through 60 are to be answered on the basis of the following paragraph.

A change in the specific problems which confront the police and in the methods for dealing with them has taken place in the last few decades. The automobile is a two-way symbol of this change in policing. It menaces every city with a complicated traffic problem and has speeded up the process of committing a crime and making a getaway, but at the same time has increased the effectiveness of police operations. However, the major concern of police departments continues to be the anti-social or criminal actions and behavior of human beings.

58. On the basis of the above paragraph, it can be stated that for the most part in the past few decades the specific problems of a police force 58.____
   A. have changed but the general problems have not
   B. as well as the general problems have changed
   C. have remained the same but the general problems have changed
   D. as well as the general problems have remained the same
   E. have caused changes in the general problems

59. According to the above paragraph, advances in science and industry have, in general, made the police 59.____
   A. operations less effective from the overall point of view
   B. operations more effective from the overall point of view
   C. abandon older methods of solving police problems
   D. concern themselves more with the anti-social acts of human beings
   E. concern themselves less with the anti-social acts of human beings

60. The automobile is a two-way symbol, according to the above paragraph, because its use 60.____
   A. has speeded up getting to, and away from, the scene of a crime
   B. both helps and hurts police operations
   C. introduces a new anti-social act—traffic violation—and does away with criminals like horse thieves
   D. both increases and decreases speed by introducing traffic problems
   E. helps people get to the city but prevents them from moving once they are there

Questions 61-80.

DIRECTIONS: In each of Questions 61 through 80, select the lettered word or phrase which means MOST NEARLY the same as, or the opposite of, the capitalized word.

61. VINDICTIVE 61.____
   A. centrifugal B. forgiving C. molten
   D. tedious E. vivacious

62. SCOPE 62.____
A. compact B detriment C. facsimile
D. potable E. range

63. HINDER 63.____
A. amplify B. aver C. method
D. observe E. retard

64. IRATE 64.____
A. adhere B. angry C. authentic
D. peremptory E. vacillate

65. APATHY 65.____
A. accessory B. availability C. fervor
D. pacify E. stride

66. LUCRATIVE 66.____
A. effective B. imperfect C. injurious
D. timely E. worthless

67. DIVERSITY 67.____
A. convection B. slip C. temerity
D. uniformity E. viscosity

68. OVERT 68.____
A. laugh B. lighter C. orifice
D. quay E. sly

69. SPORADIC 69.____
A. divide B. encumbrance C. livid
D. occasional E. original

70. RESCIND 70.____
A. annul B. deride C. extol
D. indulge E. insist

71. AUGMENT 71.____
A. alter B. decrease C. obey
D. perceive E. supersede

72. AUTONOMOUS 72.____
A. careless B. conceptual C. constant
D. defamatory E. independent

73. TRANSCRIPT 73.____
A. copy B. report C. sentence
D. termination E. verdict

74. DISCORDANT 74.____
A. astride B. comprised C. effusive
D. harmonious E. slick

75. DISTEND 75.____
A. constrict B. direct C. redeem

76. EMANATE 76.____
A. bridge B. coherency C. conquer
D. degrade E. flow

77. EXULTANT 77.____
A. easily upset B. in bad taste
C. in high spirits D. subject to moods
E. very much over-priced

78. PREVARICATE 78.____
A. hesitate B. increase C. lie
D. procrastinate E. reject

79. COGNIZANT 79.____
A. obvious B. search C. stupid
D. suspicious E. unaware

80. CREDIBLE 80.____
A. daring B. helpful C. surreptitious
D. unbelievable E. uncontrollable

81. Assume that a parking space for six cars is to be outlined with white paint. The total area to be outlined is 24 feet by 40 feet, and the space for each car, also marked off by white lines, is to be 8 feet by 20 feet. The total length of white lines to be painted is MOST NEARLY _____ feet. 81.____
A. 64 B. 128 C. 156 D. 184 E. 232

82. A police car is ordered to report to the scene of a crime 5 miles away. If the car travels at an average rate of 40 miles per hour, the length of time it will take to reach its destination is MOST NEARLY _____ minutes. 82.____
A. 3 B. 7 C. 10 D. 13 E. 16

83. A block has metered parking for 19 cars from 7 A.M. to 9 P.M. at a charge of $4 per hour. Assuming that each car that is parked remains for a full hour and that on an average for each hour of parking there is a vacancy of five minutes for each meter, the amount of revenue from the meters for a day will be MOST NEARLY 83.____
A. $400 B. $600 C. $800 D. $1000 E. $1200

84. The standard formula for the stopping distance of a car with all four wheels locked is $S = \frac{V \text{ times } V}{30W}$ where S is the stopping distance in feet, V the speed of the car in miles per hour at the moment the brakes are applied, and W is a number which depends on the friction between the tires and the road.
If the speed of a car is 50 miles per hour and W is equal to 5/3, the stopping distance will be MOST NEARLY _____ feet. 84.____
A. 30 B. 40 C. 50 D. 60 E. 70

85. The radiator of a police car contains 20 quarts of a mixture consisting of 80% water and 20% anti-freeze compound. Assume that you have been ordered to draw off some of the mixture and add pure anti-freeze compound until the mixture is 75% water and 25% anti-freeze compound.
The number of quarts of the mixture which should be removed is MOST NEARLY 85.____
A. 2 B. 3 C. 4 D. 5 E. 6

Questions 86-90.

DIRECTIONS: Questions 86 through 90 are to be answered on the basis of the following table.

FATAL HIGHWAY ACCIDENTS

	Drivers Over 18 Years of Age			Drivers 18 Years of Age & Under		
	Auto	Other Vehicles	Total	Auto	Other Vehicles	Total
January	43	0	43	4	0	4
February	52	0	52	10	0	10
March	36	0	36	8	0	8
April	50	0	50	17	0	17
May	40	2	42	5	0	5
June	26	0	26	8	0	8
July	29	0	29	6	0	6
August	29	1	30	6	0	3
September	36	0	36	4	0	4
October	45	1	46	2	1	3
November	54	1	55	3	0	3
December	66	1	67	0	0	6
TOTALS	506	6	512	76	1	77

86. The average number of fatal auto accidents per month involving drivers older than sixteen was MOST NEARLY 86.____
A. 42 B. 43 C. 44 D. 45 E. 46

87. The total number of fatal highway accidents was 87.____
A. 506 B. 512 C. 562 D. 582 E. 589

88. The month during which the LOWEST number of fatal highway accidents occurred was 88.____
A. March B. June C. July
D. August E. September

89. Of the total number of fatal highway accidents involving drivers older than 18, the percentage of accidents which took place during December is MOST NEARLY 89.____
A. 10 B. 13 C. 16 D. 19 E. 22

90. The GREATEST percentage drop in fatal accidents occurred from 90.____
A. February to March B. April to May C. June to July
D. July to August E. August to September

KEY (CORRECT ANSWERS)

1.	A	21.	B	41.	A	61.	B	81.	E
2.	C	22.	D	42.	E	62.	E	82.	B
3.	B	23.	E	43.	D	63.	E	83.	D
4.	E	24.	A	44.	E	64.	B	84.	C
5.	B	25.	C	45.	B	65.	C	85.	A
6.	A	26.	C	46.	A	66.	E	86.	A
7.	C	27.	B	47.	A	67.	D	87.	E
8.	B	28.	E	48.	C	68.	E	88.	D
9.	E	29.	A	49.	D	69.	D	89.	B
10.	C	30.	C	50.	C	70.	A	90.	B
11.	C	31.	D	51.	B	71.	B		
12.	B	32.	B	52.	E	72.	E		
13.	D	33.	B	53.	D	73.	A		
14.	A	34.	C	54.	B	74.	D		
15.	D	35.	D	55.	B	75.	A		
16.	A	36.	E	56.	A	76.	E		
17.	E	37.	D	57.	E	77.	C		
18.	D	38.	D	58.	A	78.	C		
19.	C	39.	A	59.	B	79.	E		
20.	E	40.	B	60.	B	80.	D		

EXAMINATION SECTION

TEST 1

DIRECTIONS: Each question or incomplete statement is followed by several suggested answers or completions. Select the one that BEST answers the question or completes the statement. *PRINT THE LETTER OF THE CORRECT ANSWER IN THE SPACE AT THE RIGHT.*

1. Upon arriving at the scene of an accident in which a pedestrian was struck and killed by an automobile, an officer's first action was to clear the scene of spectators. 1.____
   Of the following, the PRINCIPAL reason for this action is that
   A. important evidence may be inadvertently destroyed by the crowd
   B. this is a fundamental procedure in first aid work
   C. the operator of the vehicle may escape in the crowd
   D. witnesses will speak more freely if other persons are not present

2. In questioning witnesses, an officer is instructed to avoid leading questions or questions that will suggest the answer. 2.____
   Accordingly, when questioning a witness about the appearance of a suspect, it would be BEST for him to ask:
   A. What kind of hat did he wear?
   B. Did he wear a felt hat?
   C. What did he wear?
   D. Didn't he wear a hat?

3. The only personal description the police have of a particular criminal was made several years ago. 3.____
   Of the following, the item in the description that will be MOST useful in identifying him at the present time is the
   A. color of his eyes
   B. color of his hair
   C. number of teeth
   D. weight

4. Crime statistics indicate that property crimes such as larceny, burglary, and robbery are more numerous during winter months than in summer. 4.____
   The one of the following explanations that MOST adequately accounts for this situation is that
   A. human needs, such as clothing, food, heat, and shelter, are greater in winter
   B. criminal tendencies are aggravated by climatic changes
   C. there are more hours of darkness in winter and such crimes are usually committed under cover of darkness
   D. urban areas are more densely populated during winter months, affording greater opportunity for such crimes

5. When automobile tire tracks are to be used as evidence, a plaster cast is made of them. 5.____
Of the following, the MOST probable reason for taking a photograph is that
   A. photographs can be duplicated more easily than castings
   B. less skill is required for photographing than casting
   C. the tracks may be damaged in the casting process
   D. photographs are more easily transported than castings

6. It is generally recommended that an officer, in lifting a revolver that is to be sent to the police laboratory for ballistics tests and fingerprint examination, do so by insetting a pencil through the trigger guard rather than into the barrel of the weapon. 6.____
The reason for preferring this procedure is that
   A. every precaution must be taken not to eliminate fingerprints on the weapon
   B. there is a danger of accidentally discharging the weapon by placing the pencil in the barrel
   C. the pencil may make scratches inside the barrel that will interfere with the ballistics tests
   D. a weapon can more easily be lifted by the trigger guard

7. PHYSICIAN is to PATIENT as ATTORNEY is to 7.____
   A. court B. client C. counsel D. judge

8. JUDGE is to SENTENCE as JURY is to 8.____
   A. court B. foreman C. defendant D. verdict

9. REVERSAL is to AFFIRMANCE as CONVICTION is to 9.____
   A. appeal B. acquittal C. error D. mistrial

10. GENUINE is to TRUE as SPURIOUS is to 10.____
   A. correct B. conceived C. false D. speculative

11. ALLEGIANCE is to LOYALTY as TREASON is to 11.____
   A. felony B. faithful C. obedience D. rebellion

12. CONCUR is to AGREE as DIFFER is to 12.____
   A. coincide B. dispute C. join D. repeal

13. A person who has an uncontrollable desire to steal without need is called a 13.____
   A. dipsomaniac B. kleptomaniac
   C. monomaniac D. pyromaniac

14. In the sentence, "The placing of any inflammable substance in any building or the placing of any device or contrivence capable of producing fire, for the purpose of causing a fire is an attempt to burn," the MISSPELLED word is 14.____
   A. inflammable B. substance C. device D. contrivence

15. In the sentence, "The word 'break' also means obtaining an entrance into a building by any artifice used for that purpose, or by colussion with any person therein," the MISSPELLED word is 15.____
A. obtaining B. entrance C. artifice D. colussion

16. In the sentence, "Any person who with intent to provoke a breech of the peace causes a disturbance or is offensive to others may be deemed to have committed disorderly conduct," the MISSPELLED word is 16.____
A. breech B. disturbance C. offensive D. committed

17. In the sentence, "When the offender inflicts a grevious harm upon the person from whose possession, or in his presence, property is taken, he is guilty of robbery, the MISSPELLED word is 17.____
A. offender B. grevious C. possession D. presence

18. In the sentence, "A person who wilfully encourages or advises another person in attempting to take the latter's life is guilty of a felony," the MISSPELLED word is 18.____
A. wilfully B. encourages C. advises D. attempting

19. The treatment to be given the offender cannot alter the fact of his offense; but we can take measures to reduce the chances of similar acts in the future. We should banish the criminal, not in order to exact revenge nor directly to encourage reform, but to deter him and others from further illegal attacks on society. 19.____
According to this paragraph, the PRINCIPAL reason for punishing criminals is to
A. prevent the commission of future crimes
B. remove them safely from society
C. avenge society
D. teach them that crime does not pay

20. Even the most comprehensive and best substantiated summaries of the total volume of criminal acts would not contribute greatly to an understanding of the varied social and biological factors which are sometimes assumed to enter into crime causation, nor would they indicate with any degree of precision the needs of police forces in combating crime. 20.____
According to this statement,
A. crime statistics alone do not determine the needs of police forces in combating crime
B. crime statistics are essential to a proper understanding of the social factors of crime
C. social and biological factor which enter the crime causation have little bearing on police needs
D. a knowledge of the social and biological factors of crime is essential to a proper understanding of crime statistics

21. The police officer's art consists in applying and enforcing a multitude of laws and ordinances in such degree or proportion and in such manner that the greatest degree of social protection will be secured. The degree of enforcement and the method of application will vary with each neighborhood and community. 21.____
According to the foregoing paragraph,
   A. each neighborhood or community must judge for itself to what extent the law is to be enforced
   B. a police officer should only enforce those laws which are designed to give the greatest degree of social protection
   C. the manner and intensity of law enforcement is not necessarily the same in all communities
   D. all laws and ordinances must be enforced in a community with the same degree of intensity

22. Police control in the sense of regulating the details of police operations involves such matters as the technical means for so organizing the available personnel that competent police leadership, when secured, can operate effectively. It is concerned not so much with the extent to which popular controls can be trusted to guide and direct the course of police protection a with the administrative relationships which should exist between the component parts of the police organism. 22.____
According to the foregoing statement, police control is
   A. solely a matter of proper personnel assignment
   B. the means employed to guide and direct the course of police protection
   C. principally concerned with the administrative relationships between units of a police organization
   D. the sum total of means employed in rendering police protection

23. Two patrol cars hurry to the scene of an accident from different directions. The first proceeds at the rate of 45 miles per hour and arrives in four minutes. Although the second car travels over a route which is three-fourths of a mile longer, it arrives at the scene only a half-minute later. 23.____
The speed of the second car, expressed in miles per hour, is
   A. 50 B. 55 C. 60 D. 65

24. A motorcycle officer issued 72 traffic summonses in January, 60 in February and 83 in March. 24.____
In order to average 75 summonses per month for the four months of January, February, March, and April, during April he will have to issue _____ summonses.
   A. 80 B. 85 C. 90 D. 95

25. In a unit of the Police Department to which 40 officers are assigned, the sick report record during 2022 was as follows: 1 was absent 8 days, 5 were absent 3 days each, 4 were absent 5 days each, 10 were absent 2 days each, 8 were absent 4 days each, 5 were absent 1 day each. 25.____
The average number of days on sick report for all the members of this unit is MOST NEARLY
   A. ½ B. 1 C. 2 ½ D. 3

Questions 26-30.

DIRECTIONS: Column I lists various statements of fact. Column II is a list of crimes. Next to the numbers corresponding to the number preceding the statements of fact in Column I, place the letter preceding the crime listed in Column II with which Jones should be charged. In answering these questions, the following definitions of crimes should be applied, bearing in mind that ALL elements contained in the definitions must be present in order to charge a person with that crime.

BURGLARY is breaking and entering a building with intent to commit some crime therein. EMBEZZLEMENT is the appropriation to one's use of another's property which has been entrusted to one's care or which has come lawfully into one's possession. EXTORTION is taking or obtaining property from another with his consent, induced by a wrongful use of force or fear. LARCENY is taking and carrying away the personal property of another with intent to deprive or defraud the true owner of the use and benefit of such property. ROBBERY is the unlawful taking of the personal property of another from his person or in his presence by force or violence, or fear of injury.

COLUMN I

26. Jones, believing Smith had induced his wife to leave him, went to Smith's home armed with a knife with which he intended to assault Smith. When his knock was unanswered, he forced open the door of Smith's home and entered but, finding the house empty, he threw away the knife and left. 26.____

27. Jones was employed as a collection agent by Smith. When Smith refused to reimburse him for certain expenses he claimed to have incurred in connection with his work, Jones deducted this amount from sums he had collected for Smith. 27.____

28. Jones spent the night in a hotel. During the night he left his room, went downstairs to the desk, stole money and returned to his room. 28.____

29. Jones, a building inspector, found that the elevators in Smith's building were being operated without a permit. He threatened to report the matter and have the elevators shut down unless Smith paid him a sum of money. Smith paid the amount demanded 29.____

30. Jones held-up Smith on the street and, pointing a revolve at him, demanded his money. Smith, without resisting, handed Jones his money. When Jones was apprehended, it was discovered that the revolver was a toy. 30.____

COLUMN II

A. burglary
B. embezzlement
C. extortion
D. larceny
E. robbery
F. no crime

Questions 31-40.

DIRECTIONS: Questions 31 through 40 consist of statements from which a term is missing. Each of these statements can be completed correctly with one of the terms in the following list. In the space opposite the number corresponding to the number of the question, place the LETTER preceding the term in the following list which MOST accurately completes the statement.

A. affidavit
B. appeal
C. arraignment
D. arrest
E. bench warrant
F. habeas corpus
G. indictment
H. injunction
I. sentence
J. subpoena

31. A _____ is a writ calling witnesses to court. 31.____

32. _____ is a method used to obtain a review of a case in court of superior jurisdiction. 32.____

33. A judgment passed by a court on a person on trial as a criminal offender is called a _____. 33.____

34. _____ is a writ or order requiring a person to refrain from a particular act. 34.____

35. _____ is the name given to a writ commanding the bringing of the body of a certain person before a certain court. 35.____

36. A _____ is a court order directing that an offender be brought into court. 36.____

37. The calling of a defendant before the court to answer an accusation is called _____. 37.____

38. The accusation in writing, presented by the grand jury to a competent court charging a person with a public offense is an _____. 38.____

39. A sworn declaration in writing is an _____. 39.____

40. _____ is the taking of a person into custody for the purpose of holding him to answer a criminal charge. 40.____

Questions 41-55.

DIRECTIONS: Questions 41 through 55 consist of statements from which a term is missing. Each of these statements can be completed correctly with one of the terms in the following list. In the space opposite the number corresponding to the number of the question, place the LETTER preceding the term in the following list which MOST accurately completes the statement.

A. accessory	B. accomplice	C. alibi
D. autopsy	E. ballistics	F. capital
G. confidence man	H. commission	I. conspiracy
J. corroborated	K. grand jury	L. homicide
M. misdemeanors	N. penology	O. perjury

41. _____ is the dissection of a dead human body to determine the cause of death. 41.____

42. The general term which mean the killing of one person by another is _____. 42.____

43. _____ is the science of the punishment of crime. 43.____

44. False swearing constitutes the crime of _____. 44.____

45. A combination of two or more persons to accomplish a criminal or unlawful act is called _____. 45.____

46. By _____ is meant evidence showing that a defendant was in another place when the crime was committed. 46.____

47. _____ is a term frequently used to describe a person engaged in a kind of swindling operation. 47.____

48. A _____ offense is one for which a life sentence or death penalty is prescribed by law. 48.____

49. A violation of a law may be either an act of omission or an act of _____. 49.____

50. An _____ is a person who is liable to prosecution for the identical offense charged against a defendant on trial. 50.____

51. A person would be an _____ who after the commission of a crime aided in the escape of one he knew to be an offender. 51.____

52. An official body called to hear complaints and to determine whether there is ground for criminal prosecution is known as the _____. 52.____

53. Crimes are generally divided into two classes, namely felonies and _____. 53.____

54. _____ is the science of the motion of projectiles. 54.____

55. Testimony of a witness which is confirmed by another witness is _____. 55.____

Questions 56-60.

DIRECTIONS: Next to the question number which corresponds with the number of each item in Column I, place the letter preceding the adjective in Column II which BEST describes the persons in Column I.

COLUMN I	COLUMN II	
56. A talkative woman	A. abstemious	56.____
	B. pompous	
57. A person on a reducing diet	C. erudite	57.____
	D. benevolent	
58. A scholarly professor	E. docile	58.____
	F. loquacious	
59. A man who seldom speaks	G. indefatigable	59.____
	H. taciturn	
60. A charitable person		60.____

Questions 61-65.

DIRECTIONS: Next to the question number which corresponds with the number preceding each profession in Column I, place the letter preceding the word in Column II which BEST explains the subject of that profession.

COLUMN I	COLUMN II	
61. Geologist	A. animals	61.____
	B. eyes	
62. Oculist	C. feet	62.____
	D. fortune-telling	
63. Podiatrist	E. language	63.____
	F. rocks	
64. Palmist	G. stamps	64.____
	H. woman	
65. Zoologist		65.____

Questions 66-70.

DIRECTIONS: Next to the question number corresponding to the number of each of the words in Column I, place the letter preceding the word in Column II that is MOST NEARLY OPPOSITE to it in meaning.

COLUMN I	COLUMN II	
66. comely	A. beautiful	66.____
	B. cowardly	
67. eminent	C. kind	67.____
	D. sedate	
68. frugal	E. shrewd	68.____
	F. ugly	
69. gullible	G. unknown	69.____
	H. wasteful	
70. valiant		70.____

KEY (CORRECT ANSWERS)

1.	A	16.	A	31.	J	46.	C	61.	F
2.	C	17.	B	32.	B	47.	G	62.	B
3.	A	18.	A	33.	I	48.	F	63.	C
4.	C	19.	A	34.	H	49.	H	64.	D
5.	C	20.	A	35.	F	50.	B	65.	A
6.	C	21.	C	36.	E	51.	A	66.	F
7.	B	22.	C	37.	C	52.	L	67.	G
8.	D	23.	A	38.	G	53.	N	68.	H
9.	B	24.	B	39.	A	54.	E	69.	E
10.	C	25.	C	40.	D	55.	K	70.	B
11.	D	26.	A	41.	D	56.	F		
12.	B	27	B	42.	M	57.	A		
13.	B	28.	D	43.	O	58.	C		
14.	D	29.	C	44.	P	59.	H		
15.	D	30.	E	45.	J	60.	D		

EXAMINATION SECTION

TEST 1

DIRECTIONS: Each question or incomplete statement is followed by several suggested answers or completions. Select the one that BEST answers the question or completes the statement. *PRINT THE LETTER OF THE CORRECT ANSWER IN THE SPACE AT THE RIGHT.*

1. The delivery of an arrested person to his sureties, upon their giving security for his appearance at the time and place designated to submit to the jurisdiction and judgment of the court, is known as 1.____
   A. bail B. habeas corpus
   C. parole D. probation

2. Jones was charged with the murder of Smith. Brown, Jones' landlord, testified at the trial that Jones had in his home a well-equipped laboratory which contained all the necessary chemical for producing the poison which an autopsy showed caused Smith's death. 2.____
   Brown's testimony constitutes what is called _____ evidence.
   A. corroborative B. opinion C. hearsay D. circumstantial

3. In addressing a class of recruits, a police lieutenant remarked: "Carelessness and failure are twins." 3.____
   The one of the following that MOST NEARLY expresses his meaning is
   A. negligence seldom accompanies success
   B. incomplete work is careless work
   C. conscientious work is never attended by failure
   D. a conscientious person never makes mistakes

4. In taking a statement from a person who has been shot by an assailant and is not expected to live, police are instructed to ask the person: "Do you believe you are about to die?" 4.____
   Of the following, the MOST probable reason for this question is
   A. the theory that a person about to die will tell the truth
   B. to determine if the victim is conscious and capable of making a statement
   C. to put the victim mentally at ease and more willing to talk
   D that the statement could not be used in court if his mind was distraught by the fear of impending death

5. If, while you are on duty at a busy intersection, a pedestrian asks you for directions to a particular place, the BEST course of conduct is to 5.____
   A. ignore the question and continue directing operations
   B. tell the pedestrian to ask a patrolman on foot patrol
   C. answer the question in a brief, courteous manner
   D. leave your post only long enough to give clear and adequate directions

6. In lecturing on the law of arrest, a lieutenant remarked: "To go beyond is as bad as to fall short." 6.____
The one of the following which MOST NEARLY expresses his meaning is
   A. never undertake the impossible
   B. extremes are not desirable
   C. look before you leap
   D. too much success is dangerous

7. Suppose you are an officer assigned to a patrol precinct. While you are in the vicinity of a school, your attention is called to a man who is selling small packages to school children. You are told that this man distributes similar packages to these same children daily and that he is suspected of dealing in narcotics. 7.____
Of the following, the BEST action for you to take is to
   A. pretend to be an addict and attempt to purchase narcotics from him
   B. observe the man's action yourself for several days in order to obtain grounds for arrest
   C. stop and question one or more of the children after they have transacted business with the man
   D. stop and question the man as he leaves the children

8. In the event of a poison gas attack, civil defense authorities advise civilians to _____ door and windows and go to _____. 8.____
   A. open; upper floors
   B. close; upper floors
   C. open; the basement
   D. close; the basement

9. The procedure whereby a defendant is brought before a magistrate, informed of the charge against him, and asked how he pleads thereto, is called 9.____
   A. arraignment
   B. indictment
   C. presentment
   D. inquisition

10. A written accusation of a crime presented by a grand jury is called a(n) 10.____
   A. commitment
   B. arraignment
   C. indictment
   D. demurrer

11. The one of the following statements made by a prisoner that is correctly called an alibi is: 11.____
   A. "He struck me first."
   B. "I didn't intend to hurt him."
   C. "I was miles away from there at the time."
   D. "I don't remember what happened."

12. A person who, after the commission of a crime, conceals the defender with the intent that the latter may escape from arrest and trial, is called a(n) 12.____
   A. accessory
   B. accomplice
   C. confederate
   D. associate

13. A sworn statement of fact is called a(n) 13.____
   A. affidavit
   B. oath
   C. acknowledgment
   D. subpoena

14. The right of trial by jury in the courts of the state is PRIMARILY safeguarded by a provision of 14.____
   A. the United States Constitution
   B. the constitution of the state
   C. a state statute
   D. a Federal statute

15. The task of protecting the President and his family is entrusted PRIMARILY to the 15.____
   A. Federal Bureau of Investigation
   B. United States Secret Service
   C. Central Intelligence Agency
   D. District of Columbia Police Department

16. The coordinating organization for the various Federal agencies engaged in intelligence activities is the 16.____
   A. Federal Bureau of Investigation
   B. Federal Security Agency
   C. Mutual Security Agency
   D. Central Intelligence Agency

17. A drug addict whose arm shows many scars from the injection of a hypodermic needle is MOST apt to be addicted to 17.____
   A. heroin
   B. cocaine
   C. opium
   D. marijuana

18. All of the following drugs are derived from opium EXCEPT 18.____
   A. cocaine
   B. heroin
   C. morphine
   D. codeine

19. In addition to cases of submersion, artificial respiration is a recommended first aid procedure for 19.____
   A. sunstroke
   B. chemical poisoning
   C. electric shock
   D. apoplexy

20. An injury to a muscle or tendon brought about by severe exertion and resulting in pain and stiffness is called a 20.____
   A. strain
   B. sprain
   C. bruise
   D. fracture

21. Of the following kinds of wounds, the one in which there is the LEAST danger of infection is a(n) _____ wound. 21.____
   A. abrasive
   B. punctured
   C. lacerated
   D. incised

22. When a person is found injured on the street, it is generally advisable, pending arrival of a physician, to help prevent fainting or shock by keeping the patient 22.____
   A. in a sitting position
   B. lying down with the head level
   C. lying down with the head raised
   D. standing on his feet

23. When an injured person appears to be suffering from shock, of the following, it is MOST essential to 23.____
   A. loosen his clothing
   B. keep him warm
   C. administer a stimulant
   D. place him in a prone position

24. In the sentence, "Malice was immanent in all his remarks," the word "immanent" means MOST NEARLY 24.____
    A. elevated B. inherent C. threatening D. foreign

25. In the sentence, "The extant copies of the document were found in the safe," the word "extant" means MOST NEARLY 25.____
    A. existing B. original C. forged D. duplicate

26. In the sentence, "The recruit was more complaisant after the captain spoke to him," the word "complaisant" means MOST NEARLY 26.____
    A. calm B. affable C. irritable D. confident

27. In the sentence, "The man was captured under highly creditable circumstances," the word "creditable" means MOST NEARLY 27.____
    A. doubtful B. believable C. praiseworthy D. unexpected

28. In the sentence, "His superior officers were more sagacious than he," the word "sagacious" means MOST NEARLY 28.____
    A. shrewd B. obtuse C. absurd D. verbose

29. In the sentence, "He spoke with impunity," the word "impunity" means MOST NEARLY 29.____
    A. rashness B. caution C. without fear D. immunity

30. In the sentence, "The new patrolman displayed unusual temerity during the emergency," the word "temerity" means MOST NEARLY 30.____
    A. fear B. rashness C. calmness D. anxiety

31. In the sentence, "The portions of food were parsimoniously served," the word "parsimoniously means MOST NEARLY 31.____
    A. stingily B. piously C. elaborately D. generously

32. In the sentence, "Generally the speaker's remarks were sententious," the word "sententious means MOST NEARLY 32.____
    A. verbose B. witty
    C. argumentative D. pithy

33. In the sentence, "The prisoner was fractious when brought to the station house," the word "fractious" means MOST NEARLY 33.____
    A. penitent B. talkative C. irascible D. broken-hearted

34. In the sentence, "The judge was implacable when the attorney pleaded for leniency," the word "implacable" means MOST NEARLY 34.____
    A. inexorable B. disinterested
    C. inattentive D. indifferent

35. In the sentence, "The court ordered the mendacious statements stricken from the record," the word "mendacious" means MOST NEARLY 35.____
    A. begging B. lying C. threatening D. lengthy

36. In the sentence, "The district attorney spoke in a strident voice," the word "strident" means MOST NEARLY 36.____
A. loud
B. harsh-sounding
C. sing-song
D. low

37. In the sentence, "The speaker had a predilection for long sentences," the word "predilection" means MOST NEARLY 37.____
A. aversion
B. talent
C. propensity
D. diffidence

38. In the sentence, "The candidate wants to file his application for preference before it is too late," the word "before" is used as a(n) 38.____
A. preposition
B. subordinating conjunction
C. pronoun
D. adverb

39. The one of the following sentences which is grammatically PREFERABLE to the others is: 39.____
A. Our engineers will go over your blueprints so that you may have no problems in construction.
B. For a long time he had been arguing that we, not he, are to blame for the confusion.
C. I worked on this automobile for two hours and still cannot find out what is wrong with it.
D. Accustomed to all kinds of hardships, fatigue seldom bothers veteran policemen.

40. The plural of 40.____
A. turkey is turkies
B. cargo is cargoes
C. bankruptcy is bankruptcys
D. son-in-law is son-in-laws

41. The abbreviation "viz." means MOST NEARLY 41.____
A. namely
B. for example
C. the following
D. see

42. In the sentence, "A man in a light-grey suit waited thirty-five minutes in the ante-room for the all-important document," the word IMPROPERLY hyphenated is 42.____
A. light-grey
B. thirty-five
C. ante-room
D. all-important

43. The MOST accurate of the following sentences is: 43.____
A. The commissioner, as well as his deputy and various bureau heads, were present.
B. A new organization of employers and employees have been formed.
C. One or the other of these men have been selected.
D. The number of pages in the book is enough to discourage a reader.

44. The MOST accurate of the following sentences is: 44.____
A. Between you and me, I think he is the better man.
B. He was believed to be me.
C. Is it us that you wish to see?
D. The winners are him and her.

45. In the sentence, "The committee favored submiting the amendment to the electorate," the MISSPELLED word is 45.____
A. committee B. submiting C. amendment D. electorate

46. In the sentence, "He maliciously demurred to an ajournment of the proceedings," the MISSPELLED word is 46.____
A. maliciously B. demurred C. ajournment D. proceedings

47. In the sentence, "His innocence at that time is irrelevent in view of his more recent villainous demeanor," the MISSPELLED word is 47.____
A. innocence B. irrelevent C villainous D. demeanor

48. In the sentence, "The mischievous boys aggrevated the annoyance of their neighbor," the MISSPELLED word is 48.____
A. mischievous B. aggrevated C. annoyance D. neighbor

49. In the sentence, "While his persiverance was commendable, his judgment was debatable, the MISSPELLED word is 49.____
A. persiverance B. commendable
C. judgment D. debatable

50. In the sentence, "He was hoping the appeal would facilitate his aquittal," the MISSPELLED word is 50.____
A. hoping B. appeal C. facilitate D. aquittal

51. In the sentence, "It would be preferable for them to persue separate courses," the MISSPELLED word is 51.____
A. preferable B. persue C. separate D. courses

52. In the sentence, "The litigant was complimented on his persistance and achievement," the MISSPELLED word is 52.____
A. litigant B. complimented
C. persistance D. achievement

53. In the sentence, "Ocassionally there are discrepancies in the descriptions of miscellaneous items," the MISSPELLED word is 53.____
A. ocassionally B. discrepancies
C. descriptions D. miscellaneous

54. In the sentence, "The councilmanic seargent-at-arms enforced the prohibition," the MISSPELLED word is 54.____
A. councilmanic B. seargent-at-arms
C. enforced D. prohibition

55. In the sentence, "The teacher had an ingenious device for mantaining attendance," the MISSPELLED word is 55.____
A. ingenious B. device C. mantaining D. attendance

Questions 56-63.

DIRECTIONS: Questions 56 through 63 are to be answered on the basis of the following excerpt from a recorded annual report of the police department. This material should be read first and then referred to in answering these questions, which are to be answered SOLELY on the basis of the material herein contained.

LEGAL BUREAU

One of the more important functions of this bureau is to analyze and furnish the department with pertinent information concerning Federal and State statutes and Local Laws which affect the department, law enforcement or crime prevention. In addition, all measures introduced in the State Legislature and the City Council which may affect this department are carefully reviewed by members of the Legal Bureau and, where necessary, opinions and recommendations thereon are prepared.

Another important function of this office is the prosecution of cases in the Magistrate's Courts. This is accomplished by assignment of attorneys who are members of the Legal Bureau to appear in those cases which are deemed to raise issues of importance to the department or questions of law which require technical presentation to facilitate proper determination; and also in those cases where request is made for such appearances by a magistrate, some other official of the city, or a member of the force. Attorneys are regularly assigned to prosecute all cases in the Women's Court.

Proposed legislation was prepared and sponsored for introduction in the State Legislature and, at this writing, one of these proposals has already been enacted into law and five others are presently on the Governor's desk awaiting executive action. The new law prohibits the sale or possession of a hypodermic syringe or needle by an unauthorized person. The bureau's proposals awaiting executive action pertain to an amendment to the Code of Criminal Procedure prohibiting desk officers from taking bail in gambling cases or in cases mentioned in Section 552, Code of Criminal Procedure; including confidence men and swindlers as jostlers in the Penal Law; prohibiting the sale of switchblade knives of any size to children under 16 and bills extending the licensing period of gunsmiths.

The Legal Bureau has regularly cooperated with the Corporation Counsel and the District Attorneys in respect to matters affecting this department, and has continued to advise and represent the Police Athletic League, the Police Sports Association, the Police Relief Fund, and the Police Pension Fund.

The following is a statistical report of the activities of the bureau during the current year as compared with the previous year:

	Current Year	Previous Year
Memoranda of law prepared	68	83
Legal matters forwarded to corporation counsel	122	144
Letters requesting legal information	756	807
Letters requesting departmental records	139	111
Matters for publication	17	26
Court appearances of members of bureau	4,678	4,621
Conferences	94	103
Lectures at Police Academy	30	33
Reports on proposed legislation	194	255
Deciphering of codes	79	27
Expert testimony	31	16
Notices to court witnesses	55	81
Briefs prepared	22	18
Court papers prepared	258	--

56. One of the functions of the Legal Bureau is to 56.____
    A. review and make recommendations on proposed Federal laws affecting law enforcement
    B. prepare opinions on all measures introduced in the State Legislature and the City Council
    C. furnish the Police Department with pertinent information concerning all new Federal and State laws
    D. analyze all laws affecting the work of the Police Department

57. The one of the following that is NOT a function of the Legal Bureau is 57.____
    A. law enforcement and crime prevention
    B. prosecution of all cases in Women's Court
    C. advise and represent the Police Sports Association
    D. lecturing at the Police Academy

58. Members of the Legal Bureau frequently appear in Magistrate's Court for the purpose of 58.____
    A. defending members of the Police Force
    B. raising issues of importance to the Police Department
    C. prosecuting all offenders arrested by members of the Force
    D. facilitating proper determination of questions of law requiring technical presentation

59. The Legal Bureau sponsored a bill that would 59.____
    A. extend the licenses of gunsmiths
    B. prohibit the sale of switchblade knives to children of any size
    C. place confidence men and swindlers in the same category as jostlers in the Penal Law
    D. prohibit desk officers from admitting gamblers, confidence men, and swindlers to bail

60. From the report, it is NOT reasonable to infer that 60.____
   A. fewer bills affecting the Police Department were introduced in the current year
   B. the preparation of court papers was a new activity assumed in the current year
   C. the Code of Criminal Procedure authorizes desk officers to accept bail in certain cases
   D. the penalty for jostling and swindling is the same

61. According to the statistical report, the activity showing the GREATEST percentage of decrease in the current year as compared to the previous year was 61.____
   A. matters for publication
   B. reports on proposed legislation
   C. notices to court witnesses
   D. memoranda of law prepared

62. According to the statistical report, the activity showing the GREATEST percentage of increase in the current year as compare with the previous year was 62.____
   A. court appearances of members of the bureau
   B. giving expert testimony
   C. deciphering of codes
   D. letters requesting departmental records

63. According to the report, the percentage of bills prepared and sponsored by the Legal Bureau which were passed by the State Legislature and sent to the Governor for approval was APPROXIMATELY 63.____
   A. 3.1%
   B. 2.6%
   C. .5%
   D. not capable of determination from the data given

64. A squad of officers assigned to enforce a new parking regulation in a particular area issued tag summonses on a particular day as follows: four officers issued 16 summonses each; three issued 19 each; one issued 22; seven issued 25 each; eleven issued 28 each; ten issued 30 each; two issued 36 each; one issued 41; and three issued 45 each. 64.____
   The average number of summonses issued by a member of this squad was MOST NEARLY
   A. 6.2
   B. 17.2
   C. 21.0
   D. 27.9

65. A water storage tank is 75 feet long and 30 feet wide and has a depth of 6½ feet. Each cubic foot of the tank holds 9½ gallons. 65.____
   The TOTAL capacity of the tank is _____ gallons.
   A. 73,125½
   B. 131,625
   C. 138,937½
   D. 146,250

66. The price of admission to a PAL entertainment were $2.50 each for adults and $1.00 for children; the turnstile at the entrance showed that 358 persons entered and the gate receipts were $626.50. 66.____
The number of children who attended was
A. 170 B. 175 C. 179 D. 183

67. A patrol car travels six times as fast as a bicycle. 67.____
If the patrol car goes 168 miles in two hours less time than the bicycle requires to go 42 miles, their respective rates of speed are _____ miles per hour.
A. 36 and 6 B. 42 and 7 C. 63 and 10½ D. 126 and 21

68. The radiator of an automobile already contains six quarts of a 10% solution of alcohol. 68.____
In order to make a mixture of 20% alcohol, it will be necessary to add _____ quarts of alcohol.
A. ¾ B. 1¾ C. 2½ D. 3

69. A man received an inheritance of $80,000 and wanted to invest it so that it would produce an annual income sufficient to pay his rent of $400 a month. 69.____
In order to do this, he will have to receive interest or dividends at the rate of _____% per annum.
A. 3 B. 4 C. 5¾ D. 6

70. If the price of a bus ticket varies *directly* as the mileage involved, and a ticket to travel 135 miles costs $29.70, a ticket for a 30-mile trip will cost 70.____
A. $15.20 B. $13.40 C. $6.60 D. $2.20

71. A man owed a debt of $5,800. After a first payment of $100, he agreed to pay the balance by monthly payments in which each payment after this first would be $20 more than that of the preceding month. 71.____
If no interest charge is made, he will have to make, including the first payment, a total of _____ monthly payments.
A. 16 B. 20 C. 24 D. 28

72. The written test of a civil service examination has a weight of 30, the oral test a weight of 20, experience a weight of 20, and the physical test a weight of 30. A candidate received ratings of 76 on the written test, 84 on the oral, and 80 for experience. 72.____
In order to attain an average of 85 on the examination, his rating on the physical test must be
A. 86 B. 90 C. 94 D. 98

73. A family has an income of $3,200 per month. It spends 22% of this amount for rent, 36% for food, 16% for clothing, and 12% for additional household expenses. After meeting these expenses, 50% of the balance is deposited in the bank. 73.____
The amount deposited monthly is
A. $224.00 B. $366.00 C. $448.00 D. $520.00

74. Upon retirement last July, an officer bought a farm of 64 acres for $18,000 per acre. He made a down payment of $612,000 and agreed to pay the balance in installments of $7,500 a month commencing on August 1, 2022. Disregarding interest, he will make his LAST payment in 74.____
   A. July 2028
   B. August 2030
   C. January 2032
   D. April 2035

75. 40% of those who commit a particular crime are subsequently arrested and convicted. 75% of those committed receive sentences of 10 years or more. Assuming that those arrested for the first time serve less than 10 years, the percentage of those committing this crime who receive sentences of ten years or more is MOST NEARLY 75.____
   A. 20%
   B. 30%
   C. 40%
   D. 50%

KEY (CORRECT ANSWERS)

1.	A	21.	D	41.	A	61.	A
2.	D	22.	B	42.	C	62.	C
3.	A	23.	B	43.	D	63.	D
4.	A	24.	B	44.	A	64.	D
5.	C	25.	A	45.	B	65.	C
6.	B	26.	B	46.	C	66.	C
7.	C	27.	C	47.	C	67.	B
8.	B	28.	A	48.	B	68.	A
9.	A	29.	D	49.	A	69.	D
10.	C	30.	B	50.	D	70.	C
11.	C	31.	A	51.	B	71.	B
12.	A	32.	D	52.	C	72.	D
13.	A	33.	C	53.	A	73.	A
14.	B	34.	A	54.	B	74.	A
15.	B	35.	B	55.	C	75.	B
16.	D	36.	B	56.	D		
17.	A	37.	C	57.	A		
18.	A	38.	B	58.	D		
19.	C	39.	A	59.	C		
20.	A	40.	B	60.	D		

EXAMINATION SECTION

TEST 1

DIRECTIONS: Each question or incomplete statement is followed by several suggested answers or completions. Select the one that BEST answers the question or completes the statement. *PRINT THE LETTER OF THE CORRECT ANSWER IN THE SPACE AT THE RIGHT.*

Questions 1-4.

DIRECTIONS: Questions 1 through 4 measure your ability to recognize objects, people, events, parts of maps, or crime, accident, or other scenes to which you have been exposed.

Below and on the following pages are twenty illustrations. Study them carefully. In the test, you will be shown pairs of drawings. For each pair, you will be asked which is or are from the twenty illustrations in this part.

2 (#1)

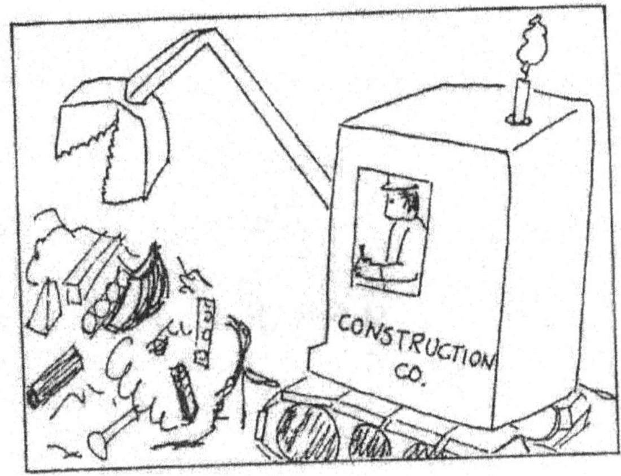

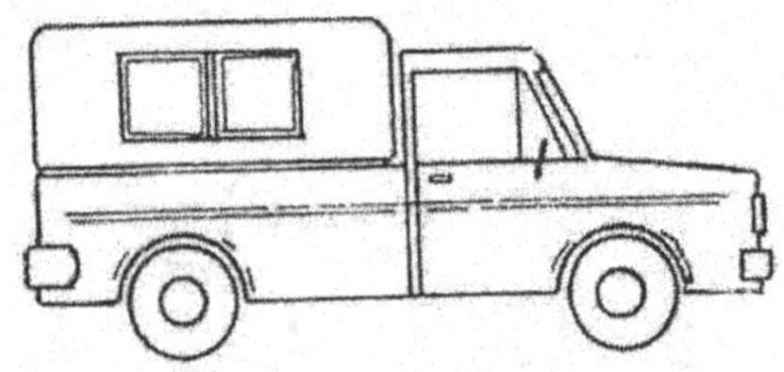

3 (#1)

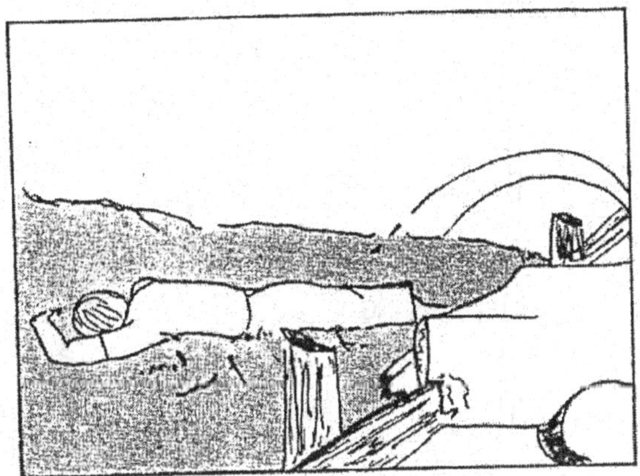

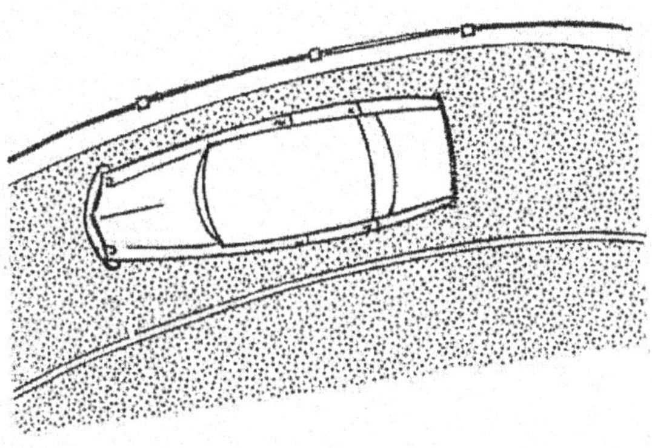

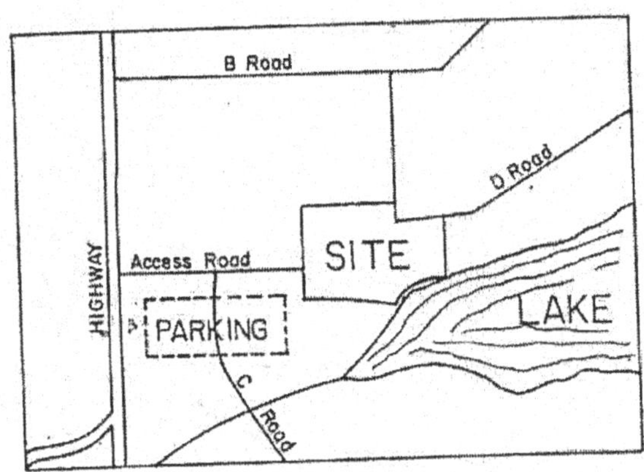
B Road
D Road
HIGHWAY
Access Road
SITE
LAKE
PARKING
C Road

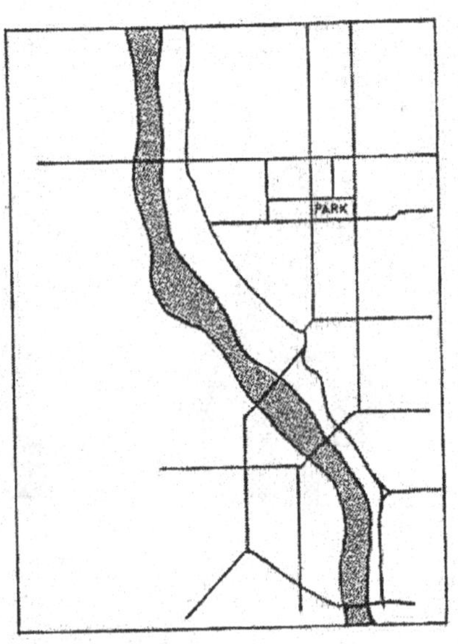
PARK

Questions 1-4.

DIRECTIONS: In Questions 1 through 4, select the choice that corresponds to the scene(s) that is(are) from the illustrations for this section. *PRINT THE LETTER OF THE CORRECT ANSWER IN THE SPACE AT THE RIGHT.*

1. I II 2.____

A. I only
B. II only
C. Both I and II
D. Neither I nor II

2. I II 2.

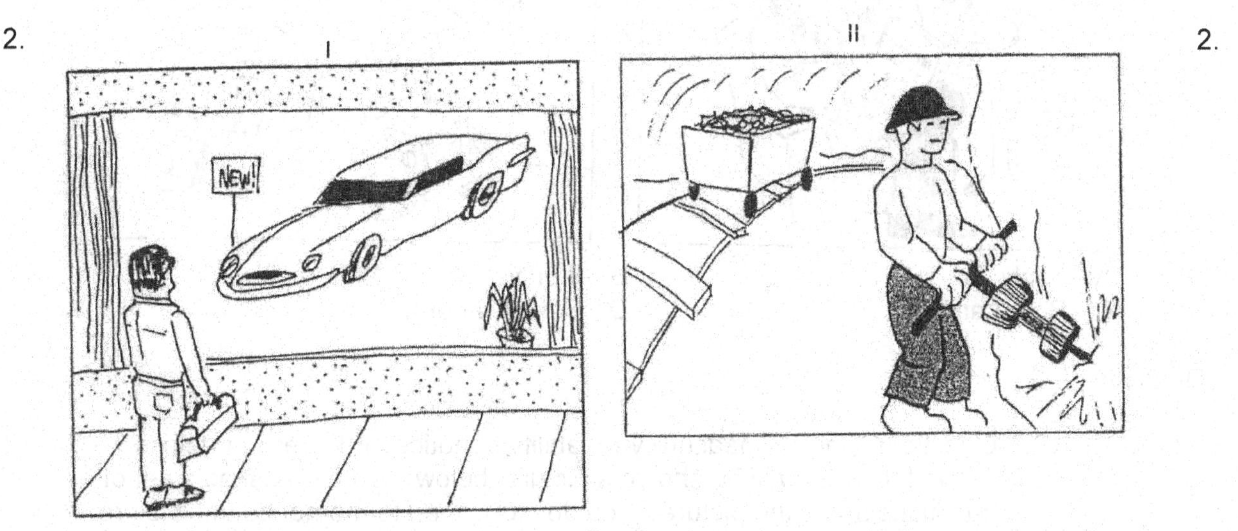

A. I only
B. II only
C. Both I and II
D. Neither I nor II

3. I II 3.____

A. I only
B. II only
C. Both I and II
D. Neither I nor II

4. I II 4.____

A. I only
B. II only
C. Both I and II
D. Neither I nor II

Questions 5-6.

DIRECTIONS: Questions 5 and 6 measure your ability to notice and interpret details accurately. You will be shown a picture, below, and then asked a set of questions about the picture. You do NOT need to memorize this picture. You may look at the picture when answering the questions.

5. 5.____

Details in the picture lend some support to or do NOT tend to contradict which of the following statements about the person who occupies the room?
I. The person is very careless.
II. The person smokes.
The CORRECT answer is:
A. I only
B. II only
C. Both I and II
D. Neither I nor II

6. The number on the piece of paper on the desk is MOST likely a 6.____
A. ZIP code
B. street number
C. social security number
D. telephone area code

Questions 7-10.

DIRECTIONS: Questions 7 through 10 measure your ability to recognize objects or people in differing views, contexts, or situations. Each question consists of three pictures; one labeled I and one labeled II. In each question, you are to determine whether A – I only, B – II only, C – Both I and II, and D – Neither I nor II COULD be the subject.

The Subject is *always* ONE person or ONE object. The Subject picture shows the object or person as it, he, or she appeared at the time of initial contact. Pictures I and II show objects from a different viewpoint than that of the Subject picture. For example, if the Subject picture presents a front view, I and II may present back views, side views, or a back and a side view. Also, art objects may be displayed differently, may have a different base or frame or method of hanging.

When the subject is a person, I or II will be a picture of a different person or will be a picture of the same person after some change has taken place. The person may have made a deliberate attempt to alter his or her appearance, such as wearing (or taking off a wig, growing (or shaving off) a beard or mustache, or dressing as a member of the opposite sex. The change may also be a natural one, such as changing a hair style, changing from work clothes to play clothes, or from play clothes to work clothes, or growing older, thinner, or fatter. None has had cosmetic surgery.

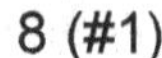

7. Subject I  II 7.____

A. I only
B. II only
C. Both I and II
D. Neither I nor II

8. Subject I  II 8.____

A. I only
B. II only
C. Both I and II
D. Neither I nor II

9. Subject I 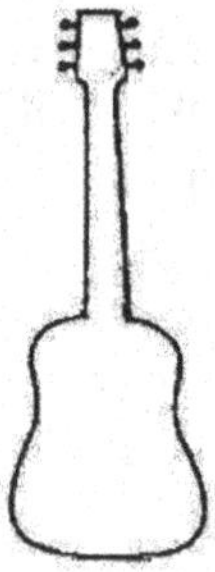 II 9.____

A. I only
B. II only
C. Both I and II
D. Neither I nor II

10. Subject I II 10.____

A. I only
B. II only
C. Both I and II
D. Neither I nor II

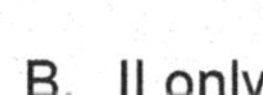

KEY (CORRECT ANSWERS)

1.	B	6.	B
2.	D	7.	D
3.	A	8.	A
4.	A	9.	D
5.	B	10.	D

EVALUATING INFORMATION AND EVIDENCE
EXAMINATION SECTION
TEST 1

DIRECTIONS: Each question or incomplete statement is followed by several suggested answers or completions. Select the one that BEST answers the question or completes the statement. *PRINT THE LETTER OF THE CORRECT ANSWER IN THE SPACE AT THE RIGHT.*

Questions 1-9.

DIRECTIONS: Questions 1 through 9 measure your ability to (1) determine whether statements from witnesses say essentially the same thing and (2) determine the evidence needed to make it reasonably certain that a particular conclusion is true.

1. Which of the following pairs of statements say essentially the same thing in two different ways? 1.____
   I. Some employees at the water department have fully vested pensions.
      At least one employee at the water department has a pension that is not fully vested.
   II. All swans are white birds.
      A bird that is not white is not a swan.

   The CORRECT answer is:
   A. I only B. I and II C. II only D. Neither I nor II

2. Which of the following pairs of statements say essentially the same thing in two different ways? 2.____
   I. If you live in Humboldt County, your property taxes are high.
      If your property taxes are high, you live in Humboldt County.
   II. All the Hutchinsons live in Lindsborg.
      At least some Hutchinsons do not live in Lindsborg.

   The CORRECT answer is;
   A. I only B. I and II C. II only D. Neither I nor II

3. Which of the following pairs of statements say essentially the same thing in two different ways? 3.____
   I. Although Spike is a friendly dog, he is also one of the most unpopular dogs on the block.
      Although Spike is one of the most unpopular dogs on the block, he is a friendly dog.
   II. Everyone in Precinct 19 is taller than Officer Banks.
      Nobody in Precinct 19 is shorter than Officer Banks.

   The CORRECT answer is:
   A. I only B. I and II C. II only D. Neither I nor II

4. Which of the following pairs of statements say essentially the same thing in two different ways? 4.____
   I. On Friday, every officer in Precinct 1 is assigned parking duty or crowd control, or both.
      If a Precinct 1 officer has been assigned neither parking duty nor crowd control, it is not Friday.
   II. Because the farmer mowed the hay fields today, his house will have mice tomorrow.
      Whenever the farmer mows his hay fields, his house has mice the next day.

   The CORRECT answer is:
   A. I only B. I and II C. II only D. Neither I nor II

5. Summary of Evidence Collected to Date: 5.____
   I. Fishing in the Little Pony River is against the law.
      Captain Rick caught an 8-inch trout and ate it for dinner.

   Prematurely Drawn Conclusion: Captain Rick broke the law.
   Which of the following pieces of evidence, if any, would make it reasonably certain that the conclusion drawn is true?
   A. Captain Rick caught his trout in the Little Pony River.
   B. There is no size limit on trout mentioned in the law.
   C. A trout is a species of fish.
   D. None of the above

6. Summary of Evidence Collected to Date: 6.____
   I. Some of the doctors in the ICU have been sued for malpractice.
   II. Some of the doctors in the ICU are pediatricians.

   Prematurely Drawn Conclusion: Some of the pediatricians in the ICU have never been sued for malpractice.
   Which of the following pieces of evidence, if any, would make it reasonably certain that the conclusion drawn is true?
   A. The number of pediatricians in the ICU is the same as the number of doctors who have been sued for malpractice.
   B. The number of pediatricians in the ICU is smaller than the number of doctors who have been sued for malpractice.
   C. The number of ICU doctors who have been sued for malpractice is smaller than the number who are pediatricians.
   D. None of the above

7. Summary of Evidence Collected to Date: 7.____
   I. Along Paseo Boulevard, there are five convenience stores.
   II. EZ-GO is east of Pop-a-Shop.
   III. Kwik-E-Mart is west of Bob's Market.
   IV. The Nightwatch is between EZ-GO and Kwik-E-Mart.

   Prematurely Drawn Conclusion: Pop-a-Shop is the westernmost convenience store on Paseo Boulevard.

Which of the following pieces of evidence, if any, would make it reasonably certain that the conclusion drawn is true?

A. Bob's Market is the easternmost convenience store on Paseo.
B. Kwik-E-Mart is the second store from the west.
C. The Nightwatch is west of the EZ-GO.
D. None of the above

8. Summary of Evidence Collected to Date: 8.____

Stark drove home from work at 70 miles an hour and wasn't breaking the law.

Prematurely Drawn Conclusion: Stark was either on an interstate highway or in the state of Montana.

Which of the following pieces of evidence, if any, would make it reasonably certain that the conclusion drawn is true?

A. There are no interstate highways in Montana.
B. Montana is the only state that allows a speed of 70 miles an hour on roads other than interstate highways.
C. Most states don't allow speed of 70 miles an hour on state highways.
D. None of the above

9. Summary of Evidence Collected to Date: 9.____

I. Margaret, owner of MetroWoman magazine, signed a contract with each of her salespeople promising an automatic $200 bonus to any employee who sells more than 60 subscriptions in a calendar month.
II. Lynn sold 82 subscriptions to MetroWoman in the month of December.

Prematurely Drawn Conclusion: Lynn received a $20 bonus.

Which of the following pieces of evidence, if any, would make it reasonably certain that the conclusion is true?

A. Lynn is a salesperson.
B. Lynn works for Margaret.
C. Margaret offered only $200 regardless of the number of subscriptions sold.
D. None of the above

Questions 10-14.

DIRECTIONS: Questions 10 through 14 refer to Map #3 and measure your ability to orient yourself within a given section of town, neighborhood or particular area. Each of the questions describes a starting point and a destination. Assume that you are driving a car in the area shown on the map accompanying the questions. Use the map as a basis for the shortest way to get from one point to another without breaking the law.

On the map, a street marked by arrows, or by arrows and the words "One Way," indicates one-way travel and should be assumed to be one-way for the entire length, even when there are breaks or jogs in the street. EXCEPTION: A street that does not have the same name over the full length.

4 (#1)

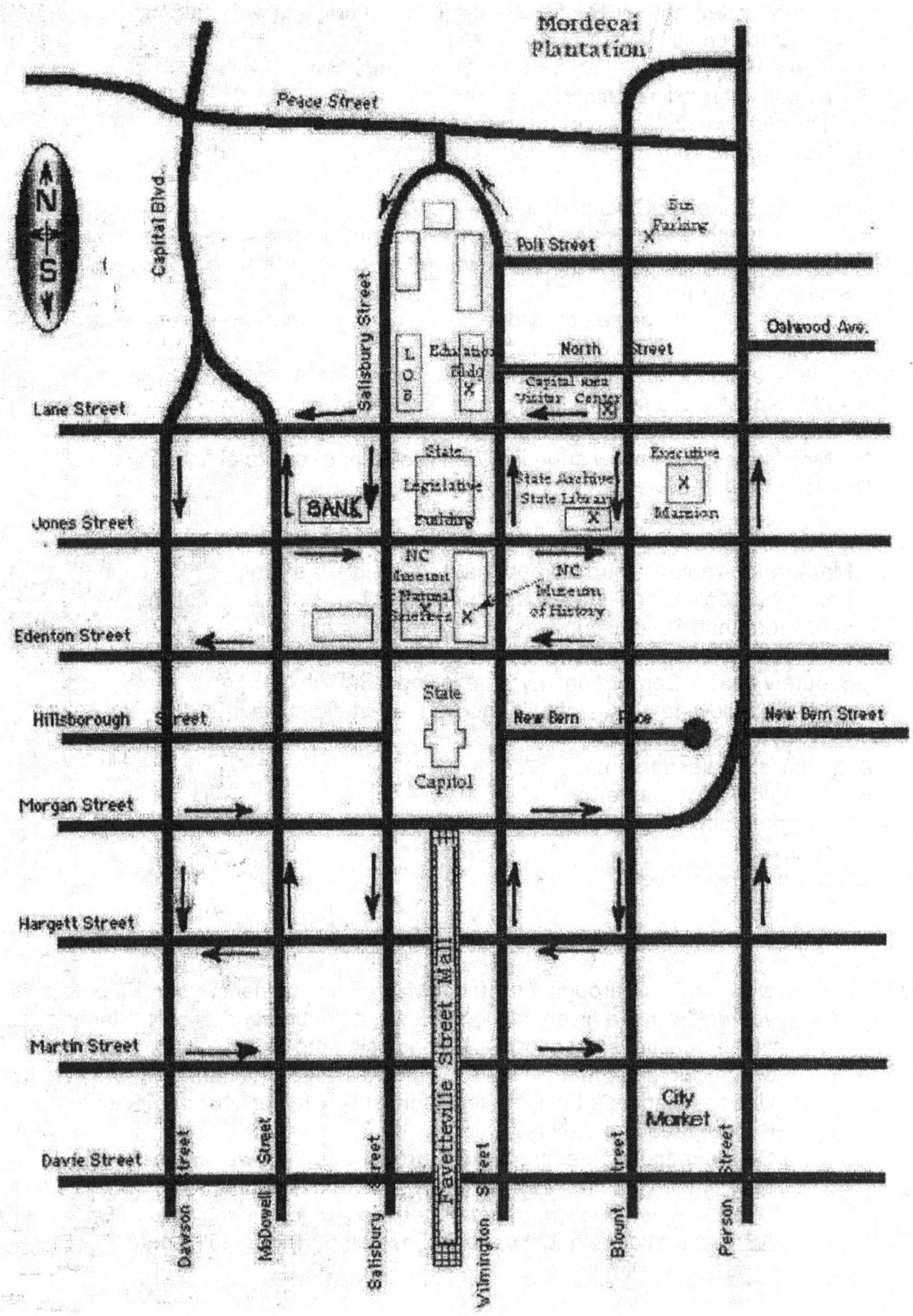
Mordecai Plantation
Peace Street
Capital Blvd.
N
S
Poll Street
Oakwood Ave.
North Street
Salisbury Street
Education Bldg
Capital Area Visitor Center
Lane Street
State Legislative Building
State Archive State Library
Executive Mansion
BANK
Jones Street
NC Museum of Natural Sciences
NC Museum of History
Edenton Street
State Capitol
Hillsborough Street
New Bern Place
New Bern Street
Morgan Street
Hargett Street
Fayetteville Street Mall
Martin Street
City Market
Davie Street
Dawson Street
McDowell Street
Salisbury Street
Wilmington Street
Blount Street
Person Street

10. The SHORTEST legal way from the south end of the Fayetteville Street Mall, at Davie Street, to the city of Raleigh Municipal Building is 10.____
   A. west on Davie, north on McDowell
   B. west on Davie, north on Dawson
   C. east on Davie, north on Wilmington, west on Morgan
   D. east on Davie, north on Wilmington, west on Hargett

11. The SHORTEST legal way from the City Market to the Education Building is 11.____
   A. north on Blount, west on North
   B. north on Person, west on Lane
   C. north on Blount, west on Lane
   D. west on Martin, north on Wilmington

12. The SHORTEST legal way from the Education Building to the State Capitol is 12.____
   A. south on Wilmington
   B. north on Wilmington, west on Peace, south on Capitol, bear west to go south on Dawson, and east on Morgan
   C. west on Lane, south on Salisbury
   D. each on North, south on Blount, west on Edenton

13. The SHORTEST legal way from the State Capitol to Peace College is 13.____
   A. north on Wilmington, jog north, east on Peace
   B. east on Morgan, north on Person, west on Peace
   C. west on Edenton, north on McDowell, north on Capitol Blvd., east on Peace
   D. east on Morgan, north on Blount, west on Peace

14. The SHORTEST legal way from the State Legislative Building to the City Market is 14.____
   A. south on Wilmington, east on Martin
   B. east on Jones, south on Blount
   C. south on Salisbury, east on Davie
   D. east on Lane, south on Blount

Questions 15-19.

DIRECTIONS: Questions 15 through 19 refer to Figure #3, on the following page, and measure your ability to understand written descriptions of events. Each question presents a description of an accident or event and asks you which of the following five drawings in Figure #3 BEST represents it.
In the drawings, the following symbols are used:
Moving vehicle ⌂ Non-moving vehicle ☗
Pedestrian or bicyclist •
The path and direction of travel of a vehicle or pedestrian is indicated by a solid line.
The path and direction of travel of each vehicle or pedestrian directly involved in a collision from the point of impact is indicated by a dotted line.

6 (#1)

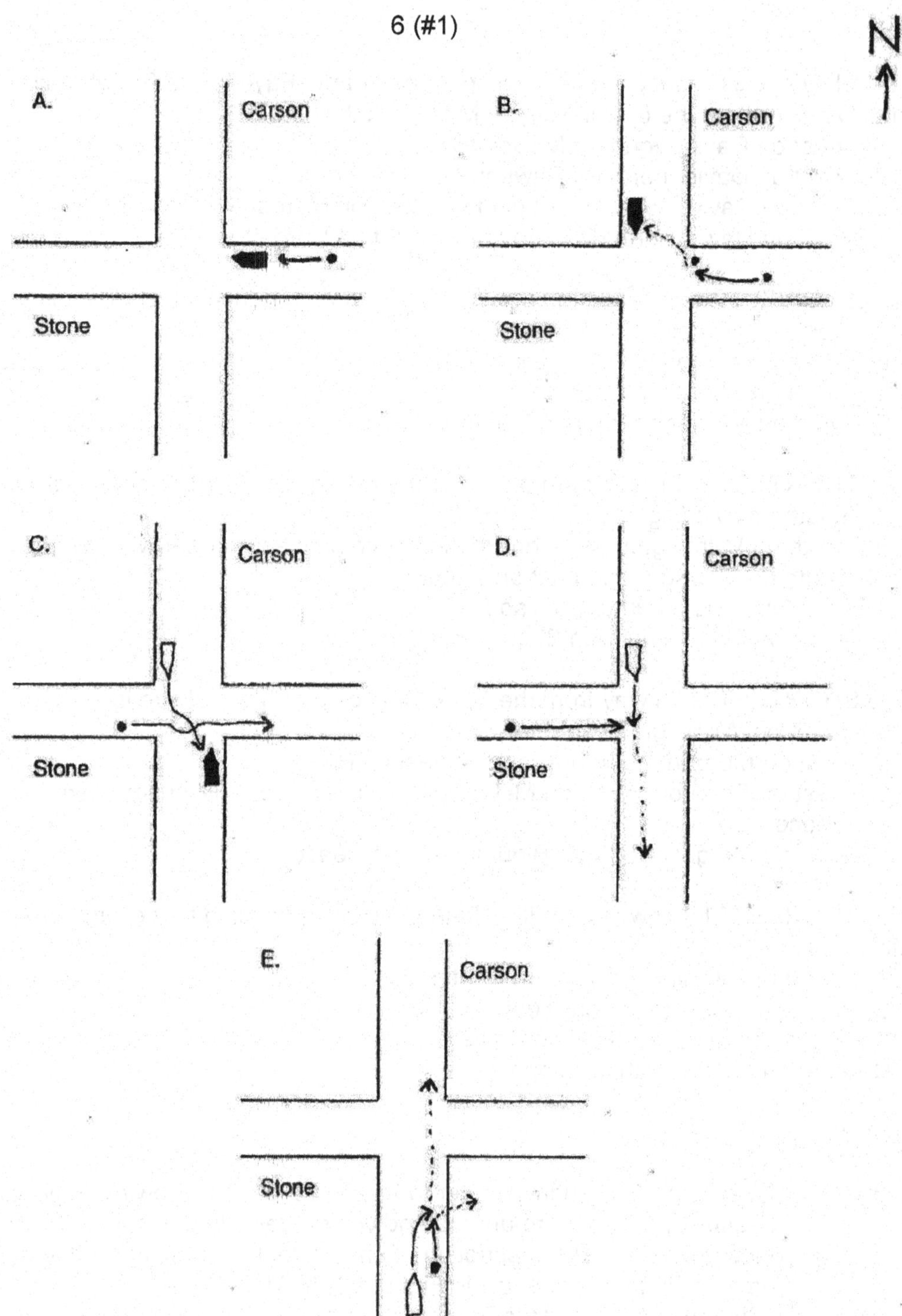

In the space at the right, print the letter of the drawing that BEST fit the descriptions written below.

15. A driver headed north on Carson veers to the right and strikes a bicyclist who is also headed north. The bicyclist is thrown from the road. The driver flees north on Carson. 15.____

16. A driver heading south on Carson runs the stop sign and barely misses colliding with an eastbound cyclist. The cyclist swerves to avoid the collision and continues traveling east. The driver swerves to avoid the collision and strikes a car parked in the northbound lane on Carson. 16.____

17. A bicyclist heading west on Stone collides with a pedestrian in the crosswalk, then veers through the intersection and collides with the front of a car parked in the southbound lane on Carson. 17.____

18. A driver traveling south on Carson runs over a bicyclist who has run the stop sign, and then flees south on Carson. 18.____

19. A bicyclist heading west on Stone collides with the rear of a car parked in the westbound lane. 19.____

Questions 20-22.

DIRECTIONS: In Questions 20 through 22, choose the word or phrase CLOSEST in meaning to the word or phrase printed in capital letters.

20. INSOLVENT 20.____
A. bankrupt B. vagrant C. hazardous D. illegal

21. TENANT 21.____
A. laborer B. occupant C. owner D. creditor

22. INFRACTION 22.____
A. portion B. violation C. remark D. detour

Questions 23-25.

DIRECTIONS: Questions 23 through 25 measure your ability to do fieldwork-related arithmetic. Each question presents a separate arithmetic problem for you to solve.

23. Officer Jones has served on the police force longer than Smith. Smith has served longer than Moore. Moore has served less time than Jones, and Park has served longer than Jones. 23.____
Which officer has served the LONGEST on the police force?
A. Jones B. Smith C. Moore D. Park

24. A car wash has raised the price of an outside-only wash from $4 to $5. The car wash applies the same percentage increase to its inside-and-out wash, which was $10. 24.____
What is the new cost of the inside-and-out wash?
A. $8 B. $11 C. $12.50 D. $15

25. Ron and James, college students, make $10 an hour working at the restaurant. Ron works 13 hours a week and James works 20 hours a week.
To make the same amount that Ron earns in a year, James would work about _____ weeks. 25.____

A. 18 B. 27 C. 34 D. 45

KEY (CORRECT ANSWERS)

1.	C	11.	B
2.	D	12.	C
3.	B	13.	A
4.	B	14.	B
5.	A	15.	E
6.	D	16.	C
7.	B	17.	B
8.	B	18.	D
9.	B	19.	A
10.	A	20.	A

21. B
22. B
23. D
24. C
25. C

SOLUTIONS TO QUESTIONS 1-9

P implies Q = original statement

Not Q implies not P = contrapositive of the original statement. A statement and its contrapositive are logically equivalent.

Q implies P = converse of the original statement

Not P implies not Q = inverse of the original statement. The converse and inverse of an original statement are logically equivalent.

P implies Q = Not P or Q.

1. The CORRECT answer is C.
   Item I is wrong because “some employees” means “at least one employee” and possibly “all employees.” If it is true that all employees have fully vested pensions, then the second statement is false. Item II is correct because the second statement is the contrapositive of the first statement.

2. The CORRECT answer is D.
   Item I is wrong because the converse of a statement does not necessarily follow from the original statement. Item II is wrong because statement I implies that there are no Hutchinson family members who live outside Lindsborg.

3. The CORRECT answer is B. Item I is correct because it is composed of the same two compound statements that are simply mentioned in a different order. Item II is correct because if each person is taller than Officer Banks, then there is no person in that precinct who can possibly be shorter than Officer Banks.

4. The CORRECT answer is B.
   Item I is correct because the second statement is the contrapositive of the first statement. Item II is correct because each statement indicates that mowing the hay fields on a particular day leads to the presence of mice the next day.

5. The CORRECT answer is A.
   If Captain Rick caught his trout in the Little Pony River, then we can conclude that he was fishing there. Since statement I says that fishing in the Little Pony Rive is against the law, we conclude that Captain Rick broke the law.

6. The CORRECT answer is D.
   The number of doctors in each group, whether the same or not, has no bearing on the conclusion. There is nothing in evidence to suggest that the group of doctors sued for malpractice overlaps with the group of doctors that are pediatricians.

7. The CORRECT answer is B.
   If we are given that Kwik-E-Mart is the second store from the west, then the order of stores from west to east, is Pop-a-Shop, Kwik-E-Mart, Nightwatch, EZ-GO, and Bob's Market.

8. The CORRECT answer is B.
We are given that Stark drove at 70 miles per hour and didn't break the law. If we also know that Montana is the only state that allows a speed of 70 miles per hour, then we can conclude that Stark must have been driving in Montana or else was driving on some interstate.

9. The CORRECT answer is B.
The only additional piece of information needed is that Lynn works for Margaret. This will guarantee that Lynn receives the promised $200 bonus.

TEST 2

DIRECTIONS: Each question or incomplete statement is followed by several suggested answers or completions. Select the one that BEST answers the question or completes the statement. *PRINT THE LETTER OF THE CORRECT ANSWER IN THE SPACE AT THE RIGHT.*

Questions 1-9.

DIRECTIONS: Questions 1 through 9 measure your ability to (1) determine whether statements from witnesses say essentially the same thing and (2) determine the evidence needed to make it reasonably certain that a particular conclusion is true.
To do well on this part of the test, you do NOT have to have a working knowledge of police procedures and techniques. Nor do you have to have any more familiarity with criminals and criminal behavior than that acquired from reading newspapers, listening to radio or watching TV. To do well in this part, you must read and reason carefully.

1. Which of the following pairs of statements say essentially the same thing in two different ways? 1.____
   I. All of the teachers at Slater Middle School are intelligent, but some are irrational thinkers.
      Although some teachers at Slater Middle School are irrational thinkers, all of them are intelligent.
   II. Nobody has no friends.
      Everybody has at least one friend.

   The CORRECT answer is:
   A. I only B. I and II C. II only D. Neither I nor II

2. Which of the following pairs of statements say essentially the same thing in two different ways? 2.____
   I. Although bananas taste good to most people, they are also a healthy food.
      Bananas are a healthy food, but most people eat them because they taste good.
   II. If Dr. Jones is in, we should call at the office.
      Either Dr. Jones is in, or we should not call at the office.

   The CORRECT answer is:
   A. I only B. I and II C. II only D. Neither I nor II

3 Which of the following pairs of statements say essentially the same thing in two different ways? 3.____
   I. Some millworker work two shifts.
      If someone works only one shift, he is probably not a millworker.
   II. If a letter carrier clocks in at nine, he can finish his route by the end of the day.
      If a letter carrier does not clock in at nine, he cannot finish his route by the end of the day.

   The CORRECT answer is:
   A. I only B. I and II C. II only D. Neither I nor II

4. Which of the following pairs of statements say essentially the same thing in two different ways? 4.____
   I. If a member of the swim team attends every practice, he will compete in the next meet.
   Either a swim team member will compete in the next meet, or he did not attend every practice.
   II. All the engineers in the drafting department who wear glasses know how to use AutoCAD.
   If an engineer wears glasses, he will know how to use AutoCAD.
   The CORRECT answer is:
   A. I only B. I and II C. II only D. Neither I nor II

5. Summary of Evidence Collected to Date: 5.____
   All of the parents who attend the weekly parenting seminars are high school graduates.
   Prematurely Drawn Conclusion: Some parents who attend the weekly parenting seminars have been convicted of child abuse.
   Which of the following pieces of evidence, if any, would make it reasonably certain that the conclusion drawn is true?
   A. Those convicted of child abuse are often high school graduates.
   B. Some high school graduates have been convicted of child abuse.
   C. There is no correlation between education level and the incidence of child abuse.
   D. None of the above

6. Summary of Evidence Collected to Date: 6.____
   I. Mr. Cantwell promised to vote for new school buses if he was reelected to the board.
   II. If the new school buses are approved by the school board, then Mr. Cantwell was not reelected to the board.
   Prematurely Drawn Conclusion: Approval of the new school buses was defeated in spite of Mr. Cantwell's vote.
   Which of the following pieces of evidence, if any, would make it reasonably certain that the conclusion drawn is true?
   A. Mr. Cantwell decided not to run for reelection.
   B. Mr. Cantwell was reelected to the board.
   C. Mr. Cantwell changed his mind and voted against the new buses.
   D. None of the above

7. Summary of Evidence Collected to Date: 7.____
   I. The station employs three detectives: Francis, Jackson, and Stern. One of the detectives is a lieutenant, one is a sergeant, and one is a major.
   II. Francis is not a lieutenant.
   Prematurely Drawn Conclusion: Jackson is a lieutenant.
   Which of the following pieces of evidence, if any, would make it reasonably certain that the conclusion drawn is true?
   A. Stern is not a sergeant. B. Stern is a major.
   C. Francis is a major. E. None of the above

8. Summary of Evidence Collected to Date: 8.____
   I. In the office building, every survival kit that contains a gas mask also contains anthrax vaccine.
   II. Some of the kits containing water purification tablets also contain anthrax vaccine.

   Prematurely Drawn Conclusion: If the survival kit near the typists' pool contains a gas mask, it does not contain water purification tablets.
   Which of the following pieces of evidence, if any, would make it reasonably certain that the conclusion drawn is true?
   A. Some survival kits contain all three items.
   B. The survival kit near the typists' pool contains anthrax vaccine.
   C. The survival kit near the typists' pool contains only two of these items.
   D. None of the above

9. Summary of Evidence Collected to Date: 9.____
   The shrink-wrap mechanism is designed to shut itself off if the heating coil temperature drops below 400 during the twin cycle.
   Prematurely Drawn Conclusion: If the machine was operating the twin cycle on Monday, it was not operating properly.
   Which of the following pieces of evidence, if any, would make it reasonably certain that the conclusion drawn is true?
   A. On Monday, the heating coil temperature reached 450.
   B. When the machine performs functions other than the twin cycle, the heating coil temperature sometimes drops below 400.
   C. The shrink-wrap mechanism did not shut itself off on Monday.
   D. None of the above

Questions 10-14.

DIRECTIONS: Questions 10 through 14 refer to Map #3 and measure your ability to orient yourself within a given section of town, neighborhood or particular area. Each of the questions describes a starting point and a destination. Assume that you are driving a car in the area shown on the map accompanying the questions. Use the map as a basis for the shortest way to get from one point to another without breaking the law.

On the map, a street marked by arrows, or by arrows and the words "One Way," indicates one-way travel and should be assumed to be one-way for the entire length, even when there are breaks or jogs in the street. EXCEPTION: A street that does not have the same name over the full length.

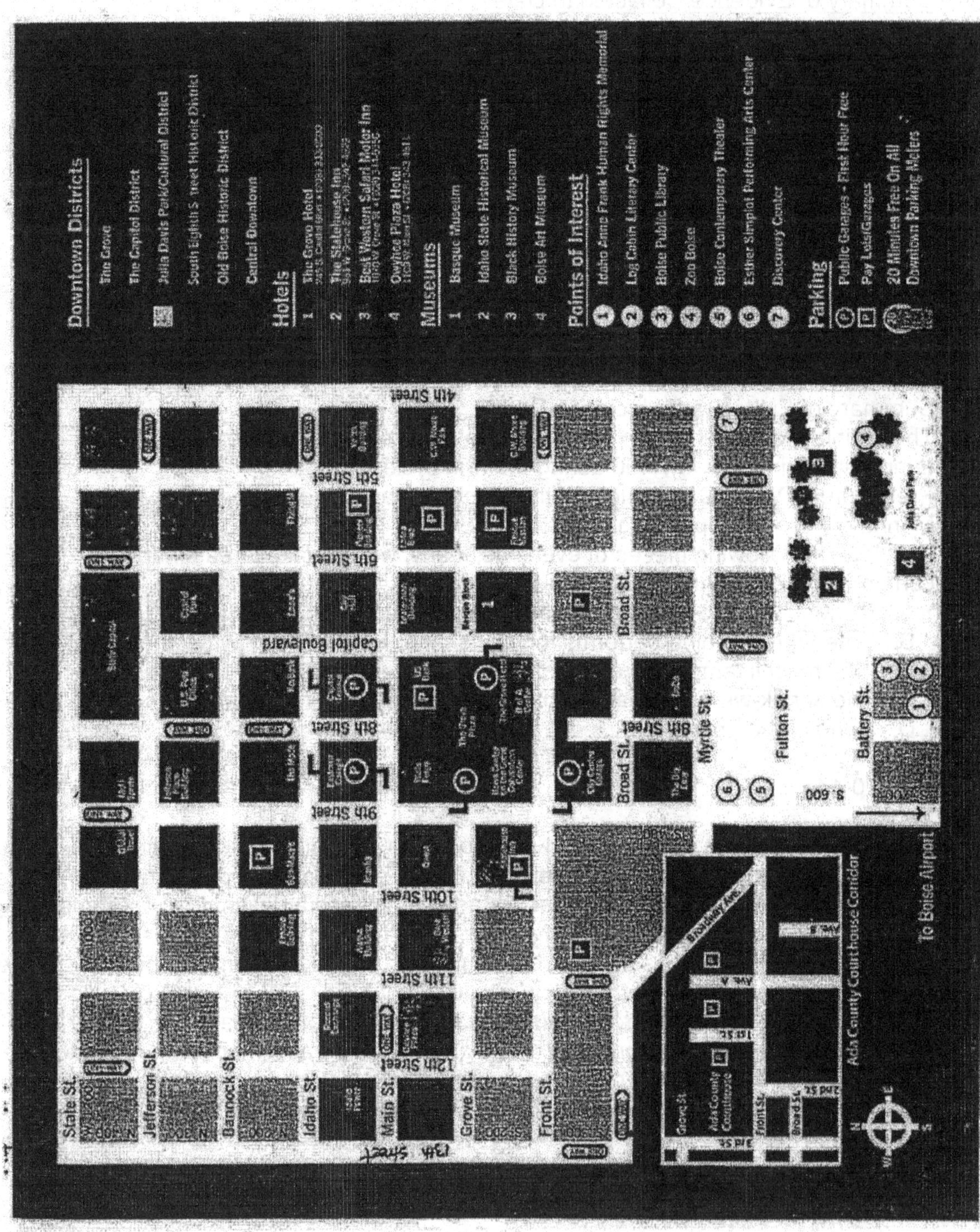

10. The SHORTEST legal way from the State Capitol to Idaho Power is 10.____
   A. south on Capitol Blvd., west on Main, north on 12th
   B. south on 8th, west on Main
   C. west on Jefferson, south on 12th
   D. south on Capitol Blvd., west on Front, north on 12th

11. The SHORTEST legal way from the Jefferson Place Building to the Statesman Building is 11.____
   A. east on Jefferson, south on Capitol Blvd.
   B. south on 8th, east on Main
   C. east on Jefferson, south on 4th, west on Main
   D. south on 9th, east on Main

12. The SHORTEST legal way from Julia Davis Park to Owyhee Plaza Hotel is 12.____
   A. north on 5th, west on Front, north on 11th
   B. north on 6th, west on Main
   C. west on Battery, north on 9th, west on Front, north on Main
   D. north on 5th, west on Front, north on 13th, east on Main

13. The SHORTEST legal way from the Big Easy to City Hall is 13.____
   A. north on 9th, east on Main
   B. east on Myrtle, north on Capitol Blvd.
   C. north on 9th, east on Idaho
   D. east on Myrtle, north on 6th

14. The SHORTEST legal way from the Boise Contemporary Theater to the Pioneer Building is 14.____
   A. north on 9th, east on Main
   B. north on 9th, east on Myrtle, north on 6th
   C. east on Fulton, north on Capitol Blvd., east on Main
   D. east on Fulton, north on 6th

Questions 15-19.

DIRECTIONS: Questions 15 through 19 refer to Figure #3, on the following page, and measure your ability to understand written descriptions of events. Each question presents a description of an accident or event and asks you which of the following five drawings in Figure #3 BEST represents it.
In the drawings, the following symbols are used:
Moving vehicle   Non-moving vehicle
Pedestrian or bicyclist •
The path and direction of travel of a vehicle or pedestrian is indicated by a solid line.
The path and direction of travel of each vehicle or pedestrian directly involved in a collision from the point of impact is indicated by a dotted line.

In the space at the right, print the letter of the drawing that BEST fit the descriptions written below.

6 (#2)

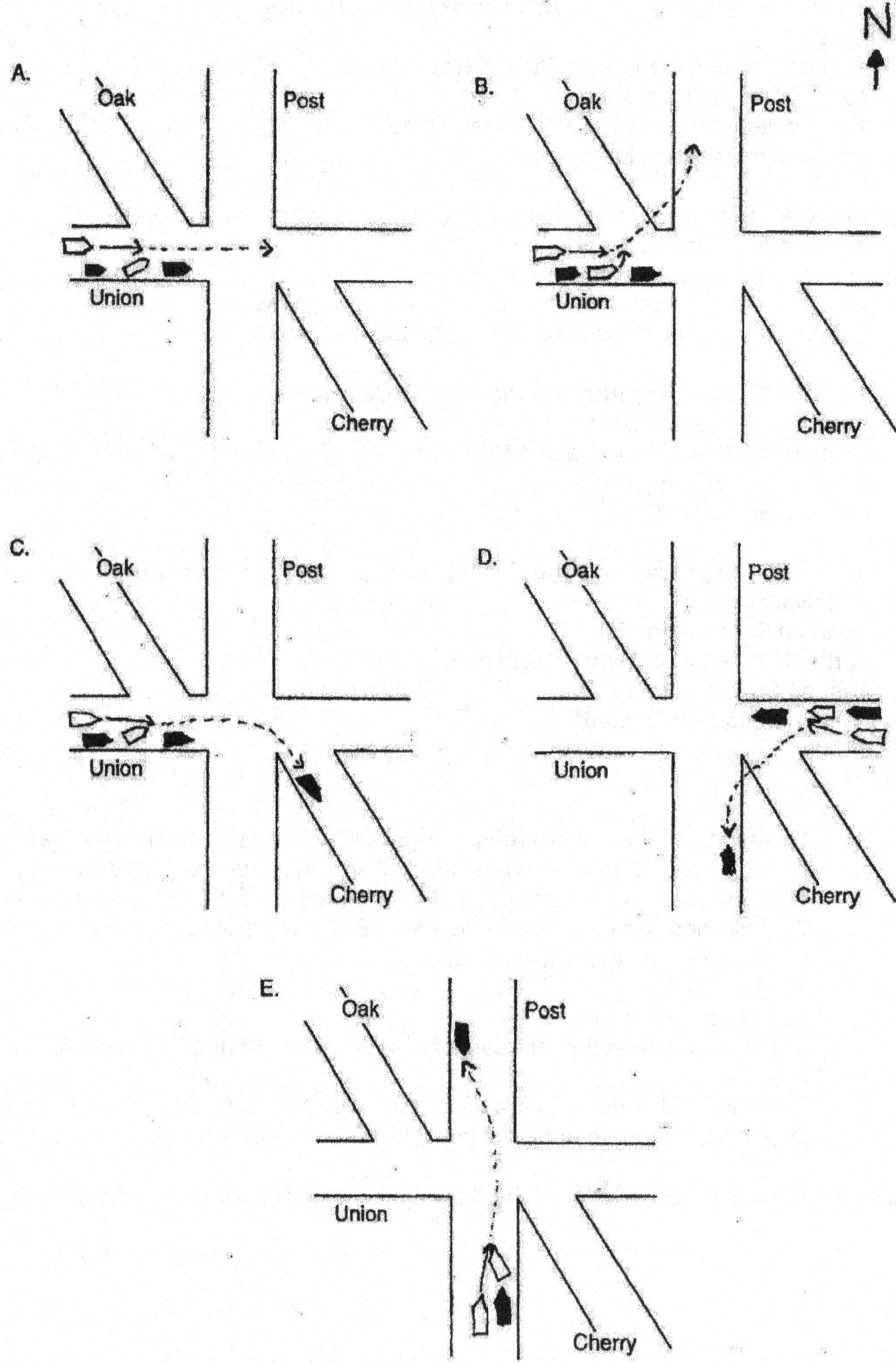
N
A.
Oak
Post
Union
Cherry
B.
Oak
Post
Union
Cherry
C.
Oak
Post
Union
Cherry
D.
Oak
Post
Union
Cherry
E.
Oak
Post
Union
Cherry

15. A driver headed east on Union strikes a car that is pulling out from between two parked cars, and then continues east. 15.____

16. A driver headed north on Post strikes a car that is pulling out from in front of a parked car, then veers into the oncoming lane and collides head-on with a car that is parked in the southbound lane of Post. 16.____

17. A driver headed east on Union strikes a car that is pulling out from two parked cars, travels through the intersection, and makes a sudden right turn onto Cherry, where he strikes a parked car in the rear. 17.____

18. A driver headed west on Union strikes a car that is pulling out from between two parked cars, and then swerves to the left. He cuts the corner and travels over the sidewalk at the intersection of Cherry and Post, and then strikes a car that is parked in the northbound lane on Post. 18.____

19. A driver headed east on Union strikes a car that is pulling out from between two parked cars, and then swerves to the left. He cuts the corner and travels over the sidewalk at the intersection of Oak and Post, and then flees north on Post. 19.____

Questions 20-22.

DIRECTIONS: In Questions 20 through 22, choose the word or phrase CLOSEST in meaning to the word or phrase printed in capital letters.

20. TITLE 20.____
   A. danger B. ownership C. description D. treatise

21. REVOKE 21.____
   A. cancel B. imagine C. solicit D. cause

22. BRIEF 22.____
   A. summary B. ruling C. plea D. motion

Questions 23-25.

DIRECTIONS: Questions 23 through 25 measure your ability to do fieldwork-related arithmetic. Each question presents a separate arithmetic problem for you to solve.

23. An investigator plans to drive from his home to Los Angeles, a trip of 2,800 miles. His car has a 24-gallon tank and gets 18 miles to the gallon. 23.____
If he starts out with a full tank of gasoline, what is the FEWEST number of stops he will have to make for gasoline to complete his trip to Los Angeles?
   A. 4 B. 5 C. 6 D. 7

24. A caseworker has 24 home visits to schedule for a week. She will visit three homes on Sunday, and on every day that follows she will visit one more home than she visited on the previous day. 24.____
At the end of the day on _____, the caseworker will have completed all of her home visits.
A. Wednesday B. Thursday C. Friday D. Saturday

25. Ms. Langhorn takes a cab from her house to the airport. The cab company charges $3.00 to start the meter and $.50 per mile after that. It's 15 miles from Ms. Langhorn's house to the airport. 25.____
How much will she have to pay for a cab?
A. $10.50 B. $11.50 C. $14.00 D. $15.50

KEY (CORRECT ANSWERS)

1. B
2. A
3. D
4. B
5. D

6. B
7. B
8. C
9. C
10. C

11. D
12. A
13. B
14. C
15. A

16. E
17. C
18. D
19. B
20. B

21. A
22. A
23. C
24. B
25. A

SOLUTIONS TO QUESTIONS 1-9

P implies Q = original statement

Not Q implies not P = contrapositive of the original statement. A statement and its contrapositive are logically equivalent.

Q implies P = converse of the original statement

Not P implies not Q = inverse of the original statement. The converse and inverse of an original statement are logically equivalent.

P implies Q = Not P or Q.

1. The CORRECT answer is B.
For Item I, the irrational thinking teachers at the Middle School belong the group of all Middle School teachers. Since all teachers at the Middle School are intelligent, this includes the subset of irrational thinkers. For item II, if no one person has no friends, this implies that each person must have at least one friend.

2. The CORRECT answer is A.
In item I, both statements state that (a) bananas are healthy and (b) bananas are eaten mainly because they taste good. In item II, the second statement is not equivalent to the first statement. An equivalent statement to the first statement would be "Either Dr. Jones is not in or we should call at the office."

3. The CORRECT answer is D.
In item I, given that a person works one shift, we cannot draw any conclusion about whether he/she is a millworker. It is possible that a millworker works one, two, or a number more than two shifts. In item II, the second statement is the inverse of the first statement; they are not logically equivalent.

4. The CORRECT answer is B.
In item I, any statement in the form "P implies Q" is equivalent to "Not P or Q." In this case, P = A member of the swim team attends practice, and Q = He will compete in the next meet. In item II, "P implies Q" is equivalent to "all P belongs to Q." In this case, P = Engineer wears glasses, and Q = He will know how to use AutoCAD.

5. The CORRECT answer is D. Because the number of high school graduates is so much larger than the number of convicted child abusers, none of the additional pieces of evidence make it reasonably certain that there are convicted abusers within this group of parents.

6. The CORRECT answer is B.
Statement II is equivalent to "If Mr. Cantwell is reelected to the school board, then school buses are not approved. Statement I assures us that Mr. Cantwell will vote for new school buses. The only logical conclusion is that in spite of Mr. Cantwell's reelection to the board and subsequent vote, approval of the buses was still defeated.

7. The CORRECT answer is B. From Statement II, we conclude that Francis is either a sergeant or a major. If we also know that Stern is a major, we can deduce that Francis is a sergeant. This means that the third person, Jackson, must be a lieutenant.

8. The CORRECT answer is C.
Given that a survival kit contains a gas mask, Statement I assures us that it also contains the anthrax vaccine. If the survival kit near the typist pool only contains two items, than we can conclude that the gas mask in this location cannot contain a third item, namely the anthrax vaccine.

9. The CORRECT answer is C.
The original statement can be written in "P implies Q" form, where P = the heating coil temperature drops below 400 during the twin cycle, and Q = the mechanism shuts itself off. The contrapositive (which must be true) would be "If the mechanism did not shut itself off then the heating coil temperature did not drop below 400." We would then conclude that the temperature was too high and, therefore, the machine did not operate properly.

EVALUATING INFORMATION AND EVIDENCE

EXAMINATION SECTION

TEST 1

DIRECTIONS: Each question or incomplete statement is followed by several suggested answers or completions. Select the one that BEST answers the question or completes the statement. *PRINT THE LETTER OF THE CORRECT ANSWER IN THE SPACE AT THE RIGHT.*

Questions 1-9.

DIRECTIONS: Questions 1 through 9 measure your ability to (1) determine whether statements from witnesses say essentially the same thing and (2) determine the evidence needed to make it reasonably certain that a particular conclusion is true.

1. Which of the following pairs of statements say essentially the same thing in two different ways? 1.____
   I. If you get your feet wet, you will catch a cold.
   If you catch a cold, you must have gotten your feet wet.
   II. If I am nominated, I will run for office.
   I will run for office only if I am nominated.
   The CORRECT answer is:
   A. I only B. I and II C. II only D. Neither I nor II

2. Which of the following pairs of statements say essentially the same thing in two different ways? 2.____
   I. The enzyme Rhopsin cannot be present if the bacterium Trilox is absent.
   Rhopsin and Trilox always appear together.
   II. A member of PENSA has an IQ of at least 175.
   A person with an IQ of less than 175 is not a member of PENSA
   The CORRECT answer is;
   A. I only B. I and II C. II only D. Neither I nor II

3. Which of the following pairs of statements say essentially the same thing in two different ways? 3.____
   I. None of Finer High School's sophomores will be going to the prom.
   No student at Finer High School who is going to the prom is a sophomore.
   II. If you have 20/20 vision, you may carry a firearm.
   You may not carry a firearm unless you have 20/20 vision.
   The CORRECT answer is:
   A. I only B. I and II C. II only D. Neither I nor II

4. Which of the following pairs of statements say essentially the same thing in two different ways? 4.____
   I. If the family doesn't pay the ransom, they will never see their son again.
      It is necessary for the family to pay the ransom in order for them to see their son again.
   II. If it is raining, I am carrying an umbrella.
      If I am carrying an umbrella, it is raining.

   The CORRECT answer is:
   A. I only B. I and II C. II only D. Neither I nor II

5. Summary of Evidence Collected to Date: 5.____
   In the county's maternity wards, over the past year, only one baby was born who did not share a birthday with any other baby.
   Prematurely Drawn Conclusion: At least one baby was born on the same day as another baby in the county's maternity wards.
   Which of the following pieces of evidence, if any, would make it reasonably certain that the conclusion drawn is true?
   A. More than 365 babies were born in the county's maternity wards over the past year.
   B. No pairs of twins were born over the past year in the county's maternity wards.
   C. More than one baby was born in the county's maternity wards over the past year.
   D. None of the above

6. Summary of Evidence Collected to Date: 6.____
   Every claims adjustor for MetroLife drives only a Ford sedan when on the job.
   Prematurely Drawn Conclusion: A person who works for MetroLife and drives a Ford sedan is a claims adjustor.
   Which of the following pieces of evidence, if any, would make it reasonably certain that the conclusion drawn is true?
   A. Most people who work for MetroLife are claims adjustors.
   B. Some people who work for MetroLife are not claims adjustors.
   C. Most people who work for MetroLife drive Ford sedans
   D. None of the above

7. Summary of Evidence Collected to Date: 7.____
   Mason will speak to Zisk if Zisk will speak to Ronaldson.
   Prematurely Drawn Conclusion: Jones will not speak to Zisk if Zisk will speak to Ronaldson.
   Which of the following pieces of evidence, if any, would make it reasonably certain that the conclusion drawn is true?
   A. If Zisk will speak to Mason, then Ronaldson will not speak to Jones.
   B. If Mason will speak to Zisk, then Jones will not speak to Zisk.
   C. If Ronaldson will speak to Jones, then Jones will speak to Ronaldson.
   D. None of the above

8. Summary of Evidence Collected to Date: 8.____
No blue lights on the machine are indicators for the belt drive status.
Prematurely Drawn Conclusion: Some of the lights on the lower panel are not indicators for the belt drive status.
Which of the following pieces of evidence, if any, would make it reasonably certain that the conclusion drawn is true?
   A. No lights on the machine's lower panel are blue.
   B. An indicator light for the machine's belt drive status is either green or red.
   C. Some lights on the machine's lower panel are blue.
   D. None of the above

9. Summary of Evidence Collected to Date: 9.____
Of the four Sweeney sisters, two are married, three have brown eyes, and three are doctors.
Prematurely Drawn Conclusion: Two of the Sweeney sisters are brown-eyed, married doctors.
Which of the following pieces of evidence, if any, would make it reasonably certain that the conclusion is true?
   A. The sister who does not have brown eyes is married.
   B. The sister who does not have brown eyes is not a doctor, and one who is not married is not a doctor.
   C. Every Sweeney sister with brown eyes is a doctor.
   D. None of the above

Questions 10-14.

DIRECTIONS: Questions 10 through 14 refer to Map #5 and measure your ability to orient yourself within a given section of town, neighborhood or particular area. Each of the questions describes a starting point and a destination. Assume that you are driving a car in the area shown on the map accompanying the questions. Use the map as a basis for the shortest way to get from one point to another without breaking the law.

On the map, a street marked by arrows, or by arrows and the words "One Way," indicates one-way travel and should be assumed to be one-way for the entire length, even when there are breaks or jogs in the street. EXCEPTION: A street that does not have the same name over the full length.

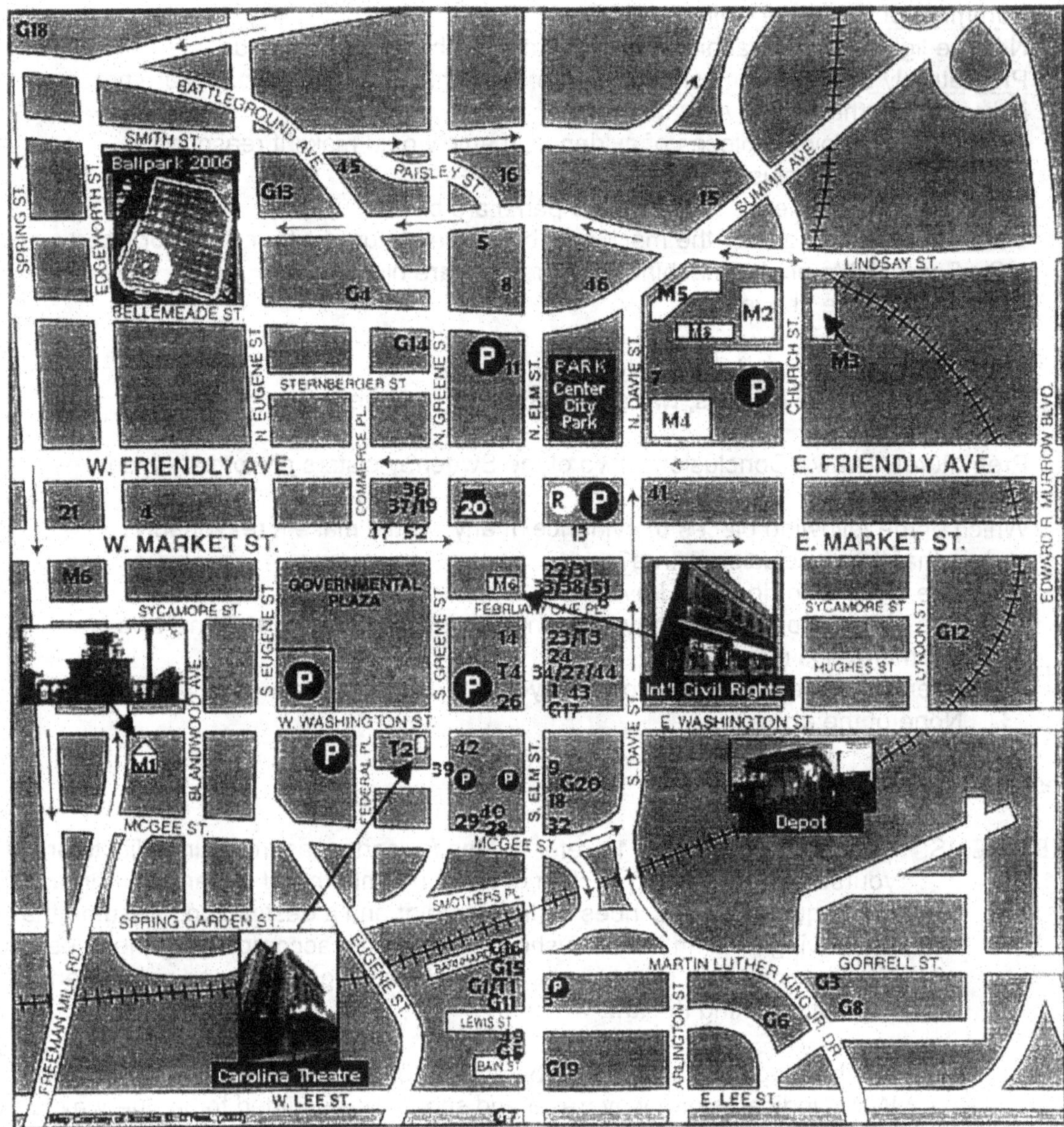

Map #5

10. The SHORTEST legal way from the depot to Center City Park is 10.____
    A. north on Church, west on Market, north on Elm
    B. east on Washington, north on Edward R. Murrow Blvd., west on Friendly Ave.
    C. west on Washington, north on Greene, east on Market, north on Davie
    D. north on Church, west on Friendly Ave.

11. The SHORTEST legal way from the Governmental Plaza to the Ballpark is 11.____
   A. west on Market, north on Edgeworth
   B. west on Market, north on Eugene
   C. north on Greene, west on Lindsay
   D. north on Commerce Place, west on Bellemeade

12. The SHORTEST legal way from the International Civil Rights Building to the building marked "M3" on the map is 12.____
   A. east on February One Place, north on Davie, east on Friendly Ave., north on Church
   B. south on Elm, west on Washington, north on Greene, east on Market, north on Church
   C. north on Elm, east on Market, north on Church
   D. north on Elm, east on Lindsay, south on Church

13. The SHORTEST legal way from the Ballpark to the Carolina Theatre is 13.____
   A. east on Lindsay, south on Greene
   B. south on Edgeworth, east on Friendly Ave., south on Greene
   C. east on Bellemeade, south on Elm, west on Washington

14. A car traveling north or south on Church Street may NOT go 14.____
   A. west onto Friendly Ave.
   B. west onto Lindsay
   C. east onto Market
   D. west onto Smith

Questions 15-19.

DIRECTIONS: Questions 15 through 19 refer to Figure #3, on the following page, and measure your ability to understand written descriptions of events. Each question presents a description of an accident or event and asks you which of the following five drawings in Figure #3 BEST represents it.
In the drawings, the following symbols are used:
Moving vehicle ⌂ Non-moving vehicle ☗
Pedestrian or bicyclist •
The path and direction of travel of a vehicle or pedestrian is indicated by a solid line.
The path and direction of travel of each vehicle or pedestrian directly involved in a collision from the point of impact is indicated by a dotted line.

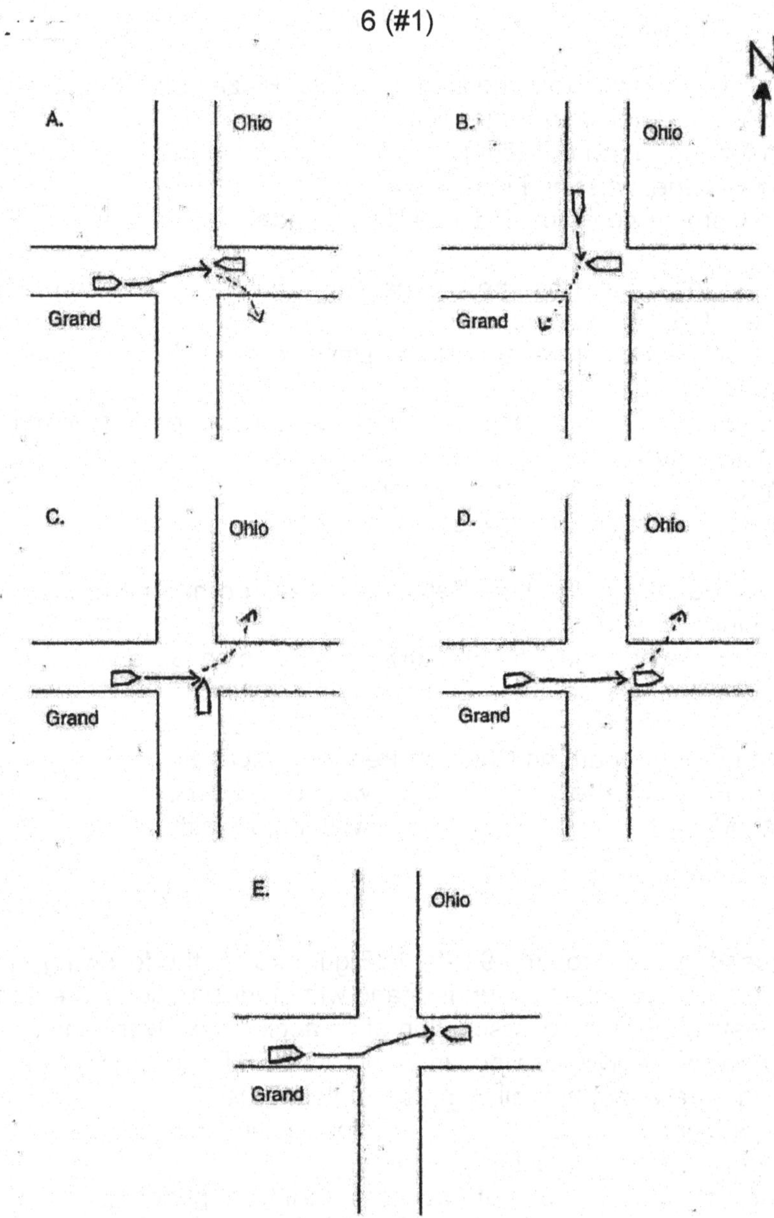

In the space at the right, print the letter of the drawing that BEST fit the descriptions written below.

15. A driver headed south on Ohio runs a red light and strikes the front of a car headed west on Grand. He glances off and leaves the roadway at the southwest corner of Grand and Ohio. 15.____

16. A driver heading east on Grand drifts into the oncoming lane as it travels through the intersection of Grand and Ohio, and strikes an oncoming car head-on 16.____

17. A driver heading east on Grand veers into the oncoming lane, sideswipes a westbound car and overcorrects as he swerves back into his lane. He leaves the roadway near the southeast corner of Grand and Ohio. 17.____

18. A driver heading east on Grand strikes the front of a car that is traveling north on Ohio and has run a red light. After striking the front of the northbound car, the driver veers left and leaves the roadway at the northeast corner of Grand and Ohio. 18.____

19. A driver heading east on Grand is traveling above the speed limit and clips the rear end of another eastbound car. The driver then veers to the left and leaves the roadway at the northeast corner of Grand and Ohio. 19.____

Questions 20-22.

DIRECTIONS: In Questions 20 through 22, choose the word or phrase CLOSEST in meaning to the word or phrase printed in capital letters.

20. PETITION 20.____
   A. appeal B. law C. oath D. opposition

21. MALPRACTICE 21.____
   A. commission B. mayhem C. error D. misconduct

22. EXONERATE 22.____
   A. incriminate B. accuse C. lengthen D. acquit

Questions 23-25.

DIRECTIONS: Questions 23 through 25 measure your ability to do fieldwork-related arithmetic. Each question presents a separate arithmetic problem for you to solve.

23. Officers Lane and Bryant visited another city as part of an investigation. Because each is from a different precinct, they agree to split all expenses. With her credit card, Lane paid $70 for food and $150 for lodging. Bryant wrote checks for gas ($50) and entertainment ($40). How much does Bryant owe Lane? 23.____
   A. $65 B. $90 C. $155 D. $210

24. In a remote mountain pass, two search-and-rescue teams, one from Silverton and one from Durango, combine to look for a family that disappeared in a recent snowstorm. The combined team is composed of 20 members. Which of the following statements could NOT be true? 24.____
   A. The Durango team has a dozen members.
   B. The Silverton team has only one member.
   C. The Durango team has two more members than the Silverton team.
   D. The Silverton team has one more member than the Durango team.

25. Three people in the department share a vehicle for a period of one year. The average number of miles traveled per month by each person is 150. How many miles will be added to the car's odometer at the end of the year? 25.____
    A. 1,800 B. 2,400 C. 3,600 D. 5,400

KEY (CORRECT ANSWERS)

1. D
2. C
3. A
4. A
5. A

6. A
7. B
8. C
9. B
10. D

11. D
12. C
13. D
14. D
15. B

16. E
17. A
18. C
19. D
20. A

21. D
22. D
23. A
24. D
25. D

SOLUTIONS TO QUESTIONS 1-9

P implies Q = original statement

Not Q implies not P = contrapositive of the original statement. A statement and its contrapositive are logically equivalent.

Q implies P = converse of the original statement

Not P implies not Q = inverse of the original statement. The converse and inverse of an original statement are logically equivalent.

P implies Q = Not P or Q.

1. The CORRECT answer is D.
   In items I and II, each statement is the converses of the other. A converse of a statement is not equivalent to its original statement.

2. The CORRECT answer is C.
   In item I, the first statement is equivalent to "If Trilox is absent, then Rhopsin is also absent." But this does NOT imply that if Trilox is present, so too must Rhopsin be present. In item II, each statement is the contrapositive of the other. Thus, they are equivalent.

3. The CORRECT answer is A.
   In item I, the first sentence tells us that if a student is a sophomore, he/she will not go the prom. The second statement is equivalent to "If a student does attend the prom, he/she is not a sophomore." This is the contrapositive of the first statement, (so it is equivalent to it).

4. The CORRECT answer is A.
   In item I, the second statement can be written as "If the family sees their son again, then they must have paid the ransom." This is the contrapositive of the first statement. In item II, these statements are converses of each other; thus, they are not equivalent.

5. The CORRECT answer is A.
   If more than 365 babies were born in the county in one year, then at least two babies must share the same birthday.

6. The CORRECT answer is A.
   Given that most people who work for MetroLife are claims adjustors, plus the fact that all claims adjustors drive only a Ford sedan, it is a reasonable conclusion that any person who drives a Ford sedan and works for MetroLife is a claims adjustor.

7. The CORRECT answer is B.
   Jones will not speak to Zisk if Zisk will speak to Ronaldson, which will happen if Mason will speak to Zisk.

8. The CORRECT answer is C.
We are given that blue lights are never an indicator for the drive belt status. If some of the lights on the lower panel of the machine are blue, then it is reasonable to conclude that some of the lights on the lower panel are not indicators for the drive belt status.

9. The CORRECT answer is B.
There is only one sister that does not have brown eyes and only one sister that is not a doctor, and if the information in answer B is correct, then we learn that the same sister is a non-doctor without brown eyes. We also learn that this same non-doctor is not married. Since this all describes the same sister, we can conclude that two of the other sisters must be married doctors with brown eyes.

TEST 2

DIRECTIONS: Each question or incomplete statement is followed by several suggested answers or completions. Select the one that BEST answers the question or completes the statement. *PRINT THE LETTER OF THE CORRECT ANSWER IN THE SPACE AT THE RIGHT.*

Questions 1-9.

DIRECTIONS: Questions 1 through 9 measure your ability to (1) determine whether statements from witnesses say essentially the same thing and (2) determine the evidence needed to make it reasonably certain that a particular conclusion is true.
To do well on this part of the test, you do NOT have to have a working knowledge of police procedures and techniques. Nor do you have to have any more familiarity with criminals and criminal behavior than that acquired from reading newspapers, listening to radio or watching TV. To do well in this part, you must read and reason carefully.

1. Which of the following pairs of statements say essentially the same thing in two different ways? 1.____
   I. If there is life on Mars, we should fund NASA.
   Either there is life on Mars, or we should not fund NASA.
   II. All Eagle Scouts are teenage boys.
   All teenage boy are Eagle Scouts.
   The CORRECT answer is:
   A. I only B. I and II C. II only D. Neither I nor II

2. Which of the following pairs of statements say essentially the same thing in two different ways? 2.____
   I. If that notebook is missing its front cover, it definitely belongs to Carter.
   Carter's notebook is the only one missing its front cover.
   II. If it's hot, the pool is open.
   The pool is open if it's hot.
   The CORRECT answer is:
   A. I only B. I and II C. II only D. Neither I nor II

3 Which of the following pairs of statements say essentially the same thing in two different ways? 3.____
   I. Nobody who works at the mill is without benefits.
   Everyone who works at the mill has benefits.
   II. We will fund the program only if at least 100 people sign the petition.
   Either we will fund the program or at least 100 people will sign the petition.
   The CORRECT answer is:
   A. I only B. I and II C. II only D. Neither I nor II

4. Which of the following pairs of statements say essentially the same thing in two different ways? 4.____

   I. If the new parts arrive, Mr. Luther's request has been answered.
   Mr. Luther requested new parts to arrive.

   II. The machine's test cycle will not run unless the operation cycle is not running.
   The machine's test cycle must be running in order for the operation cycle to run.

   The CORRECT answer is:

   A. I only B. I and II C. II only D. Neither I nor II

5. Summary of Evidence Collected to Date: 5.____

   I. To become a member of the East Side Crips, a kid must be either "jumped in" or steal a squad car without getting caught.

   II. Sid, a kid on the East Side, was caught stealing a squad car.

   Prematurely Drawn Conclusion: Sid did not become a member of the East Side Crips.

   Which of the following pieces of evidence, if any, would make it reasonably certain that the conclusion drawn is true?

   A. "Jumping in" is not allowed in prison.
   B. Sid was not "jumped in."
   C. Sid's stealing the squad car had nothing to do with wanting to join the East Side Crips.
   D. None of the above

6. Summary of Evidence Collected to Date: 6.____

   I. Jones, a Precinct 8 officer, has more arrests than Smith.

   II. Smith and Watson have exactly the same number of arrests.

   Prematurely Drawn Conclusion: Watson is not a Precinct 8 officer.

   Which of the following pieces of evidence, if any, would make it reasonably certain that the conclusion drawn is true?

   A. All the officers in Precinct 8 have more arrests than Watson.
   B. All the officers in Precinct 8 have fewer arrests than Watson.
   C. Watson has fewer arrests than Jones.
   D. None of the above

7. Summary of Evidence Collected to Date: 7.____

   I. Twenty one-dollar bills are divided among Frances, Kerry, and Brian.

   II. If Kerry gives her dollar bills to Frances, then Frances will have more money than Brian.

   Prematurely Drawn Conclusion: Frances has twelve dollars.

   Which of the following pieces of evidence, if any, would make it reasonably certain that the conclusion drawn is true?

   A. If Brian gives his dollars to Kerry, then Kerry will have more money than Frances.
   B. Brian has two dollars.
   C. If Kerry gives her dollars to Brian, Brian will still have less money than Frances.
   D. None of the above

8. Summary of Evidence Collected to Date: 8.____
I. The street sweepers will be here at noon today.
II. Residents on the west side of the street should move their cars before noon.
Prematurely Drawn Conclusion: Today is Wednesday.
Which of the following pieces of evidence, if any, would make it reasonably certain that the conclusion drawn is true?
A. The street sweepers never sweep the east side of the street on Wednesday.
B. The street sweepers arrive at noon every other day.
C. There is no parking allowed on the west side of the street on Wednesday.
D. None of the above

9. Summary of Evidence Collected to Date: 9.____
The only time the warning light comes on is when there is a power surge.
Prematurely Drawn Conclusion: The warning light does not come on if the air conditioner is not running.
Which of the following pieces of evidence, if any, would make it reasonably certain that the conclusion drawn is true?
A. The air conditioner does not turn on if the warning light is on.
B. Sometimes a power surge is caused by the dishwasher.
C. There is only a power surge when the air conditioner turns on.
D. None of the above

Questions 10-14.

DIRECTIONS: Questions 10 through 14 refer to Map #3 and measure your ability to orient yourself within a given section of town, neighborhood or particular area. Each of the questions describes a starting point and a destination. Assume that you are driving a car in the area shown on the map accompanying the questions. Use the map as a basis for the shortest way to get from one point to another without breaking the law.
On the map, a street marked by arrows, or by arrows and the words "One Way," indicates one-way travel and should be assumed to be one-way for the entire length, even when there are breaks or jogs in the street. EXCEPTION: A street that does not have the same name over the full length.

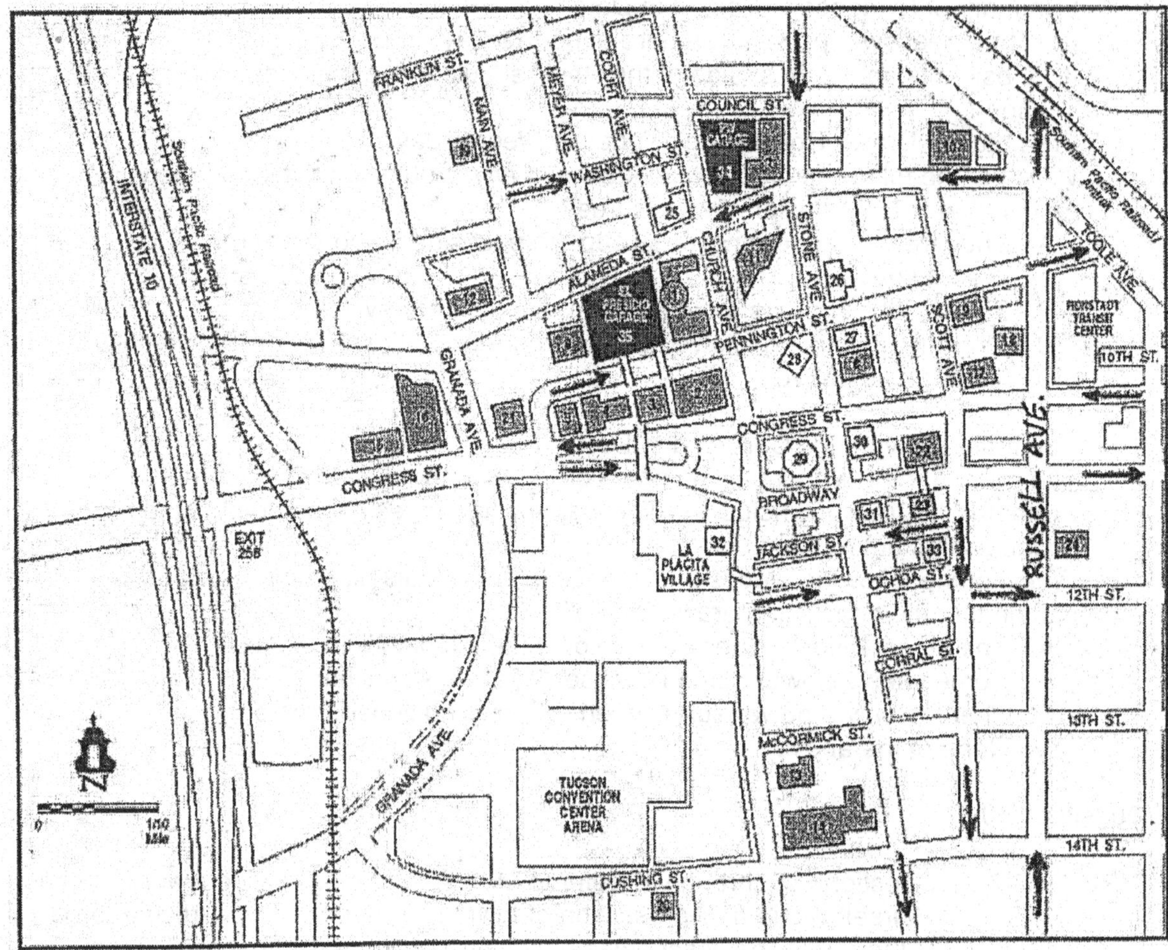

PIMA COUNTY
1 Old Courthouse
2. Superior Court Building
3. Administration Building
4. Health and Welfare Building
5. Mechanical Building
6. Legal Services Building
7. County/City Public Works Center

CITY OF TUCSON
8. City Hall
9. City Hall Annex
10. Alameda Plaza City Court Building
11. Public Library – Main Branch
12. Tucson Water Building
13. Fire Department Headquarters
14. Police Department Building

10. The SHORTEST legal way from the Public Library to the Alameda Plaza City Court Building is 10.____
   A. north on Stone Ave., east of Alameda
   B. south on Stone Ave., east on Congress, north on Russell Ave., west on Alameda
   C. south on Stone Ave., east on Pennington, north on Russell Ave., west on Alameda
   D. south on Church Ave., east on Pennington, north on Russell Ave., west on Alameda

11. The SHORTEST legal way from City Hall to the Police Department is 11.____
    A. east on Congress, south on Scott Ave., west on 14th
    B. east on Pennington, south on Stone Ave.
    C. east on Congress, south on Stone Ave.
    D. east on Pennington, south on Church Ave.

12. The SHORTEST legal way from the Tucson Water Building to the Legal Service Building is 12.____
    A. south on Granada Ave., east on Congress, north to east on Pennington, south on Stone Ave.
    B. east on Alameda, south on Church Ave., east on Pennington, south on Stone Ave.
    C. north on Granada Ave., east on Washington, south on Church Ave., east on Pennington, south on Stone Ave.
    D. south on Granada Ave., east on Cushing, north on Stone Ave.

13. The SHORTEST legal way from the Tucson Convention Center Arena to the City Hall Annex is 13.____
    A. west on Cushing, north on Granada Ave., east on Congress east on Broadway
    B. east on Cushing, north on Church Ave., east on Pennington
    C. east on Cushing, north on Russel Ave., west on Pennington
    D. east on Cushing, north on Stone Ave., east on Pennington

14. The SHORTEST legal way from Ronstadt Transit Center to the Fire Department is 14.____
    A. west on Pennington, south on Stone Ave., west on McCormick
    B. west on Congress, south on Russell Ave., west on 13th
    C. west on Congress, south on Church Ave.
    D. west on Pennington, south on Church Ave.

Questions 15-19.

DIRECTIONS: Questions 15 through 19 refer to Figure #3, on the following page, and measure your ability to understand written descriptions of events. Each question presents a description of an accident or event and asks you which of the following five drawings in Figure #3 BEST represents it.
In the drawings, the following symbols are used:
Moving vehicle ⇧ Non-moving vehicle ⬆
Pedestrian or bicyclist •
The path and direction of travel of a vehicle or pedestrian is indicated by a solid line.
The path and direction of travel of each vehicle or pedestrian directly involved in a collision from the point of impact is indicated by a dotted line.

In the space at the right, print the letter of the drawing that BEST fit the descriptions written below.

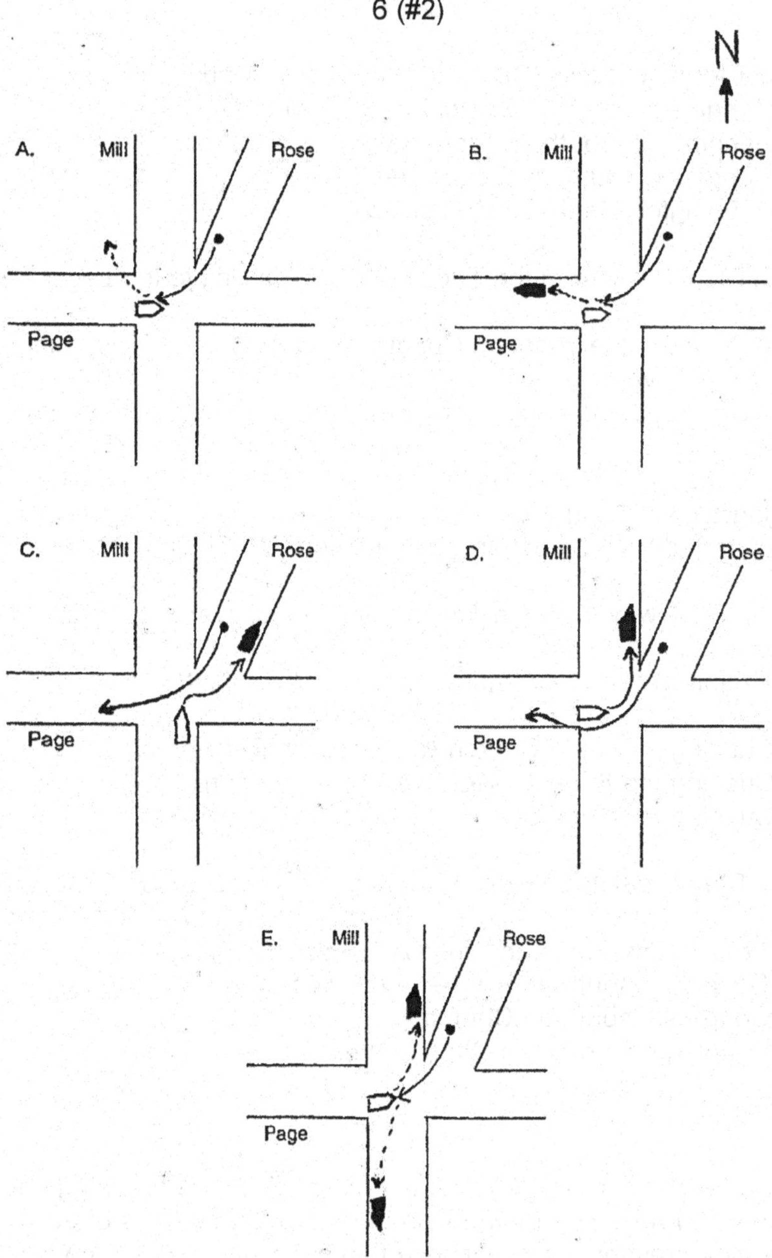

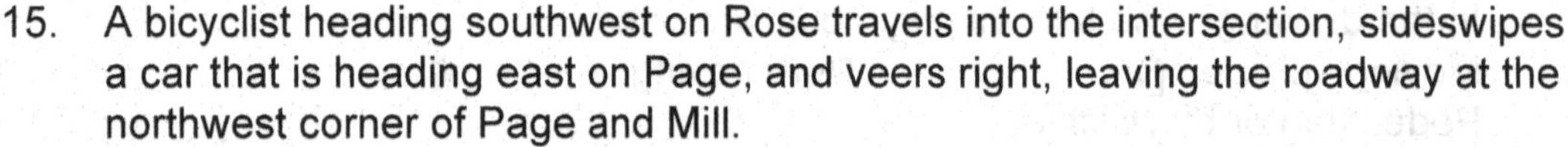

15. A bicyclist heading southwest on Rose travels into the intersection, sideswipes a car that is heading east on Page, and veers right, leaving the roadway at the northwest corner of Page and Mill. 15.____

16. A driver traveling north on Mill swerves right to avoid a bicyclist that is traveling southwest on Rose. The driver strikes the rear end of a car parked on Rose. The bicyclist continues through the intersection and travels west on Page. 16.____

17. A bicyclist heading southwest on Rose travels into the intersection, sideswipes a car that is heading east on Page, and veers right, striking the rear end of a car parked in the westbound lane on Page. 17.____

18. A driver traveling east on Page swerves left to avoid a bicyclist that is traveling southwest on Rose. The driver strikes the rear end of a car parked on Mill. The bicyclist continues through the intersection and travels west on Page. 18.____

19. A bicyclist heading southwest on Rose enters the intersection and sideswipes a car that is swerving left to avoid her. The bicyclist veers left and collides with a car parked in the southbound lane on Mill. The driver of the car veers left and collides with a car parked in the northbound lane on Mill. 19.____

Questions 20-22.

DIRECTIONS: In Questions 20 through 22, choose the word or phrase CLOSEST in meaning to the word or phrase printed in capital letters.

20. WAIVE 20.____
A. cease B. surrender C. prevent D. die

21. DEPOSITION 21.____
A. settlement B. deterioration C. testimony D. character

22. IMMUNITY 22.____
A. exposure B. accusation C. protection D. exchange

Questions 23-25.

DIRECTIONS: Questions 23 through 25 measure your ability to do fieldwork-related arithmetic. Each question presents a separate arithmetic problem for you to solve.

23. Dean, a claims investigator, is reading a 445-page case record in his spare time at work. He has already read 157 pages. 23.____
If Dean reads 24 pages a day, he should finish reading the rest of the record in ____ days.
A. 7 B. 12 C. 19 D. 24

24. The Fire Department owns four cars. The Department of Sanitation owns twice as many cars as the Fire Department. The Department of Parks and Recreation owns one fewer car than the Department of Sanitation. The Department of Parks and Recreation is buying new tires for each of its cars. Each tire costs $100. 24.____
How much is the Department of Parks and Recreation going to spend on tires?
A. $400 B. $2,800 C. $3,200 D. $4,900

25. A dance hall is about 5,000 square feet. The local ordinance does not allow more than 50 people per every 100 square feet of commercial space. 25.____
The maximum capacity of the hall is
A. 500 B. 2,500 C. 5,000 D. 25,000

KEY (CORRECT ANSWERS)

1. D
2. B
3. A
4. D
5. B

6. D
7. D
8. A
9. C
10. C

11. D
12. A
13. B
14. C
15. A

16. C
17. B
18. D
19. E
20. B

21. C
22. C
23. B
24. B
25. B

SOLUTIONS TO QUESTIONS 1-9

P implies Q = original statement

Not Q implies not P = contrapositive of the original statement. A statement and its contrapositive are logically equivalent.

Q implies P = converse of the original statement

Not P implies not Q = inverse of the original statement. The converse and inverse of an original statement are logically equivalent.

P implies Q = Not P or Q.

1. The CORRECT answer is D.
   For item I, the second statement should be "Either there is no life on Mars or we should fund NASA" in order to be logically equivalent to the first statement. For item II, the statements are converses of each other; thus, they are not equivalent.

2. The CORRECT answer is B.
   In item I, this is an example of P implies Q and Q implies P. In this case, P = the notebook is missing its cover and Q = the notebook belongs to Carter. In item II, the ordering of the words is changed, but the If P then Q is exactly the same. P = it is hot and Q = the pool is open.

3. The CORRECT answer is A.
   For item I, if nobody is without benefits, then everybody has benefits. For item II, the second equivalent statement should be "either we will not fund the program or at least 100 people will sign the petition."

4. The CORRECT answer is D.
   For item I, the first statement is an implication, whereas the second statement mentions only one part of the implication (new parts are requested) and says nothing about the other part. For item II, the first statement is equivalent to "if the operating cycle is not running, then the test cycle will run." The second statement is equivalent to "if the operating cycle is running, then the test cycle will run." So, these statements in item II are not equivalent.

5. The CORRECT answer is B.
   Since Sid did not steal a car and avoid getting caught, the only other way he could become a Crips member would be "jumped in." Choice B tells us that Sid was not "jumped in," so we conclude that he did not become a member of the Crips.

6. The CORRECT answer is D.
   Since Smith and Watson have the same number of arrests, Watson must have fewer arrests than Jones. This means that each of choices A and B is impossible. Choice C would also not reveal whether or not Watson is a Precinct 8 officer.

7. The CORRECT answer is D.
Exact dollar amounts still cannot be ascertained by using any of the other choices.

8. The CORRECT answer is A.
The street sweepers never sweep on the east side of the street on Wednesday; however, they will be here at noon today. This implies that they will sweep on the west side of the street. Since the residents should move their cars before noon, we can conclude that today is Wednesday.

9. The CORRECT answer is C.
We start with W implies P, where W = warning light comes on and P = power surge. Choice C would read as P implies A, where A = air conditioning is running. Combining these statements leads to W implies A. The conclusion can be read as: Not A implies Not W, which is equivalent to W implies A.

WORD MEANING COMMENTARY

DESCRIPTION OF THE TEST

On many examinations, you will have questions about the meaning of words or vocabulary.

In this type of question, you have to state what a word or phrase means. (A phrase is a group of words.) This word or phrase is in capital letters in a sentence. You are also given for each question five other words or groups of words—lettered A, B, C, D, and E—as possible answers. One of these words or groups of words means the same as the word or group of words in CAPITAL letters. Only one is right. You are to pick out the one that is right and select the letter of your answer.

HINTS FOR ANSWERING WORD-MEANING QUESTIONS

Read each question carefully.

Choose the best answer of the five choices even though it is not the word you might use yourself.

Answer first those that you know. Then do the others.

If you know that some of the suggested answers are not right, pay no more attention to them.

Be sure that you have selected an answer for every question, even if you have to guess.

SAMPLE QUESTIONS

DIRECTIONS: For the following questions, select the word or group of words lettered A, B, C, D, or E that means MOST NEARLY the same as the word in capital letters. Indicate the letter of the CORRECT answer for each question.

SAMPLE QUESTIONS 1 AND 2

1. The letter was SHORT. SHORT means MOST NEARLY 1.____

   A. tall B. wide C. brief D. heavy E. dark

EXPLANATION

SHORT is a word you have used to describe something that is small, or not long, or little, etc. Therefore, you would not have to spend much time figuring out the right answer. You would choose C. brief.

2. The young man is VIGOROUS. VIGOROUS means MOST NEARLY 2.____

   A. serious B. reliable C. courageous

   D. strong E. talented

EXPLANATION

VIGOROUS is a word that you have probably used yourself or read somewhere. It carries with it the idea of being active, full of pep, etc. Which one of the five choices comes closest to meaning that? Certainly not A. serious, B. reliable, or E. talented; C. courageous—maybe, D. strong—maybe. But between courageous or strong, you would have to agree that strong is the better choice. Therefore, you would choose D.

WORD MEANING

EXAMINATION SECTION

TEST 1

DIRECTIONS: For the following questions, select the word or group of words lettered A, B, C, D, or E that means MOST NEARLY the same as the word in capital letters. *PRINT THE LETTER OF THE CORRECT ANSWER IN THE SPACE AT THE RIGHT.*

1. To SULK means MOST NEARLY to 1.____
   A. cry B. annoy C. lament D. be sullen E. scorn

2. To FLOUNDER means MOST NEARLY to 2.____
   A. investigate B. label C. struggle
   D. consent E. escape

3. PARLEY means MOST NEARLY 3.____
   A. discussion B. thoroughfare C. salon
   D. surrender E. division

4. MAESTRO means MOST NEARLY 4.____
   A. official B. ancestor C. teacher
   D. watchman E. alien

5. MEANDERING means MOST NEARLY 5.____
   A. cruel B. adjusting C. winding
   D. smooth E. combining

6. GNARLED means MOST NEARLY 6.____
   A. angry B. bitter C. twisted
   D. ancient E. embroidered

7. TEMPERANCE means MOST NEARLY 7.____
   A. moderation B. climate C. carelessness
   D. disagreeableness E. rigidity

8. A PRECARIOUS position is one that is 8.____
   A. foresighted B. careful C. modest
   D. headstrong E. uncertain

9. COVETOUS means MOST NEARLY 9.____
   A. undisciplined B. grasping C. timid
   D. insincere E. secretive

10. PRIVATION means MOST NEARLY 10.____
    A. reward B. superiority in rank
    C. hardship D. suitability of behavior
    E. solitude

TEST 2

DIRECTIONS: For the following questions, select the word or group of words lettered A, B, C, D, or E that means MOST NEARLY the same as the word in capital letters. *PRINT THE LETTER OF THE CORRECT ANSWER IN THE SPACE AT THE RIGHT.*

1. To INFILTRATE means MOST NEARLY to 1.____
   A. pass through B. stop C. consider
   D. challenge openly E. meet secretly

2. REVOCATION means MOST NEARLY 2.____
   A. certificate B. repeal C. animation
   D. license E. plea

3. LOQUACIOUS means MOST NEARLY 3.____
   A. grim B. stern C. talkative
   D. lighthearted E. liberty-loving

4. APERTURE means MOST NEARLY 4.____
   A. basement B. opening C. phantom
   D. protective coloring E. light refreshment

5. A PUNGENT odor is one that is 5.____
   A. biting B. smooth C. quarrelsome
   D. wrong E. proud

6. To CORROBORATE means MOST NEARLY to 6.____
   A. deny B. elaborate C. confirm
   D. gnaw E. state

7. BENEVOLENCE means MOST NEARLY 7.____
   A. good fortune B. well-being C. inheritance
   D. violence E. charitableness

8. PETULANT means MOST NEARLY 8.____
   A. rotten B. fretful C. unrelated
   D. weird E. throbbing

9. DERELICT means MOST NEARLY 9.____
   A. abandoned B. widowed C. faithful
   D. insincere E. hysterical

10. INCISIVE means MOST NEARLY 10.____
   A. stimulating B. accidental C. brief
   D. penetrating E. final

TEST 3

DIRECTIONS: For the following questions, select the word or group of words lettered A, B, C, D, or E that means MOST NEARLY the same as the word in capital letters. *PRINT THE LETTER OF THE CORRECT ANSWER IN THE SPACE AT THE RIGHT.*

1. To LAUD means MOST NEARLY to 1.____
   A. praise B. cleanse C. replace
   D. squander E. frown upon

2. To TAUNT means MOST NEARLY to 2.____
   A. jeer at B. tighten C. rescue
   D. interest E. ward off

3. DEITY means MOST NEARLY 3.____
   A. renown B. divinity C. delicacy
   D. destiny E. futility

4. GRAVITY means MOST NEARLY 4.____
   A. displeasure B. thankfulness C. suffering
   D. roughness E. seriousness

5. A CONTEMPTUOUS author is one that is 5.____
   A. thoughtful B. soiled C. dishonorable
   D. scornful E. self-satisfied

6. To WAIVE means MOST NEARLY to 6.____
   A. exercise B. swing C. claim
   D. give up E. wear out

7. To ASPIRE means MOST NEARLY to 7.____
   A. fade away B. excite C. desire earnestly
   D. breathe heavily E. roughen

8. PERTINENT means MOST NEARLY 8.____
   A. related B. saucy C. quick
   D. impatient E. excited

9. DEVASTATION means MOST NEARLY 9.____
   A. desolation B. displeasure C. dishonor
   D. neglect E. religious fervor

10. IMMINENT means MOST NEARLY 10.____
    A. sudden B. important C. delayed
    D. threatening E. forceful

TEST 4

DIRECTIONS: For the following questions, select the word or group of words lettered A, B, C, D, or E that means MOST NEARLY the same as the word in capital letters. *PRINT THE LETTER OF THE CORRECT ANSWER IN THE SPACE AT THE RIGHT.*

1. CONTROVERSAL means MOST NEARLY 1.____
   A. faultfinding B. pleasant C. debatable
   D. ugly E. talkative

2. GHASTLY means MOST NEARLY 2.____
   A. hasty B. furious C. breathless
   D. deathlike E. spiritual

3. A BELLIGERENT attitude is one that is 3.____
   A. worldly B. warlike C. loudmouthed
   D. furious E. artistic

4. PROFICIENCY means MOST NEARLY 4.____
   A. wisdom B. oversupply C. expertness
   D. advancement E. sincerity

5. COMPASSION means MOST NEARLY 5.____
   A. rage B. strength of character
   C. forcefulness D. sympathy
   E. uniformity

6. DISSENSION means MOST NEARLY 6.____
   A. treatise B. pretense C. fear
   D. lineage E. discord

7. To INTIMATE means MOST NEARLY to 7.____
   A. charm B. hint C. disguise
   D. frighten E. hum

8. To BERATE means MOST NEARLY to 8.____
   A. classify B. scold C. underestimate
   D. take one's time E. evaluate

9. DEARTH means MOST NEARLY 9.____
   A. scarcity B. width C. affection
   D. wealth E. warmth

10. To MEDIATE means MOST NEARLY to 10.____
    A. rest B. stare C. doze
    D. make peace E. reflect

TEST 5

DIRECTIONS: For the following questions, select the word or group of words lettered A, B, C, D, or E that means MOST NEARLY the same as the word in capital letters. *PRINT THE LETTER OF THE CORRECT ANSWER IN THE SPACE AT THE RIGHT.*

1. BONDAGE means MOST NEARLY 1.____
   A. poverty B. redemption C. slavery
   D. retirement E. complaint

2. AGILITY means MOST NEARLY 2.____
   A. wisdom B. nimbleness C. agreeable
   D. simplicity E. excitement

3. To ABDICATE means MOST NEARLY to 3.____
   A. achieve B. protest C. renounce
   D. demand E. steal

4. To STIFLE means MOST NEARLY to 4.____
   A. talk nonsense B. sidestep C. depress
   D. smother E. stick

5. EDICT means MOST NEARLY 5.____
   A. abbreviation B. lie C. carbon copy
   D. correction E. decree

6. AMITY means MOST NEARLY 6.____
   A. ill will B. hope C. pity
   D. friendship E. pleasure

7. COERCION means MOST NEARLY 7.____
   A. force B. disgust C. suspicion
   D. pleasure E. criticism

8. To ABASH means MOST NEARLY to 8.____
   A. embarrass B. encourage C. punish
   D. surrender E. overthrow

9. TACITURN means MOST NEARLY 9.____
   A. weak B. evil C. tender
   D. silent E. sensitive

10. REMISS means MOST NEARLY 10.____
    A. memorable B. neglectful C. useless
    D. prompt E. exact

TEST 6

DIRECTIONS: For the following questions, select the word or group of words lettered A, B, C, D, or E that means MOST NEARLY the same as the word in capital letters. *PRINT THE LETTER OF THE CORRECT ANSWER IN THE SPACE AT THE RIGHT.*

1. STAGNANT means MOST NEARLY 1.____
   A. inactive B. alert C. selfish
   D. difficult E. scornful

2. MANDATORY means MOST NEARLY 2.____
   A. instant B. obligatory C. evident
   D. strategic E. unequaled

3. INFERNAL means MOST NEARLY 3.____
   A. immodest B. incomplete C. domestic
   D. second-rate E. fiendish

4. To EXONERATE means MOST NEARLY to 4.____
   A. free from blame B. warn C. drive out
   D. overcharge E. plead

5. ARBITER means MOST NEARLY 5.____
   A. friend B. judge C. drug
   D. tree surgeon E. truant

6. ENMITY means MOST NEARLY 6.____
   A. boredom B. puzzle C. ill will
   D. offensive language E. entanglement

7. To DISCRIMINATE means MOST NEARLY to 7.____
   A. fail B. delay C. accuses
   D. distinguish E. reject

8. DERISION means MOST NEARLY 8.____
   A. disgust B. ridicule C. fear
   D. anger E. heredity

9. EXULTANT means MOST NEARLY 9.____
   A. essential B. elated C. praiseworthy
   D. plentiful E. high-priced

10. OSTENSIBLE 10.____
    A. vibrating B. odd C. apparent
    D. standard E. ornate

TEST 7

DIRECTIONS: For the following questions, select the word or group of words lettered A, B, C, D, or E that means MOST NEARLY the same as the word in capital letters. *PRINT THE LETTER OF THE CORRECT ANSWER IN THE SPACE AT THE RIGHT.*

1. To ABHOR means MOST NEARLY 1.____
   A. hate B. admire C. taste
   D. skip E. resign

2. DUTIFUL means MOST NEARLY 2.____
   A. lasting B. sluggish C. required
   D. soothing E. obedient

3. ZEALOT means MOST NEARLY 3.____
   A. breeze B. enthusiast C. vault
   D. wild animal E. musical instrument

4. A MAGNANIMOUS attitude is one that is 4.____
   A. high-minded B. faithful C. concerned
   D. individual E. small

5. To CITE means MOST NEARLY to 5.____
   A. protest B. depart C. quote
   D. agitate E. perform

6. OBLIVION means MOST NEARLY 6.____
   A. hindrance B. accident C. courtesy
   D. forgetfulness E. old age

7. CARDINAL means MOST NEARLY 7.____
   A. independent B. well-organized C. subordinate
   D. dignified E. chief

8. To DEPLETE means MOST NEARLY to 8.____
   A. restrain B. corrupt C. despair
   D. exhaust E. spread out

9. To SUPERSEDE means MOST NEARLY to 9.____
   A. retire B. replace C. overflow
   D. bless E. oversee

10. SPORADIC means MOST NEARLY 10.____
    A. bad-tempered B. infrequent C. radical
    D. reckless E. humble

TEST 8

DIRECTIONS: For the following questions, select the word or group of words lettered A, B, C, D, or E that means MOST NEARLY the same as the word in capital letters. *PRINT THE LETTER OF THE CORRECT ANSWER IN THE SPACE AT THE RIGHT.*

1. To NEUTRALIZE means MOST NEARLY to 1.____
   A. entangle B. strengthen C. counteract
   D. combat E. converse

2. To INSINUATE means MOST NEARLY to 2.____
   A. destroy B. hint C. do wrong
   D. accuse E. release

3. DIMINUTIVE means MOST NEARLY 3.____
   A. proud B. slow C. small
   D. watery E. puzzling

4. PLIGHT means MOST NEARLY 4.____
   A. departure B. weight C. conspiracy
   D. predicament E. stamp

5. An ILLICIT relationship is one that is 5.____
   A. unlawful B. overpowering C. ill-advised
   D. small-scale E. unreadable

6. A BENIGN manner is one that is 6.____
   A. contagious B. fatal C. ignorant
   D. kindly E. decorative

7. REVERIE means MOST NEARLY 7.____
   A. abusive language B. love song C. backward step
   D. daydream E. holy man

8. APPREHENSIVE means MOST NEARLY 8.____
   A. quiet B. firm C. curious
   D. sincere E. fearful

9. To RECOIL means MOST NEARLY to 9.____
   A. shrink B. attract C. electrify
   D. adjust E. fear

10. GUISE means MOST NEARLY 10.____
    A. trickery B. request C. innocence
    D. misdeed E. appearance

TEST 9

DIRECTIONS: For the following questions, select the word or group of words lettered A, B, C, D, or E that means MOST NEARLY the same as the word in capital letters. *PRINT THE LETTER OF THE CORRECT ANSWER IN THE SPACE AT THE RIGHT.*

1. To RELINQUISH means MOST NEARLY to 1.____
   A. regret B. abandon C. pursue
   D. secure E. penetrate

2. INJUNCTION means MOST NEARLY 2.____
   A. error B. attack C. injustice
   D. suggestion E. order

3. ADVENT means MOST NEARLY 3.____
   A. attachment B. reference C. arrival
   D. excitement E. vent

4. BICAMERAL means MOST NEARLY 4.____
   A. dealing with life forms B. meeting on alternate years
   C. over-sweet D. having two legislative branches
   E. having two meanings

5. A PERVERSE attitude is one that is 5.____
   A. contrary B. stingy C. unfortunate
   D. hereditary E. easygoing

6. To THWART means MOST NEARLY to 6.____
   A. assist B. whimper C. slice
   D. escape E. block

7. DEVOID means MOST NEARLY 7.____
   A. empty B. illegal C. affectionate
   D. pious E. annoying

8. A BLAND manner is one that is 8.____
   A. gentle B. guilty C. salty
   D. unfinished E. majestic

9. To OSTRACIZE means MOST NEARLY to 9.____
   A. flatter B. scold C. show off
   D. banish E. vibrate

10. CANDOR means MOST NEARLY 10.____
    A. sociability B. outspokenness C. grief
    D. light E. flattery

TEST 10

DIRECTIONS: For the following questions, select the word or group of words lettered A, B, C, D, or E that means MOST NEARLY the same as the word in capital letters. *PRINT THE LETTER OF THE CORRECT ANSWER IN THE SPACE AT THE RIGHT.*

1. ACQUIT means MOST NEARLY 1.____
   A. increase B. harden C. clear
   D. sharpen E. sentence

2. DEXTERITY means MOST NEARLY 2.____
   A. conceit B. skill C. insistence
   D. embarrassment E. guidance

3. ASSIMILATE means MOST NEARLY 3.____
   A. absorb B. imitate C. maintain
   D. outrun E. curb

4. DESPONDENCY means MOST NEARLY 4.____
   A. relief B. gratitude C. dejection
   D. hatred E. poverty

5. A BUOYANT manner is one that is 5.____
   A. conceited B. cautioning C. youthful
   D. musical E. cheerful

6. CULINARY means MOST NEARLY 6.____
   A. having to do with cooking B. pertaining to dressmaking
   C. fond of eating D. loving money
   E. tending to be secretive

7. CAPRICE means MOST NEARLY 7.____
   A. wisdom B. ornament C. pillar
   D. whim E. energy

8. DETERRENT means MOST NEARLY 8.____
   A. restraining B. cleansing C. deciding
   D. concluding E. crumbling

9. A PUGNACIOUS attitude is one that is 9.____
   A. sticky B. cowardly C. precise
   D. vigorous E. quarrelsome

10. ABSCOND means MOST NEARLY 10.____
    A. detest B. reduce C. swallow up
    D. dismiss E. flee

TEST 11

DIRECTIONS: For the following questions, select the word or group of words lettered A, B, C, D, or E that means MOST NEARLY the same as the word in capital letters. *PRINT THE LETTER OF THE CORRECT ANSWER IN THE SPACE AT THE RIGHT.*

1. DOLDRUMS means MOST NEARLY 1.____
   A. delirium B. rage C. saturation
   D. incarceration E. listlessness

2. DOUR means MOST NEARLY 2.____
   A. gloomy B. cowardly C. untidy
   D. stingy E. doubtful

3. DRAGOON means MOST NEARLY 3.____
   A. defy B. enlist C. surrender
   D. lead E. persecute

4. EMPIRICAL means MOST NEARLY 4.____
   A. experiential B. undeniable C. melancholy
   D. territorial E. traditional

5. ENCOMIUM means MOST NEARLY 5.____
   A. antidote B. adage C. anteroom
   D. eulogy E. bombast

6. ENTOMOLOGIST means MOST NEARLY student of 6.____
   A. insects B. fish C. words
   D. fossils E. reptiles

7. EPHEMERAL means MOST NEARLY 7.____
   A. persistent B. useless C. effete
   D. visionary E. short-lived

8. ETIOLOGY means MOST NEARLY 8.____
   A. epitome B. inertia C. astronomy
   D. disease E. cause

9. FETISH means MOST NEARLY 9.____
   A. tuft of hair above horse's foot B. embryo of an animal
   C. object of excessive devotion D. spirit of a festival
   E. feast of the Haitians

10. GAMUT means MOST NEARLY 10.____
    A. gamble B. alphabet C. keys
    D. chess move E. range

TEST 12

DIRECTIONS: For the following questions, select the word or group of words lettered A, B, C, D, or E that means MOST NEARLY the same as the word in capital letters. *PRINT THE LETTER OF THE CORRECT ANSWER IN THE SPACE AT THE RIGHT.*

1. HALLOW means MOST NEARLY 1.____
   A. shout aloud B. make sacred C. haunt
   D. reveal E. hole out

2. HEGEMONY means MOST NEARLY 2.____
   A. flight B. restraint C. nationalism
   D. autonomy E. leadership

3. HERMETIC means MOST NEARLY 3.____
   A. air-tight B. protruding C. sequestered
   D. briskly E. ascetic

4. IBID means MOST NEARLY 4.____
   A. that is B. as an example C. the same
   D. see above E. and so forth

5. IMPUGN means MOST NEARLY 5.____
   A. enhance B. attribute C. assail
   D. compromise E. defend

6. INCIPIENT means MOST NEARLY 6.____
   A. tasteless B. annoying C. unyielding
   D. ultimate E. commencing

7. INEXORABLE means MOST NEARLY 7.____
   A. hateful B. conciliatory C. unresponsive
   D. relentless E. pliant

8. INTREPID means MOST NEARLY 8.____
   A. awesome B. bellicose C. undisciplined
   D. courageous E. pacific

9. INVECTIVE means MOST NEARLY 9.____
   A. self study B. geometrical analysis C. verbal abuse
   D. hard-won victory E. indecision

10. INVEIGLED means MOST NEARLY 10.____
    A. ensnared B. terrified C. coerced
    D. corrupted E. incarcerated

TEST 13

DIRECTIONS: For the following questions, select the word or group of words lettered A, B, C, D, or E that means MOST NEARLY the same as the word in capital letters. *PRINT THE LETTER OF THE CORRECT ANSWER IN THE SPACE AT THE RIGHT.*

1. ITERANT means MOST NEARLY 1.____
   A. distant B. repeating C. directed
   D. wandering E. errant

2. LAMPOON means MOST NEARLY 2.____
   A. magazine B. satire C. clown
   D. lament E. shade

3. LAPIDARY means MOST NEARLY one who 3.____
   A. collects butterflies B. breaks up large estates
   C. indulges the senses D. judges the quality of beverages
   E. cuts precious stones

4. MERETRICIOUS means MOST NEARLY 4.____
   A. according to the metric system B. deserving
   C. scholarly D. indigent
   E. tawdry

5. MITIGATE means MOST NEARLY 5.____
   A. exonerate B. handicap C. aggravate
   D. appease E. defile

6. MORES means MOST NEARLY 6.____
   A. beginnings B. conglomerations C. curses
   D. mutations E. customs

7. NOSTRUM means MOST NEARLY 7.____
   A. ocean sea B. paternity C. remedy
   D. pungency E. family

8. OBJURGATE means MOST NEARLY 8.____
   A. chide B. sacrifice C. oppose
   D. purge E. repeat

9. OSSIFY means MOST NEARLY 9.____
   A. vacillate B. harden C. categorize
   D. tipple E. abstain

10. PARLOUS means MOST NEARLY 10.____
    A. wise B. bargaining C. talkative
    D. dangerous E. partial

TEST 14

DIRECTIONS: For the following questions, select the word or group of words lettered A, B, C, D, or E that means MOST NEARLY the same as the word in capital letters. *PRINT THE LETTER OF THE CORRECT ANSWER IN THE SPACE AT THE RIGHT.*

1. ADVENTITIOUS means MOST NEARLY 1.____
   A. opportunistic B. daring C. helpful
   D. deceptive E. extrinsic

2. AMBIVALENT means MOST NEARLY 2.____
   A. helpful in walking B. equally skillful with both hands
   C. simultaneously hating and loving D. ambiguous in origin
   E. equivalent

3. AMORPHOUS means MOST NEARLY 3.____
   A. inelegant B. clamorous C. quiescent
   D. ardent E. formless

4. ANATHEMA means MOST NEARLY 4.____
   A. despair B. benevolence C. disputation
   D. anomaly E. curse

5. APIARY means MOST NEARLY 5.____
   A. bee house B. pear-shaped figure C. main-traveled road
   D. monkey cage E. bird house

6. APORYPHAL means MOST NEARLY of 6.____
   A. scholarly pursuits B. sacred origin C. ancient beginnings
   D. ecclesiastical power E. doubtful authenticity

7. APOSTASY means MOST NEARLY 7.____
   A. confirmation B. detection C. supposition
   D. canonization E. deification

8. ASCETIC means MOST NEARLY 8.____
   A. exclusive B. sharp C. fragrant
   D. austere E. authentic

9. BADINAGE means MOST NEARLY 9.____
   A. indifference B. song C. banter
   D. mucilage E. autarchy

10. BOGGLE means MOST NEARLY 10.____
    A. dampen B. hesitate C. undermine
    D. disarrange E. haggle

TEST 15

DIRECTIONS: For the following questions, select the word or group of words lettered A, B, C, D, or E that means MOST NEARLY the same as the word in capital letters. *PRINT THE LETTER OF THE CORRECT ANSWER IN THE SPACE AT THE RIGHT.*

1. BUCOLIC means MOST NEARLY 1.____
   A. rustic B. flatulent C. angry
   D. loud E. bureaucratic

2. CAESURA means MOST NEARLY 2.____
   A. genesis B. referring to Caesar C. tyranny
   D. domain E. break

3. CAREEN means MOST NEARLY 3.____
   A. lurch B. wail C. pour
   D. contain E. corrode

4. CARET means MOST NEARLY 4.____
   A. measure of weight B. sign of omission C. technique in ballet
   D. growth of root E. notice for caution

5. CARIES means MOST NEARLY 5.____
   A. treatment B. convalescent C. decay
   D. chemicals E. roots

6. CASIOST means MOST NEARLY 6.____
   A. sophistical reasoner B. careless worker C. innocent victim
   D. habitual late-comer E. frenzied lawyer

7. CHIMERICAL means MOST NEARLY 7.____
   A. scientific B. debasing C. well-ordered
   D. maniacal E. fanciful

8. CLABBER means MOST NEARLY 8.____
   A. gossip B. climb C. crop
   D. entwine E. curdle

9. COMME IL FAUT means MOST NEARLY 9.____
   A. unnecessary B. erroneous C. proper
   D. mixed E. illegal

10. CRYPTIC means MOST NEARLY 10.____
    A. succinct B. astringent C. death-like
    D. crotchety E. occult

TEST 16

DIRECTIONS: For the following questions, select the word or group of words lettered A, B, C, D, or E that means MOST NEARLY the same as the word in capital letters. *PRINT THE LETTER OF THE CORRECT ANSWER IN THE SPACE AT THE RIGHT.*

1. CYNOSURE means MOST NEARLY 1.____
   A. act of completion B. occupation of ease C. attitude of doubt
   D. center of attraction E. cynical statement

2. DEBENTURE means MOST NEARLY 2.____
   A. written acknowledgment of debt B. sale of preferred stock
   C. illegal sale of securities D. dividend on stocks or bonds
   E. disclaimer in a prospectus

3. DEMURRER means MOST NEARLY 3.____
   A. promotion B. objection C. interrogation
   D. retainer E. demerit

4. DERELICTION means MOST NEARLY 4.____
   A. general decline B. damaging criticism C. probable cause
   D. abandoned vessel E. failure in duty

5. DESCRIED means MOST NEARLY 5.____
   A. delimned B. defined C. rejected
   D. erred E. discerned

6. DESIDERATUM means MOST NEARLY 6.____
   A. final outcome B. hearty approval C. last remnant
   D. desired object E. prescribed treatment

7. DISCRETE means MOST NEARLY 7.____
   A. separate B. reserved C. foresighted
   D. unbounded E. tactful

8. DISINGENUOUS means MOST NEARLY 8.____
   A. unsophisticated B. skillful C. apathetic
   D. naïve E. insincere

9. DISSIDENT means MOST NEARLY 9.____
   A. malodorous B. amoral C. discordant
   D. unfeeling E. divisive

10. EGREGIOUS means MOST NEARLY 10.____
    A. debased B. inconsequential C. incorrigible
    D. egotistical E. prominent

TEST 17

DIRECTIONS: For the following questions, select the word or group of words lettered A, B, C, D, or E that means MOST NEARLY the same as the word in capital letters. *PRINT THE LETTER OF THE CORRECT ANSWER IN THE SPACE AT THE RIGHT.*

1. EMPATHY means MOST NEARLY 1.____
   A. comatose condition
   B. sympathetic understanding
   C. depressed feeling
   D. political subdivision
   E. patriotic devotion

2. ESOTERIC means MOST NEARLY 2.____
   A. abstruse
   B. intestinal
   C. lively
   D. joining
   E. essential

3. ESPERANTO means MOST NEARLY 3.____
   A. fabled country
   B. artificial language
   C. European peace manifesto
   D. place of abandoned hope
   E. pertaining to the Elysian Fields

4. EUPHEMISM means MOST NEARLY 4.____
   A. pleasant sight
   B. right direction
   C. verbal platitude
   D. buoyant feeling
   E. inoffensive expression

5. FINICAL means MOST NEARLY 5.____
   A. blundering
   B. fastidious
   C. conclusive
   D. maniacal
   E. extravagant

6. GUERDON means MOST NEARLY 6.____
   A. debacle
   B. shield
   C. fruit
   D. obstacle
   E. recompense

7. GYVES means MOST NEARLY 7.____
   A. gallows
   B. chains
   C. barbs
   D. vegetables
   E. jives

8. HEDONIST means MOST NEARLY 8.____
   A. reviler
   B. recluse
   C. pleasure-seeker
   D. savage
   E. hermit

9. HIATUS means MOST NEARLY 9.____
   A. flower
   B. gap
   C. mistake
   D. digression
   E. hearsay

10. IMBROGLIO means MOST NEARLY 10.____
    A. secluded dwelling
    B. impassioned plea
    C. rampant destruction
    D. petit point
    E. complicated situation

TEST 18

DIRECTIONS: For the following questions, select the word or group of words lettered A, B, C, D, or E that means MOST NEARLY the same as the word in capital letters. *PRINT THE LETTER OF THE CORRECT ANSWER IN THE SPACE AT THE RIGHT.*

1. IMPALPABLE means MOST NEARLY not 1.____
   A. truthful B. concrete C. throbbing
   D. deviating E. suggestive

2. IMPECUNIOUS means MOST NEARLY 2.____
   A. poor B. wayward C. troublesome
   D. inordinate E. ingenuous

3. IMPORTUNATE means MOST NEARLY 3.____
   A. critical B. empty-handed C. disastrous
   D. pusillanimous E. pressing

4. IMPRIMIS means MOST NEARLY 4.____
   A. church dignitary B. sanction C. manuscript
   D. sacred song E. in the first place

5. INURED means MOST NEARLY 5.____
   A. belligerent B. hardened C. apprehensive
   D. irreverent E. injured

6. INVIDIOUS means MOST NEARLY 6.____
   A. obscure B. unconquerable C. offensive
   D. niggardly E. invariable

7. JOCOSE means MOST NEARLY 7.____
   A. intemperate B. contemptuous C. morose
   D. nugatory E. facetious

8. LACHRYMOSE means MOST NEARLY 8.____
   A. milky B. disdainful C. comic
   D. tearful E. comatose

9. LISSOME means MOST NEARLY 9.____
   A. nimble B. comely C. laughable
   D. lackadaisical E. aggressive

10. MERCURIAL means MOST NEARLY 10.____
    A. thermal B. coy C. volatile
    D. ponderous E. unchangeable

KEYS (CORRECT ANSWERS)

TEST 1

1. D 6. C
2. C 7. A
3. A 8. E
4. C 9. B
5. C 10. C

TEST 2

1. A 6. C
2. B 7. E
3. C 8. B
4. B 9. A
5. A 10. D

TEST 3

1. A 6 D
2. A 7. C
3. B 8. A
4. E 9. A
5. D 10. D

TEST 4

1. C 6. E
2. D 7. B
3. B 8. B
4. C 9. A
5. D 10. E

TEST 5

1. C 6. D
2. B 7. A
3. C 8. A
4. D 9. D
5. E 10. B

TEST 6

1. A 6. D
2. B 7. D
3. E 8. B
4. A 9. B
5. B 10. C

TEST 7

1. A 6. D
2. E 7. E
3. B 8. D
4. A 9. B
5. C 10. B

TEST 8

1. C 6. D
2. B 7. D
3. C 8. E
4. D 9. A
5. A 10. E

TEST 9

1. B 6. E
2. E 7. A
3. C 8. A
4. D 9. D
5. A 10. B

TEST 10

1. C 6. A
2. B 7. D
3. A 8. A
4. C 9. E
5. E 10. E

TEST 11

1. E 6. A
2. A 7. E
3. E 8. E
4. A 9. C
5. D 10. E

TEST 12

1. B 6. E
2. E 7. D
3. A 8. D
4. C 9. C
5. C 10. A

TEST 13

1. B 6. E
2. B 7. C
3. E 8. A
4. E 9. B
5. D 10. D

TEST 14

1. E 6. E
2. C 7. B
3. E 8. D
4. E 9. C
5. A 10. B

TEST 15

1. A 6. A
2. E 7. E
3. A 8. E
4. B 9. C
5. C 10. E

TEST 16

1. D 6. D
2. A 7. A
3. B 8. E
4. E 9. C
5. E 10. E

TEST 17

1. B 6. E
2. A 7. B
3. B 8. C
4. E 9. B
5. B 10. E

TEST 18

1. B 6. C
2. A 7. E
3. E 8. D
4. E 9. A
5. B 10. C
